I08105634

IMAGES
of America

PLYMOUTH AND WASHINGTON COUNTY

ON THE COVER: The Roanoke River has been a source of livelihood and recreation for residents of Washington County, North Carolina, for hundreds of years. In this photograph taken in November 1945, hunters and their dogs are heading to a hunting spot on the river near the Washington County seat of Plymouth. (State Archives of North Carolina.)

IMAGES
of America

PLYMOUTH AND WASHINGTON COUNTY

Willie Drye

ARCADIA
PUBLISHING

ISBN 978-1-4671-2124-8

Published by Arcadia Publishing
Charleston, South Carolina

Printed in the United States of America

Library of Congress Control Number: 2013946732

For all general information, please contact Arcadia Publishing:
Telephone 843-853-2070
Fax 843-853-0044
E-mail sales@arcadiapublishing.com
For customer service and orders:
Toll-Free 1-888-313-2665

Visit us on the Internet at www.arcadiapublishing.com

This book is dedicated to the late Harry Thompson, who epitomized the best of northeastern North Carolina—generous, gracious, unpretentious, and brimming with history.

Contents

Acknowledgments

I could not have done this without lots of help.

Kim Andersen, Vann Evans, and Mathew Wehner at the State Archives of North Carolina were always willing to look for one more photograph. Eric Blevins at the North Carolina Museum of History found some wonderful images. Linda Wise in the North Carolina Secretary of State's office dug up photographs of people from Washington County who had served in the North Carolina state legislature.

Chandrea Burch provided photographs from the North Carolina State Historic Preservation Office, and Sarah Downing contributed a photograph from the Outer Banks History Center.

Keith Longiotti at the University of North Carolina at Chapel Hill found unusual photographs in the North Carolina and Southern Historical collections. And archivist Jean Bischoff at Elizabeth City State University turned up photographs of an esteemed late-19th-century African American educator from Washington County.

Dana Kane in Brooklyn ran an emergency errand to the New York Public Library. DiAnne Bryant, a tenacious researcher, kept me fascinated with the information she found in census records and public files at the Washington County Courthouse.

Beth Price provided photographs of Plymouth United Methodist Church, and Diane Minton provided photographs of Grace Episcopal Church.

Plymouth photographer and writer Doward Jones contributed photographs and added his knowledge and insight to my research. Librarians Amy O'Neal, Rita Asby, and Doris Hoggard steered me to resources in the Washington County Public Library.

C.J. Belch provided information about fishing and hunting on the Roanoke River. Marvin Spencer of Plymouth's Brush Creek Yachts provided information about boats in the photographs. Mary Cotten Davenport of Mackeys offered wonderful old photographs.

Kim McCray, curator at the Port o' Plymouth Civil War Museum, provided terrific Civil War photographs, and Jimmy Hardison of the Washington County Historical Society helped me keep my facts straight.

I also had lots of help identifying people in old photographs, including Undine Cordon, Merion Anderson, Deborah Brown, Ray and Kitty Styons, George and Kathy Waters, Lib and Carter Bennett, Larry Jones, Archie Riddle Jr., and Shelton McNair. Tom Harrison helped with the expenses of collecting the photographs.

Unless otherwise noted, images appear courtesy of the following sources: Elizabeth City State University Archives (ECSUA), North Carolina Collection (NCC), North Carolina Museum of History (NCMH), North Carolina Secretary of State's Office (NCSSO), North Carolina State Historic Preservation Office (NCSHPO), North Carolina State University Libraries (NCSUL), State Archives of North Carolina (SANC), Outer Banks History Center (OBXHC), Port o' Plymouth Civil War Museum (PPCWM), Roanoke River Maritime Museum (RRMM), Somerset Place State Historic Site (SPSHS), and Washington County Library (WCL).

Introduction

It takes about two hours to drive the 120 miles from Plymouth to Raleigh on US 64, a major highway that spans North Carolina from the mountains to the sea. But a century ago, there was only a tenuous land link from Raleigh across the rivers, swamps, and wetlands of northeastern North Carolina to Plymouth. Traveling in an automobile on narrow, unpaved, and sometimes all-but-impassable roads and crossing rivers on ferries, it could take days to make the trip.

The Native Americans who lived in the area thousands of years ago and the European settlers who came later encountered much the same difficulty when they tried to go from place to place on land. So the rivers and sounds became northeastern North Carolina's first roads, and the Roanoke River became a superhighway and a conduit for maritime commerce. The people who lived there became seafarers.

The Roanoke River begins in the mountains of southwestern Virginia, near the small town of Lafayette, and flows about 410 miles eastward to the Albemarle Sound. Along the way, the river drains almost 10,000 square miles of land, and in a 24-hour span, an average of about six billion gallons of water flows past Plymouth—enough to cover one square mile of land in water 33 feet deep.

Some historians think Vikings might have been the first Europeans to explore the Roanoke, around 1000 AD. But it is more likely that English explorers under Capt. Philip Amadas and Capt. Arthur Barlowe were the first Europeans to sail up the Roanoke in 1584. They were looking for a place to plant a colony in the New World.

England tried to establish a colony on Roanoke Island—in the Albemarle Sound about 65 miles east of present-day Plymouth—in 1587. But that colony mysteriously disappeared in 1590, becoming history's famous "Lost Colony."

England's first permanent colony in the New World was established in 1607 in Jamestown, Virginia, about 140 miles north of Plymouth. European settlers did not return to the Albemarle Sound region until around 1650. Tired of paying taxes to England, settlers left Virginia and came to the north shore of the sound. Settlements eventually encircled the Albemarle Sound and became Albemarle County. Washington County would be one of the counties formed within the original boundaries of Albemarle County, which ceased to exist in the late 17th century.

The first settlements around the Albemarle Sound struggled to survive. In their classic work of history, *North Carolina: The History of a Southern State*, authors Hugh T. Lefler and Albert R. Newsom noted that the early days of settlement were marred by unrest, confusion, and slow economic growth. Lefler and Newsom attribute this difficult period in part to the isolation imposed by the region's rivers and swamps that made the area "largely out of touch with the outside world. . . . Communication by land was almost impossible except with Virginia, and even this was difficult because of forests, swamps, and rivers that made travel a 'jungle experience,' " they wrote.

And although the Roanoke River is very deep in some places, it dumps tons of silt into the Albemarle Sound. The silt and the slender Outer Banks barrier islands that form the sound's eastern shore make the sound too shallow to accommodate the deep-draft vessels needed for a thriving maritime commercial trade.

The Albemarle Assembly, the governing body of Albemarle County, tried to lure settlers to the area by offering newcomers a one-year exemption from all taxes. The assembly also declared that new settlers were excused from paying all debts from outside Albemarle County for five years.

The anti-tax sentiments were deeply ingrained among Albemarle colonists. Tobacco was a major cash crop in the area, and tons of tobacco were shipped to New England every year. British authorities taxed the shipments, but Albemarle shippers refused to pay the tax and even resorted to deception to avoid it. When they packed the tobacco for shipment, they labeled it as bait for New England fishermen. Since bait was exempted from taxation, the tobacco merchants avoided the levy. King Charles ordered colonial officials to enforce the tax laws in 1673. But one governor of Albemarle resigned rather than enforce the taxation, and his successor simply ignored the decree.

Maritime commerce came to the Roanoke River in 1685, when traders built a post on the southern shore of the Roanoke, near a Moratoc Indian town on Welch's Creek, a tributary of the Roanoke just west of present-day Plymouth. To protect themselves and their goods, the traders built a sturdy, windowless log cabin on what is now Water Street in downtown Plymouth.

An even sturdier brick house replaced the log cabin in 1700, and this building gave the name to the settlement that eventually became Plymouth—Brick House Landing. That name began appearing on maps drawn in the early 18th century. By 1771, a shipbuilding operation had been established where the trading post once stood. The settlement was called Plymouth Landing, perhaps taking the name from Plymouth, England.

Logging and lumber operations were established in the Albemarle region as the 17th century drew to a close, and in 1709, Thomas Lee built Lee's Mill, a sawmill in what is now Roper. In the three centuries since Lee's Mill began operation, the lumber industry has become a fixture in Washington County and northeastern North Carolina.

In the early 1730s, Thomas Bell established a ferry on the southern shore of the sound on what is now Mackey's Creek. Bell sold the ferry to his nephew William Mackey in 1735. A settlement grew around the ferry, and for two centuries, a ferry there linked the southern shore of the Albemarle with Edenton on the northern shore.

Meanwhile, military and political leaders were trying to find a way to overcome the economic handicaps caused by the dense swamps and shallow sound. One of those tangled wetlands, the Dismal Swamp, straddles the North Carolina–Virginia border.

The swamp posed a paradox for those who wanted to bring commerce to the area. It contained huge stands of valuable timber. But the swamp made it difficult to get to the timber and impossible to get that timber to market.

For years, North Carolina and Virginia had argued about the boundary between their colonies. Finally, the governors of the two colonies agreed that the line should run due west of the north shore of Currituck Inlet, which has since closed, and in 1728, a surveying party set out to establish the border.

The surveyors had to run the boundary through the Great Dismal Swamp. William Byrd II, a Virginian who was a member of the surveying party, described the Dismal as "a vast body of mire and nastiness." But he also realized the swamp's potential and suggested that a canal should be built through the swamp to connect the Albemarle Sound with the Elizabeth River, near Norfolk, Virginia. Such a canal would give northeastern North Carolina a link to a deepwater harbor and an outlet to the world's markets.

The Dismal Swamp Canal Company was formed in 1784, and work started on the canal in 1793. Slaves doing what author David Cecelski called "the cruelest, most dangerous, unhealthy, and exhausting labor in the American South" dug the canal through 22 miles of swamp to link the Pasquotank River—which empties into the Albemarle Sound—with the Elizabeth River just south of Norfolk. Pressure to complete the canal increased after a hurricane in 1795 closed Roanoke Inlet, cutting off the Albemarle Sound's only access to the Atlantic Ocean.

The same year the Dismal Swamp Canal Company was formed, Edenton businessman Josiah Collins Sr. and two partners bought 100,000 acres bordering Lake Phelps in what was then Tyrrell County. Collins and his partners formed the Lake Company and used slave labor to dig a six-mile canal from Lake Phelps to the Scuppernong River, which flows into the Albemarle Sound.

Collins named his farm Somerset Place after his birthplace in England, but he continued to live in Edenton. Using hired overseers and slave labor, the Lake Company began growing rice and other crops on the fertile land around the lake.

Washington County was formed from Tyrrell County in 1797, and Somerset and the Lake Phelps canal were just within the new county. Lee's Mill was the first seat of Washington County.

When the Dismal Swamp Canal opened in 1805, Plymouth and other river towns around the Albemarle Sound finally had a link to a deepwater harbor. But the canal's full potential was not realized until 1815, when William J. Lewis and other adventurers traveled the full 410-mile length of the Roanoke River in small flat-bottomed boats. The daring journey demonstrated that goods could be shipped to Plymouth—which became the Washington County seat in 1823—from hundreds of miles away.

The canal was deepened in 1829 to accommodate larger boats, and by the mid-19th century, barges towed by steamboats regularly left Plymouth carrying bacon, brandy, cotton, cypress shingles, tobacco, and other goods to Norfolk. The canal improvements increased maritime traffic so much that, in 1835, Congress provided money for a lightship, essentially a floating lighthouse, to be anchored in the Albemarle Sound at the mouth of the Roanoke. Thomas Clifton Jr. of Plymouth was assistant keeper aboard the ship.

Commercial fishing continued to grow, and by the mid-19th century, there were dozens of fish packinghouses on the river and the sound.

By 1835, the Collins family had acquired all of the land that had belonged to the Lake Company, and Josiah Collins III and his new wife moved to Somerset Place. Collins became one of only four planters in North Carolina to own more than 300 slaves.

The issue of slavery and its expansion into new states was tearing apart the United States in 1860. Although North Carolina was a slaveholding state, many residents had deep misgivings about joining six other Deep South states that left the Union to form the Confederate States of America in December 1860. This reluctance was especially strong in Plymouth, where maritime commerce had forged strong ties to the North among residents who had business interests and bank deposits in Philadelphia and Baltimore.

But civil war was unavoidable when Confederate forces fired on Fort Sumter in Charleston, South Carolina, on April 12, 1861. On April 27, the port of Plymouth was closed by a federal blockade. North Carolina left the Union on May 21, 1861.

Soon after North Carolina's secession, officials in the Confederate capital at Richmond, Virginia, ordered that the lightship at the mouth of the Roanoke River be removed so it would not aid Union warships operating in the Albemarle Sound. The lightship was towed upriver to Williamston and disappeared sometime during the war. Many historians think Confederate military leaders had the ship sunk in the Roanoke to prevent Union warships from steaming up the river.

Union military leaders immediately saw the strategic advantage of maintaining a presence in the Albemarle Sound. Union troops seized Roanoke Island in the eastern Albemarle Sound in February 1862 and occupied Plymouth a few months later. Plymouth became a base of operations and supply for Union troops. Escaped slaves and free blacks came to Plymouth seeking safety, and many of them enlisted in the Union army.

But Confederates were determined to retake the town.

In April 1864, the CSS *Albemarle*, an ironclad ram built in a Halifax County cornfield upriver from Plymouth, steamed down the Roanoke and attacked Union vessels in Plymouth, sinking one and chasing the others into the Albemarle Sound. A few days later, Confederate forces retook Plymouth.

But the Confederates did not hold the town very long. In October 1864, raiders led by Union Navy lieutenant William Cushing sank the *Albemarle* while the ironclad was anchored in the

Roanoke near Plymouth. Union forces then retook Plymouth and held it until the war ended in April 1865.

The town had taken a severe battering during the war. Only 11 buildings had somehow escaped damage or destruction during the fighting. Years later, author George Nowitzky wrote, "There is no town or city in the United States that shows more scars of war than Plymouth, N.C."

Plymouth and other communities in the former Confederate states had to rebuild economies that had been shattered by the war. Federal officials reopened the port of Plymouth in July 1865. To help restart maritime commerce in the area, the US Congress approved funds to build a small lighthouse at the mouth of the Roanoke River and designated Plymouth as a port of entry.

The new lighthouse went into operation in December 1866, and in 1870, the Roanoke River Lighthouse became part of the newly formed US Lighthouse Service. Thomas Clifton Jr., who had served as assistant keeper aboard the prewar lightship, was appointed keeper of the light, and for more than 60 years, a beacon guided ships navigating the Roanoke and western Albemarle Sound. When Thomas Clifton retired, his son William Benjamin Clifton succeeded him.

The construction of railroads helped Washington and other counties around the Albemarle recover from the ruins of the war. Plymouth eventually had two train stations: one for the Norfolk and Southern Railroad, the other for the Atlantic Coast Line Railroad.

The railroads made it easier—and cheaper—to haul timber to sawmills and then move the finished products to markets. In 1889, the John L. Roper Company built a large sawmill in Lee's Mill, and the town changed its name to Roper.

The trains also allowed farmers to ship crops to market and brought the first tourists to Washington County in the late 19th century. Towns with a railroad running through them, such as Plymouth, started growing more rapidly than towns without railroad connections.

Today, Plymouth is a small town in a county that retains much of its natural coastal beauty. During summer months, thousands of tourists daily pass through the town on US 64 en route to the nearby beaches of the Outer Banks. And Plymouth and Washington County attract tourists eager to go bass fishing or bird watching on the Roanoke River, where they can see unspoiled wilderness that looks much as it did when that first trading post was established in the 17th century.

Plymouth and Washington County also are destinations for history buffs wanting to visit the Port o' Plymouth Civil War Museum, the Roanoke River Lighthouse and Maritime Museum, and God's Creation Natural History Museum.

One

History Travels on the Water

History travels on water, and the Albemarle Sound and Roanoke River have brought a rich and colorful history to Plymouth and Washington County.

More than one-fifth of Washington County's surface area is covered by water. For thousands of years, people have used the water as their highways and a source of livelihood. Archaeologists have found dugout canoes used by Native Americans living around Lake Phelps that are as old as the pyramids of Egypt.

Before the Civil War, Plymouth was a busy river town where as many as 200 ships a day arrived and departed. Commercial fishing also had a major presence, with many big seine-fishing houses on the river and the sound.

But as the 1850s ended, slavery had driven a wedge into the nation. In April 1861, the nation broke apart when Confederate troops fired on Fort Sumter in Charleston, South Carolina. Eleven slaveholding Southern states, including North Carolina, left the Union and formed the Confederate States of America.

Union military leaders almost immediately realized that holding the rivers and sounds of coastal North Carolina would give them a big advantage in fighting the war. In early 1862, they seized control of Plymouth and other nearby towns. Plymouth became a Union stronghold, and many young men in Washington County enlisted in the Union army.

Confederates were determined to regain control of Plymouth. In April 1864, they launched a dreadnought, the ironclad CSS *Albemarle*, to break the Union hold on the Roanoke. Confederate troops teamed up with the *Albemarle* to defeat Union forces at the Battle of Plymouth.

Union strategists were equally determined to retake the town. In October 1864, a daring commando-style raid led by Navy lieutenant William Cushing sank the *Albemarle* in Plymouth. With the ironclad gone, Union forces quickly retook Plymouth and held it until the end of the war.

After the war, the federal government reopened the port of Plymouth and built a lighthouse in the Albemarle Sound at the mouth of the Roanoke to restart maritime commerce. Timber, fishing, and agriculture became the foundation of the local economy.

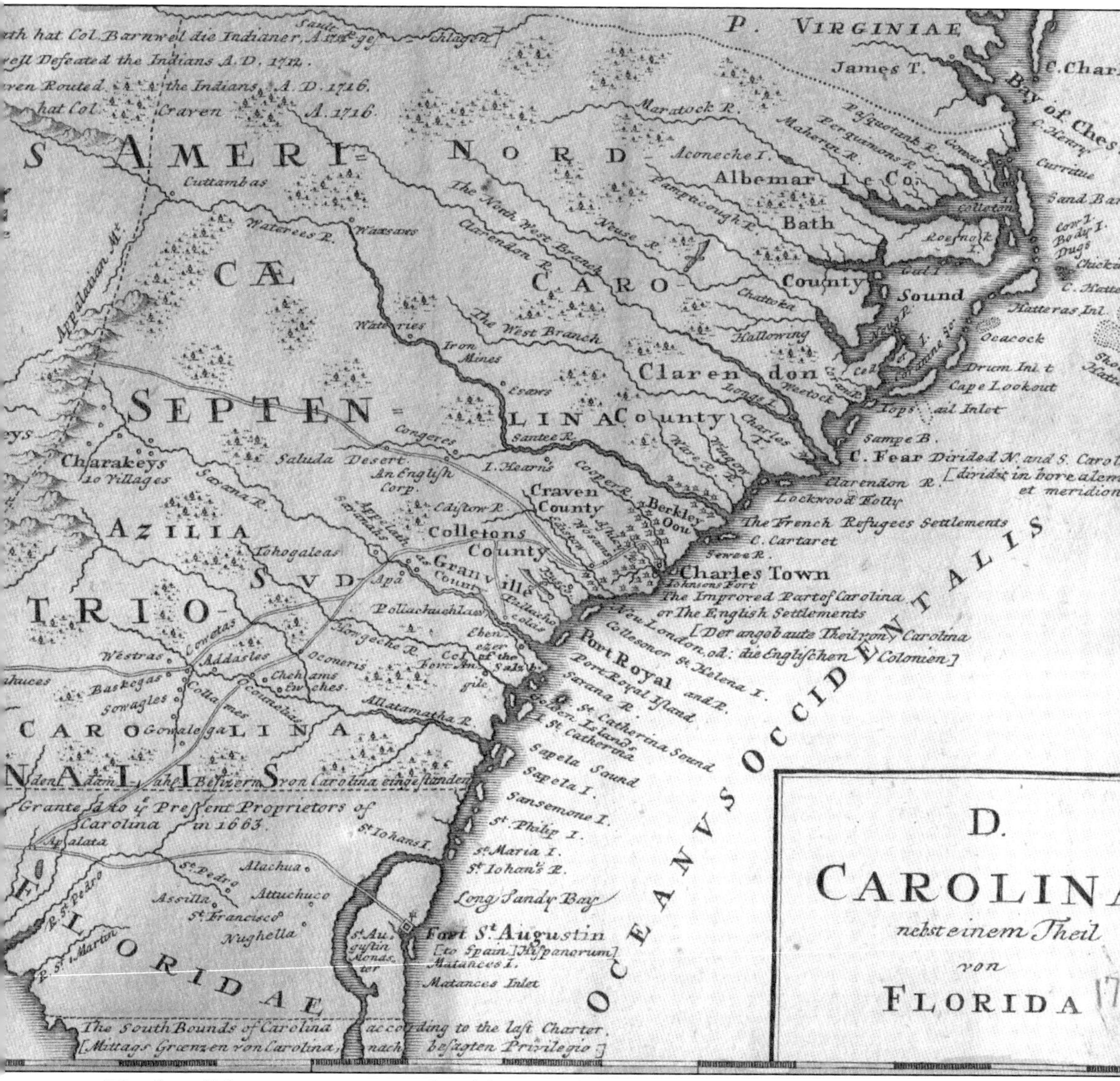

This late-17th-century map translated from English to German shows Albemarle County, formed in 1684, in the upper-right corner. Other counties were carved out of North Carolina's first county, and by the early 18th century, Albemarle County no longer existed. Washington County, established in 1799 from part of Tyrrell County, was the last to be formed from what had been Albemarle County. (NCC.)

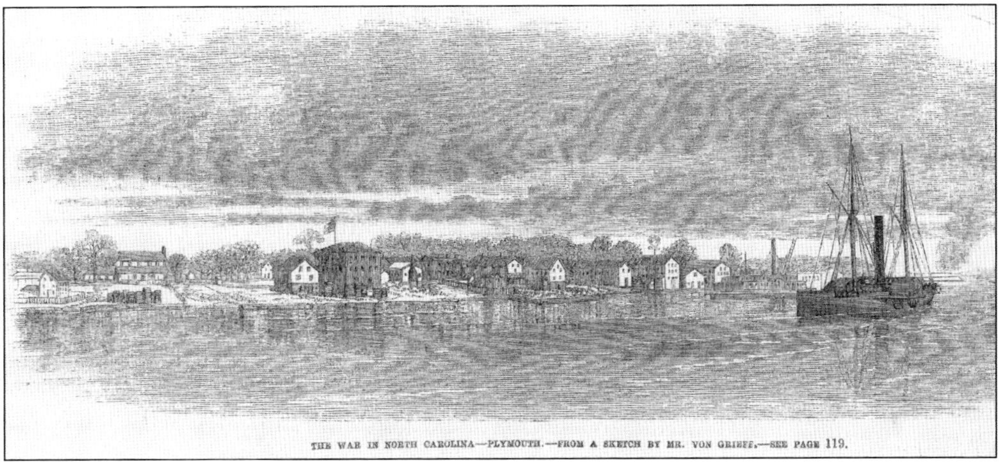

At the start of the Civil War in 1861, Plymouth was a busy river town near the Albemarle Sound in northeastern North Carolina. Union military commanders moved quickly to seize Plymouth in early 1862, using it as a base of operations and supply. Plymouth, caught between two hostile armies, was the scene of fierce fighting. The town changed hands several times during the war. (NCMH.)

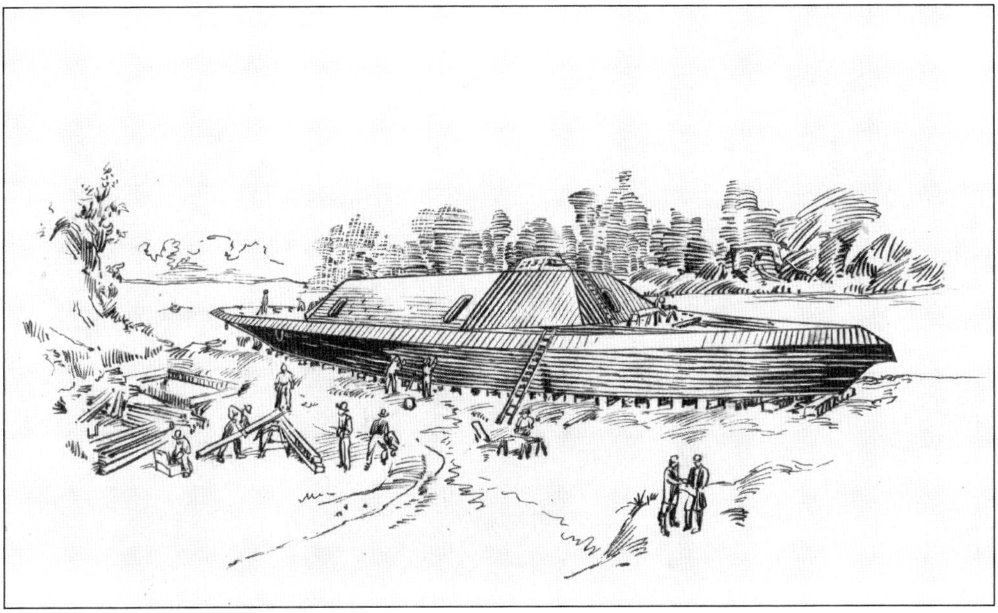

In the summer of 1863, the Confederacy began building an ironclad ram in a cornfield in Halifax County, upriver from Plymouth. The CSS *Albemarle*'s design specifications were done by John Porter, who directed the conversion of the USS *Merrimac* into the ironclad CSS *Virginia*. Gilbert Elliott, a precocious young engineer in Elizabeth City, supervised the final design and construction of the *Albemarle*. (NCMH.)

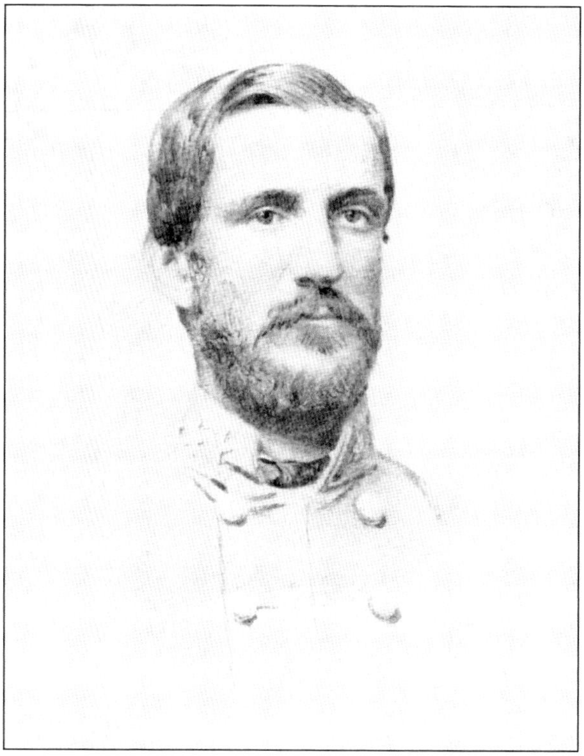

Confederate general Robert F. Hoke (pictured) was ordered by Gen. Robert E. Lee to retake the North Carolina coast. Hoke decided that retaking Plymouth was the first step and pushed vigorously for the completion of the ironclad CSS *Albemarle*. The *Albemarle* was launched on April 16, 1864. Many of its crewmen were volunteers from Hoke's command. (NCMH.)

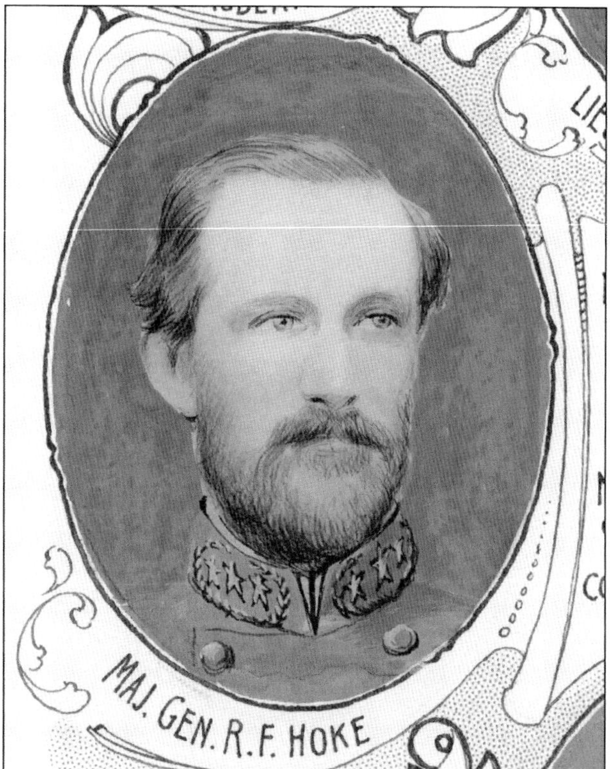

General Hoke, a native of Lincolnton, North Carolina, was considered one of General Lee's most able subordinates. As part of his plan to retake the North Carolina coast, Hoke decided to attack Plymouth first, because it was an important Union supply site and a victory there would boost Confederate morale. His plan of attack included the *Albemarle*. (NCMH.)

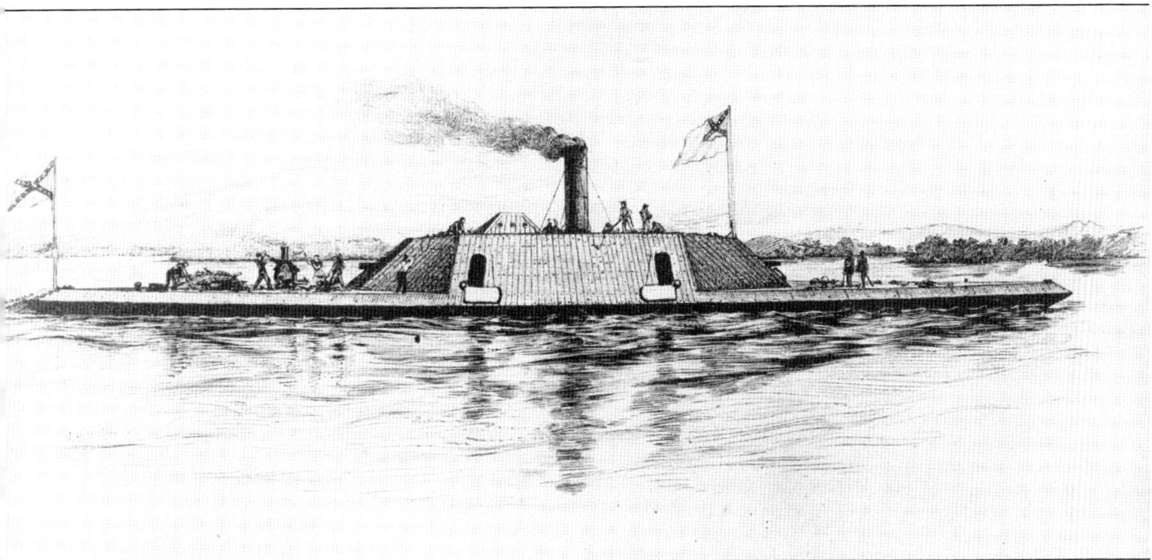

Engineers were still working on the *Albemarle* as it steamed down the Roanoke River from Halifax to Plymouth. Union commanders in Plymouth knew the Confederates were building an ironclad upriver, and they deployed barriers in an attempt to block the *Albemarle* as it steamed downriver. But the ironclad avoided the traps and continued its journey to Plymouth. (NCMH.)

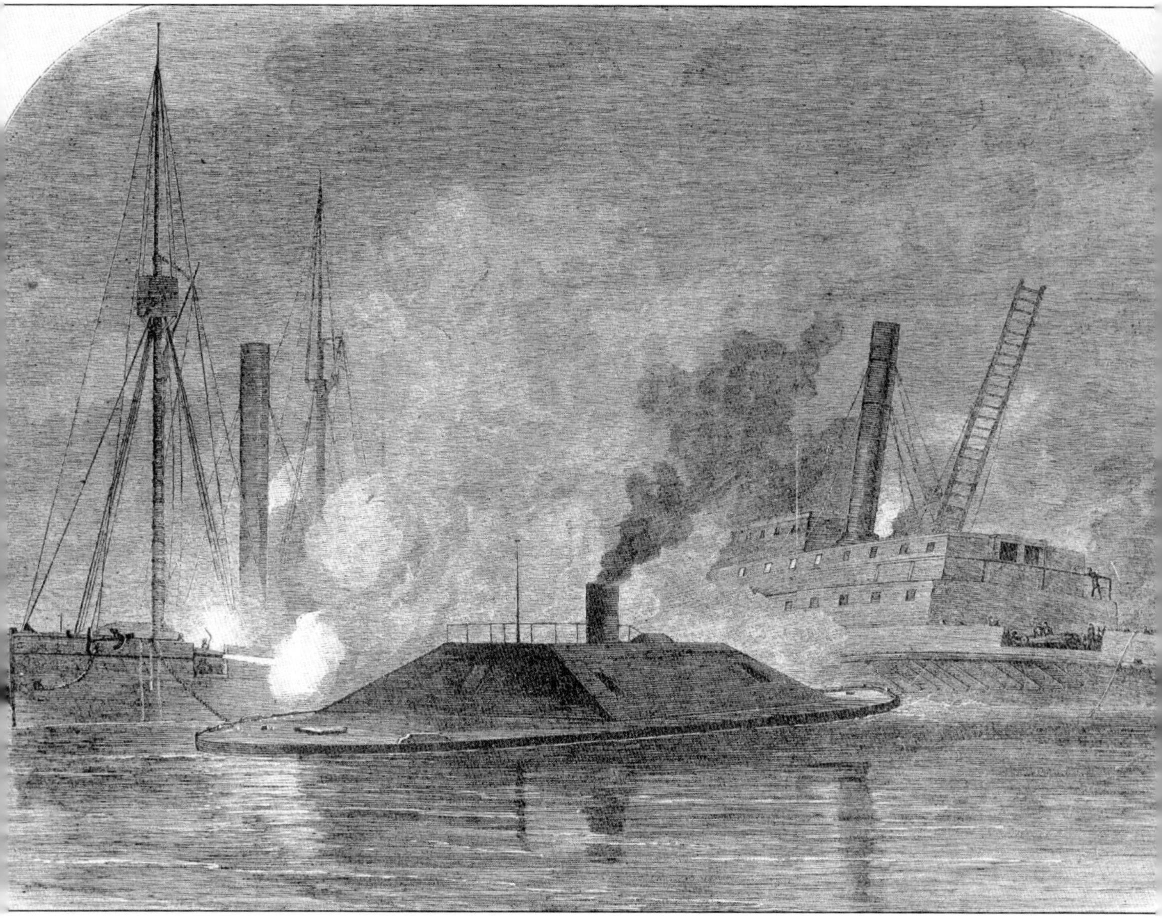

The CSS *Albemarle* reached Plymouth at dawn on April 18, 1864. This engraving shows the *Albemarle* ramming the USS *Southfield* while the USS *Miami* fires at the ironclad. But the *Miami*'s shell rebounded onto the Union ship and exploded, killing its commander. The *Southfield* sank, and the remaining Union ships fled down the Roanoke. Without naval support, Union forces surrendered on April 20. (SANC.)

The 16th Connecticut Volunteer Infantry was among the Union units that surrendered to General Hoke on April 20, 1864. Losing a regimental battle flag was considered disgraceful, so Lt. Col. John H. Burnham (pictured) ordered his unit's flags destroyed rather than allowing them to fall into enemy hands. Burnham gave pieces of the flags to his men. (PPCWM.)

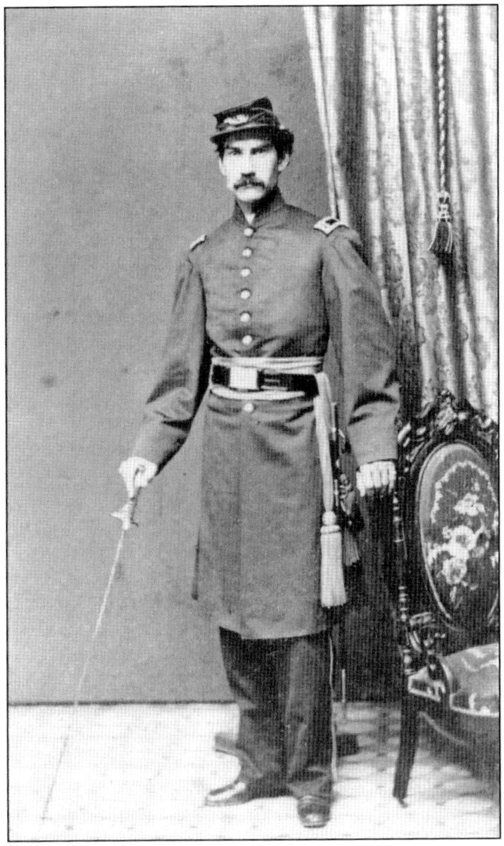

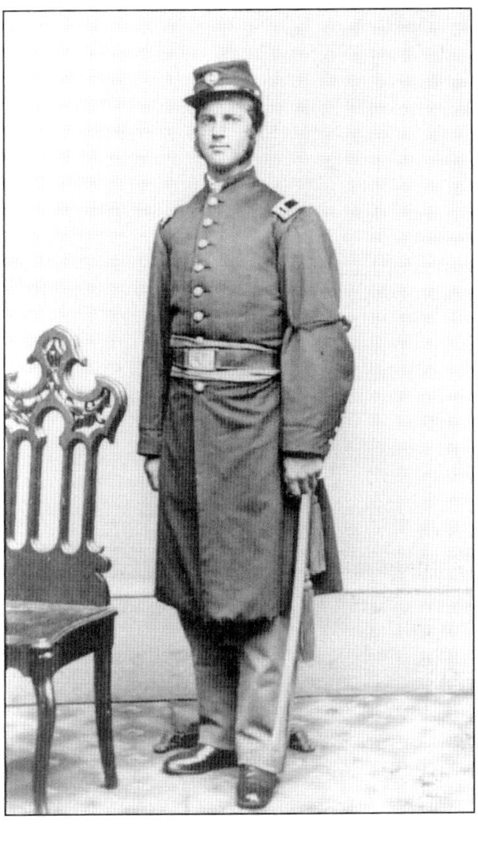

Adjutant John B. Clapp of the 16th Connecticut Volunteer Infantry received a piece of the regiment's flag before the unit surrendered at the Battle of Plymouth in April 1864. When the flags of Connecticut's Civil War units were moved in 1879, Clapp refused to return his piece of the 16th's flag, saying he did not want it to end up in a basement somewhere. (PPCWM.)

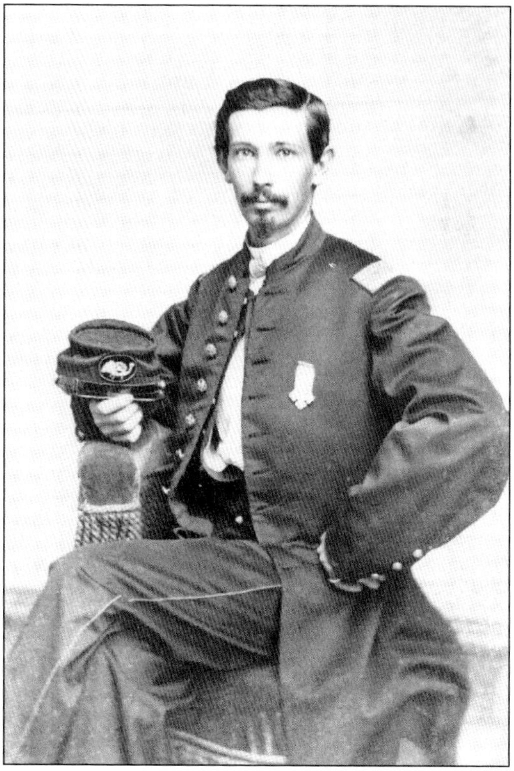

Also of the 16th Connecticut Volunteer Infantry, 2nd Lt. Bernard Blakeslee fought at the Battles of Antietam and Fredericksburg before being captured in April 1864 at the Battle of Plymouth. He was sent to Confederate prisoner of war (POW) camps in Georgia, South Carolina, and North Carolina. Blakeley, who was from Hartford, Connecticut, wrote his unit's regimental history in 1875. (PPCWM.)

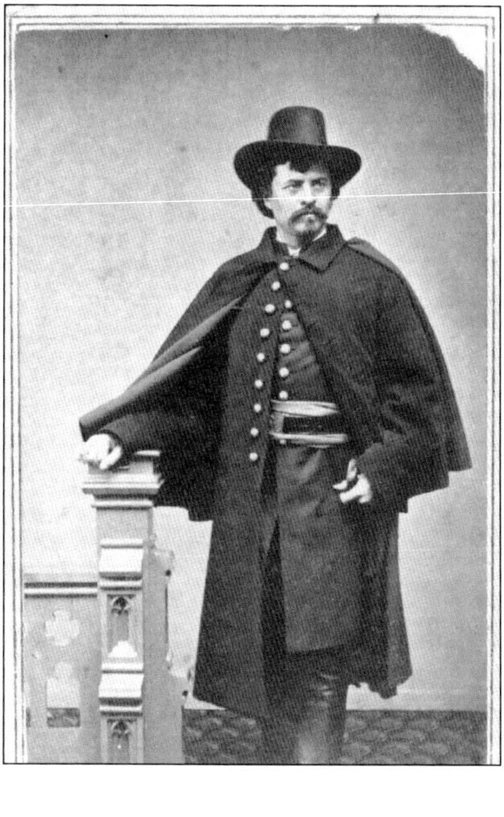

Capt. Thomas F. Burke of the 16th Connecticut Volunteer Infantry saw action at the Battles of Fredericksburg and Antietam. He was wounded in the shoulder at the Battle of Plymouth in April 1864, then taken prisoner. Eventually, he was sent to a POW camp in Columbia, South Carolina. He escaped from that camp in November 1864. (PPCWM.)

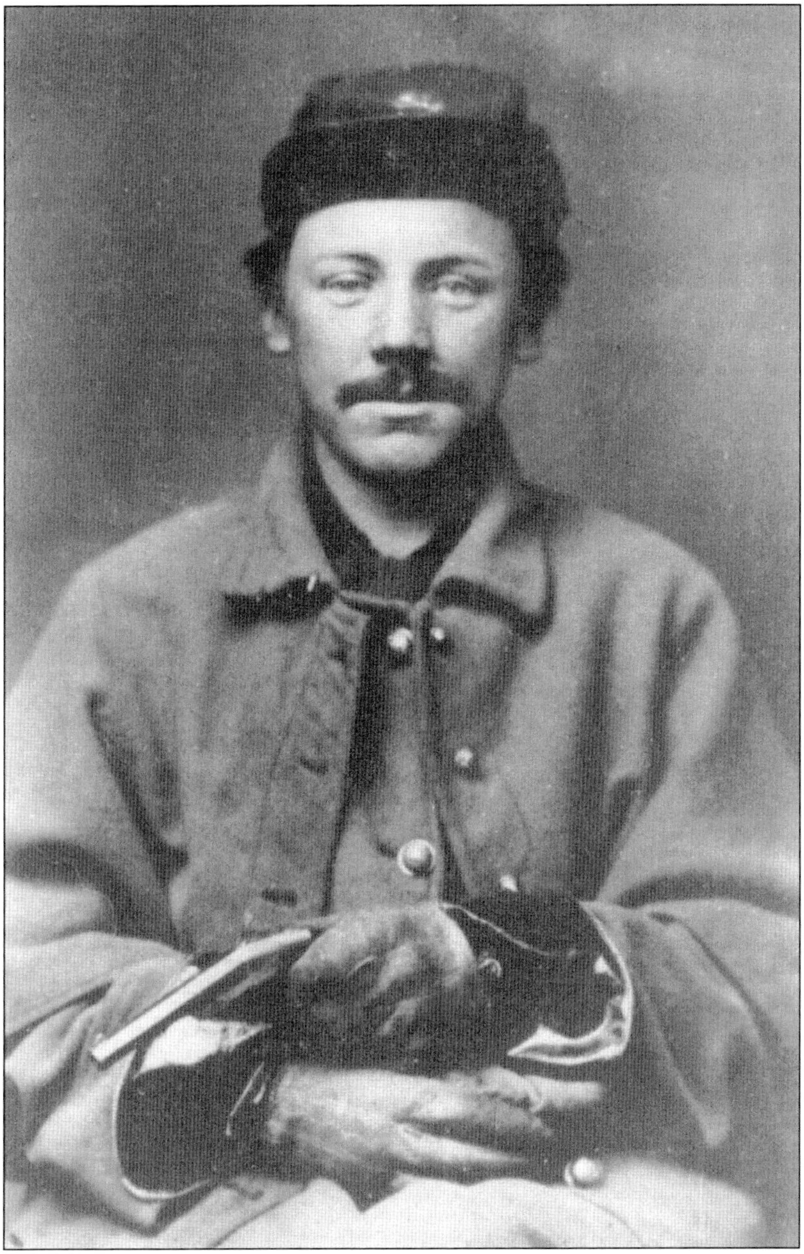

Pvt. Jared Jewel Upham of the 85th New York Infantry was taken prisoner during the Battle of Plymouth in April 1864. This photograph, taken by a commercial photographer before his capture, shows him wearing a newly issued winter uniform with gloves. The small-caliber pistol Upham is holding is not the type issued by the Union Army. It may have been a prop provided by the photographer. After the Battle of Plymouth, Upham was sent to the Confederate POW camp at Andersonville, Georgia. Although conditions at Andersonville were notoriously bad, Upham apparently survived. His descendants have found payroll records and other documents from his service, and those records show he was released from Andersonville. But he never returned to his home in Allegheny County, New York, a rural county on the border with Pennsylvania. His descendants assume he died trying to return home. (Ralph Compton.)

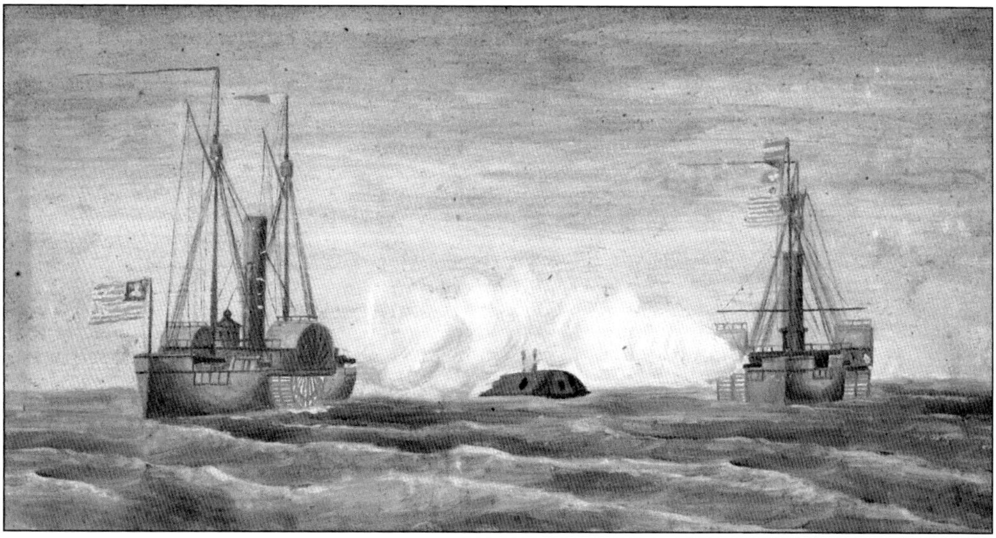

This painting shows Union warships attacking the CSS *Albemarle* in the Albemarle Sound on May 5, 1864. General Hoke had hoped to have the *Albemarle* steam from Plymouth to New Bern to help him drive Union forces out of that town as part of his plan to retake the North Carolina coast from Union forces. (NCMH.)

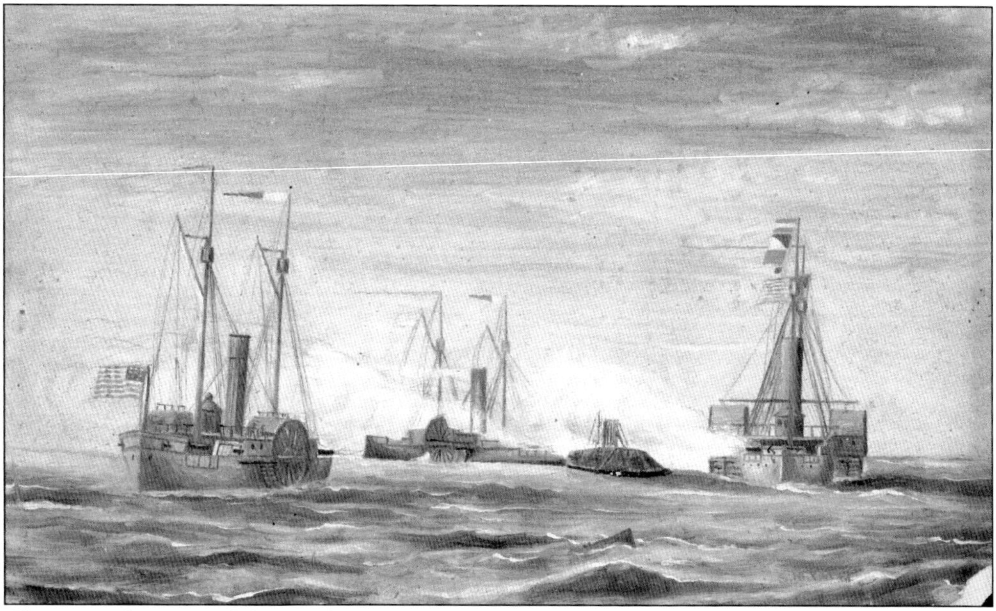

This is another view of the naval action in the Albemarle Sound on May 5, 1864. Union warships could not sink the *Albemarle* but still prevented the ironclad from taking part in General Hoke's effort to retake New Bern. Hoke still might have recaptured New Bern without the ironclad, but General Lee had ordered him to Petersburg, Virginia. (NCMH.)

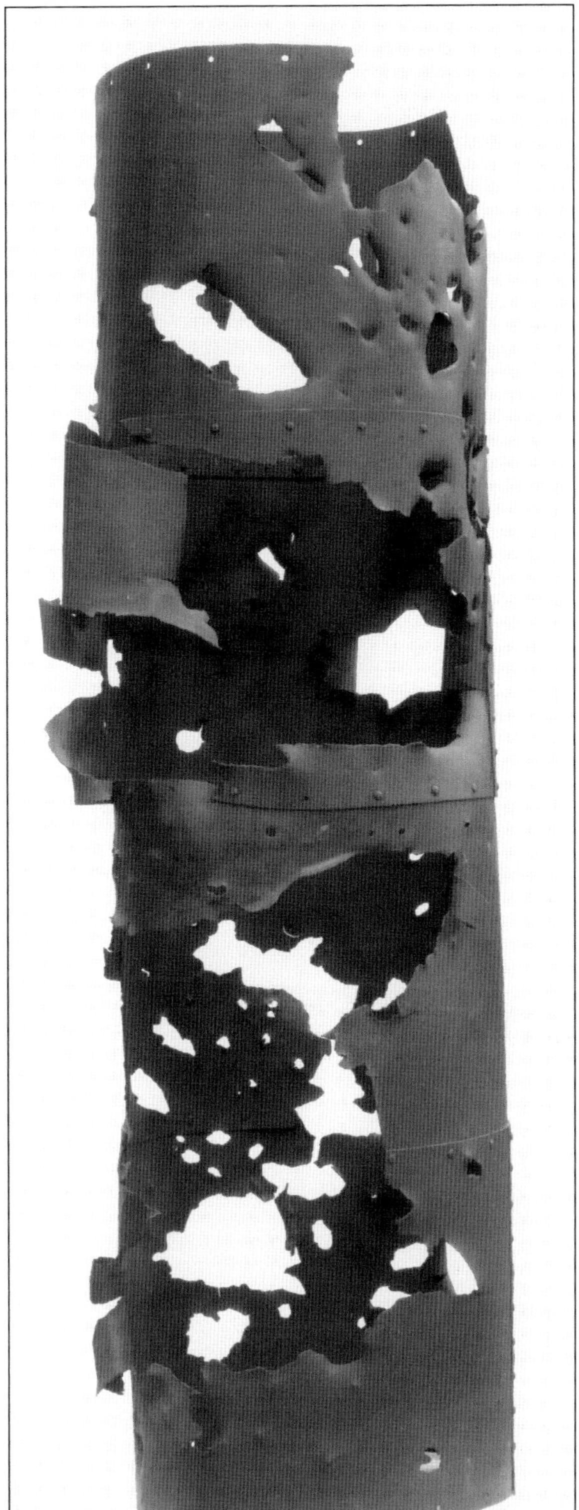

Union gunboats had so riddled the CSS *Albemarle*'s smokestack (pictured) that the fires providing the steam to power the vessel nearly went out. Had that happened, Union sailors likely would have boarded the Confederate vessel and captured her. Confederate captain James Cooke ordered that bacon, butter, and fat be thrown onto the *Albemarle*'s fires to keep them burning. He returned to Plymouth, unable to sail to New Bern. (NCMH.)

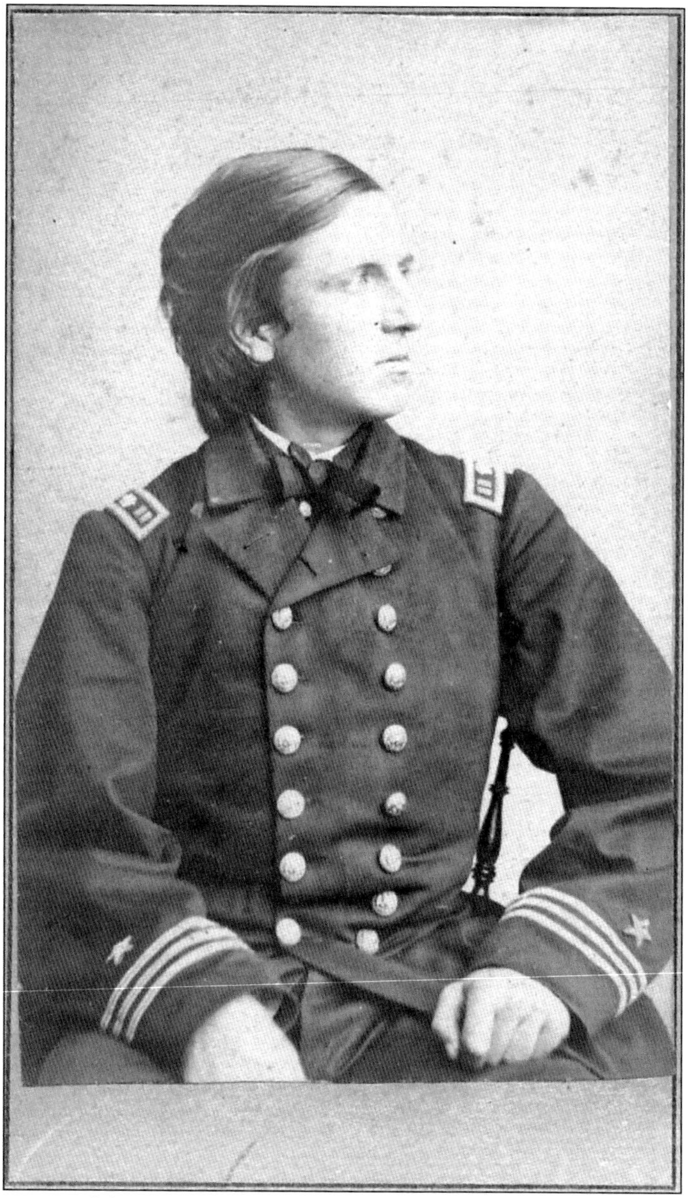

Although Union naval forces in the Albemarle Sound prevented the CSS *Albemarle* from leaving Plymouth, the ironclad's presence kept Plymouth in Confederate hands. Union naval commanders decided that the *Albemarle* must be destroyed. US Navy lieutenant William Cushing was assigned the daunting task of eliminating the Confederate warship. Cushing's naval career had been checkered. Fond of practical jokes and less fond of studying, he was expelled from the US Naval Academy for a series of infractions in early 1861. But when war came, he entered the Navy and, eventually, was entrusted with the command of ships. On October 27, 1864, Cushing led a daring raid to sink the *Albemarle*. Commanding a small steam-powered launch, Cushing put a high-explosive torpedo beneath the *Albemarle* and detonated it, sinking the ironclad in shallow water near the Plymouth waterfront. Although his launch was sunk, Cushing miraculously escaped and, with the aid of a friendly slave in Plymouth, made his way downriver to the safety of the Union flotilla in the Albemarle Sound. (Tom Harrison.)

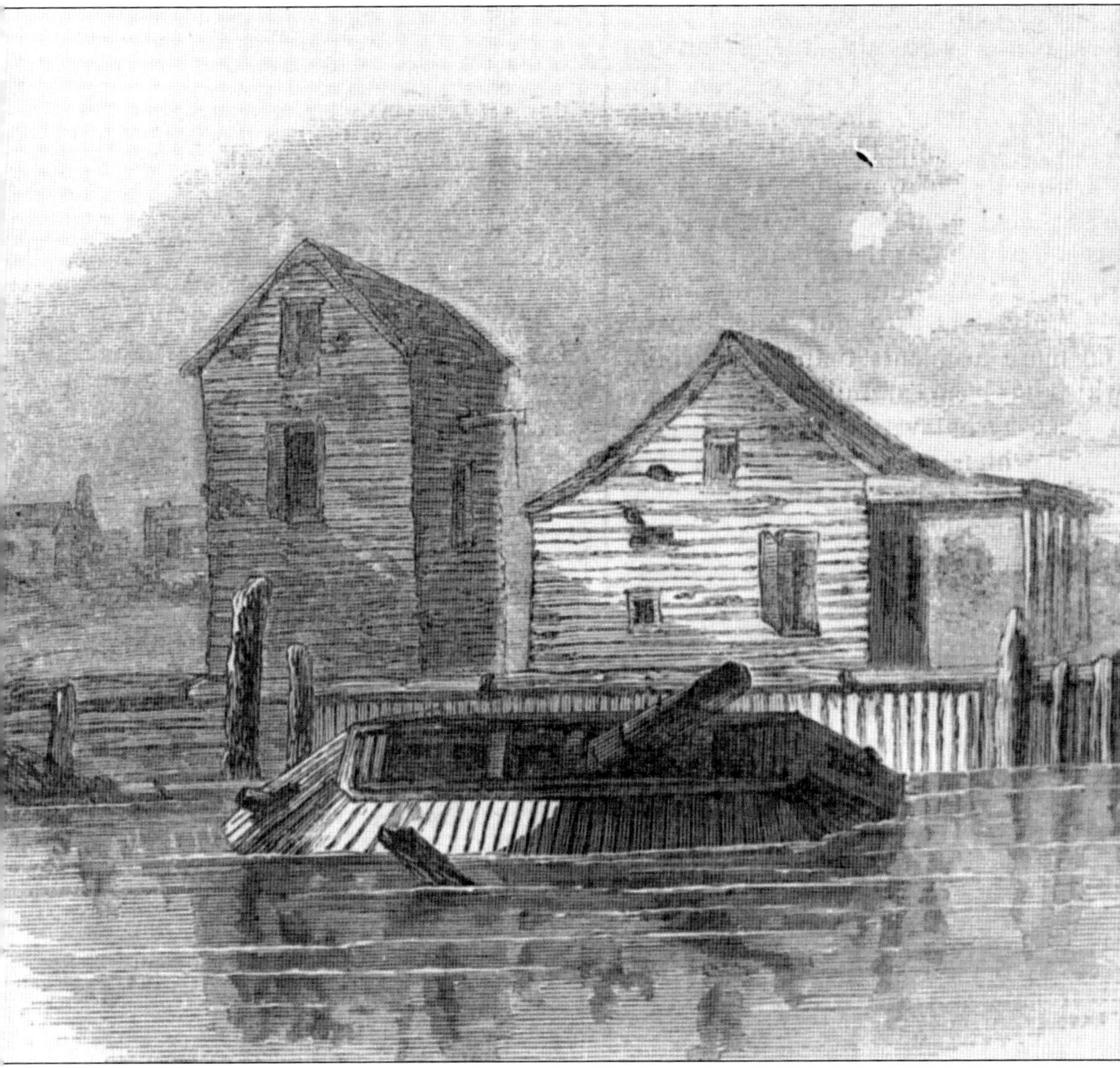

The sinking of the CSS *Albemarle*, in a raid led by Lieutenant Cushing on October 27, 1864, made newspaper headlines across the United States and Confederacy and as far away as Europe. This drawing shows the *Albemarle* lying in shallow water in the Roanoke River, near the Plymouth waterfront. (SANC.)

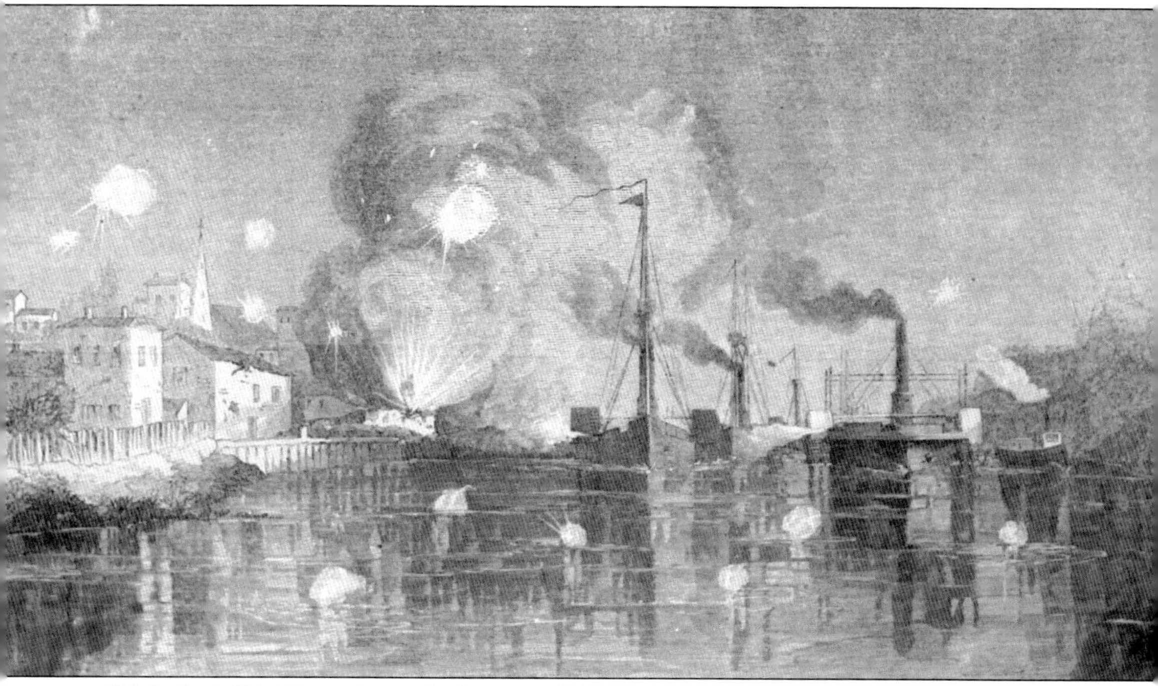

With the CSS *Albemarle* on the bottom of the Roanoke River, Union warships steamed into Plymouth and shelled Confederate forces on October 31, 1864. The church spire rising above the other buildings at left is Grace Episcopal Church, still in use today. To the right of the church, a Confederate powder magazine is exploding, which would cause several fires in the town. (SANC.)

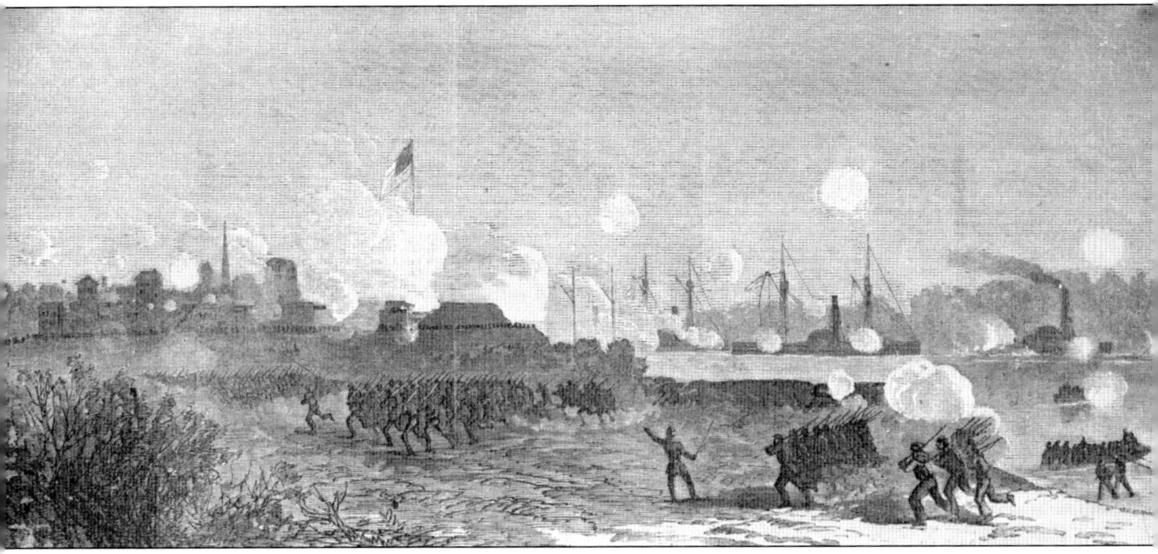

The terrific explosion of a Confederate store of powder and ammunition near the Plymouth waterfront allowed Union troops to land and drive Confederate forces out of town. Around 12:30 p.m. on October 31, 1864, Union forces raised the US flag over Plymouth, and the town was again a Union stronghold. It remained in Union hands for the rest of the war. (SANC.)

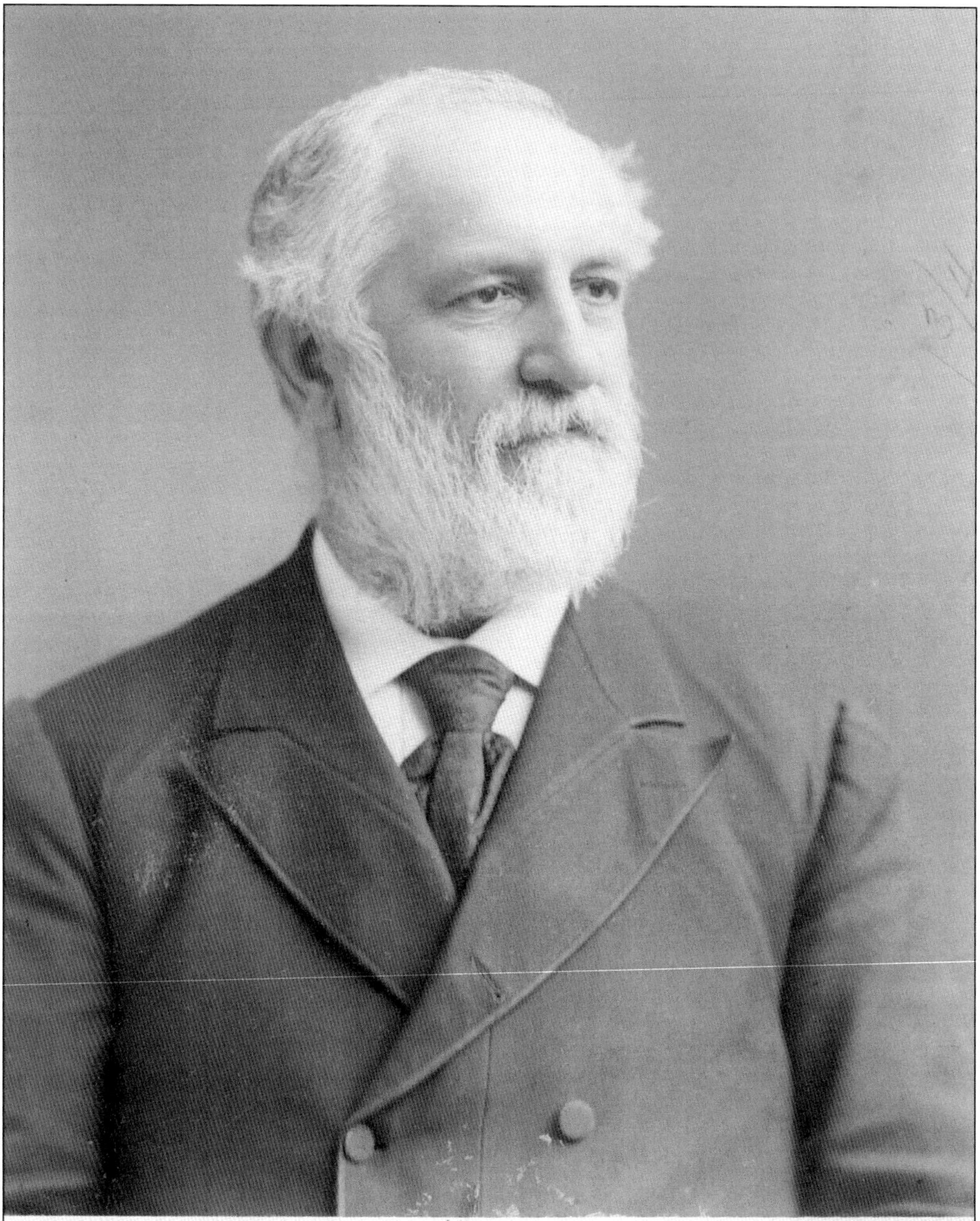

After the Civil War, Robert F. Hoke, who had led Confederate troops to victory at the Battle of Plymouth, married a woman from New York City and entered business in North Carolina. Hoke was a very private man who did not like the limelight. But during his travels through the South, he was frequently mistaken for the revered former Confederate general Robert E. Lee. (NCMH.)

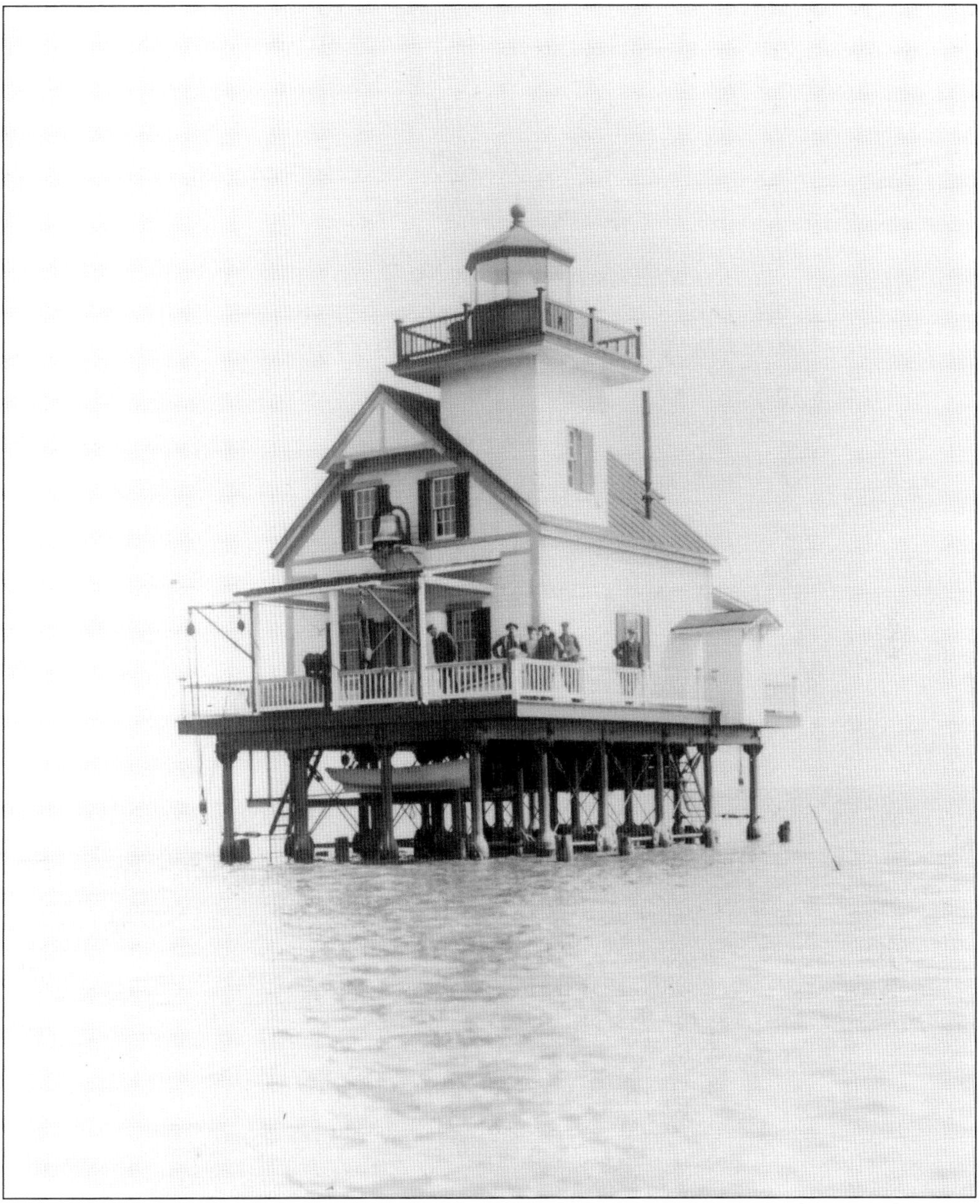

After the Civil War, federal officials wanted to restart maritime commerce on the Roanoke River and the Albemarle Sound. The lightship that had aided mariners before the war was gone. So a new lighthouse was built in the sound at the mouth of the Roanoke. The new light was completed in December 1866. Thomas Clifton, who had served as an assistant aboard the old lightship, was appointed keeper. Plymouth was designated a port of entry for northeastern North Carolina. On March 21, 1885, the Roanoke River Lighthouse was destroyed by fire. Wanting to replace the light as quickly as possible, federal officials decided to replace it with a lighthouse intended for another location. The new lighthouse was lit in August 1885. But in January 1886, during an exceptionally cold winter, ice damaged the supports of the lighthouse and caused it to collapse after only five months of service. On February 12, 1887, the third Roanoke River Lighthouse went into service. That lighthouse is shown in this photograph, taken in 1914. (OBXHC.)

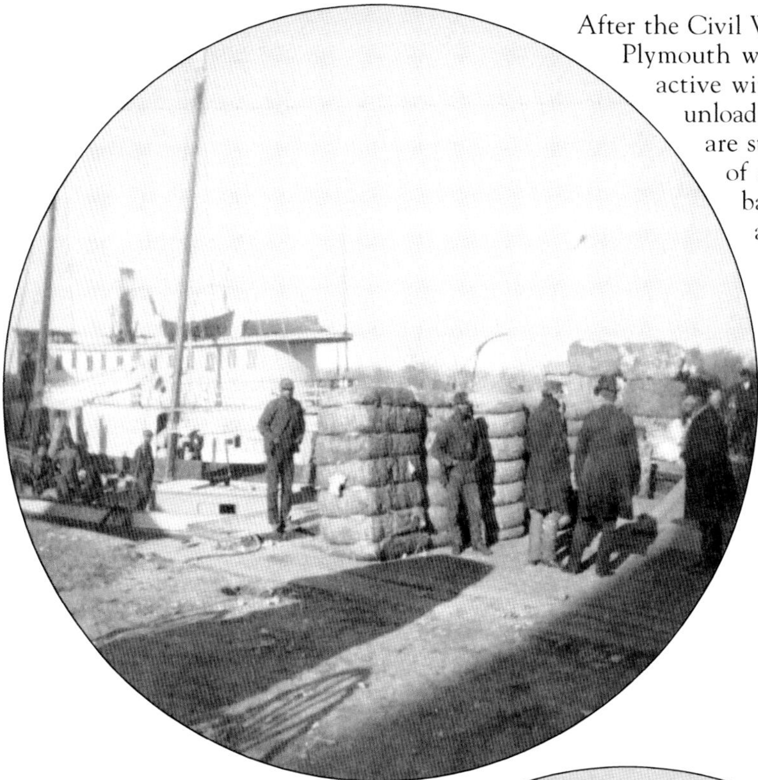

After the Civil War, the docks on the Plymouth waterfront again were active with boats loading and unloading freight. Here, men are standing next to bales of cotton, while in the background to the left, a steamboat is docked. The round frame of the photograph indicates that it was taken with an early Kodak camera, introduced in 1888. (NCMH.)

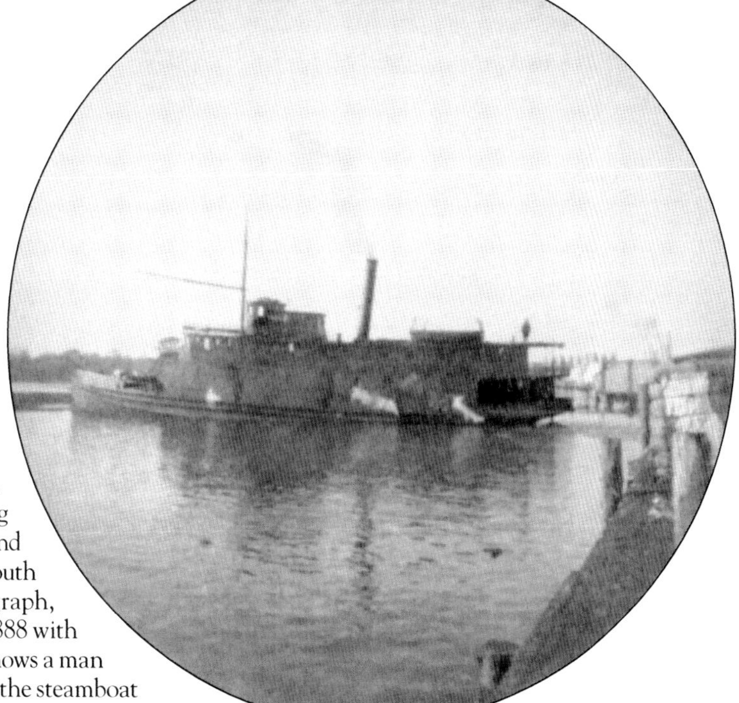

In the late 19th and early 20th centuries, traveling by water was the preferred and easiest way to get from place to place in northeastern North Carolina. Steamboats and sailing schooners hauled freight and passengers from the Plymouth waterfront. This photograph, taken sometime around 1888 with an early Kodak camera, shows a man standing near the stern of the steamboat *Plymouth*. (NCMH.)

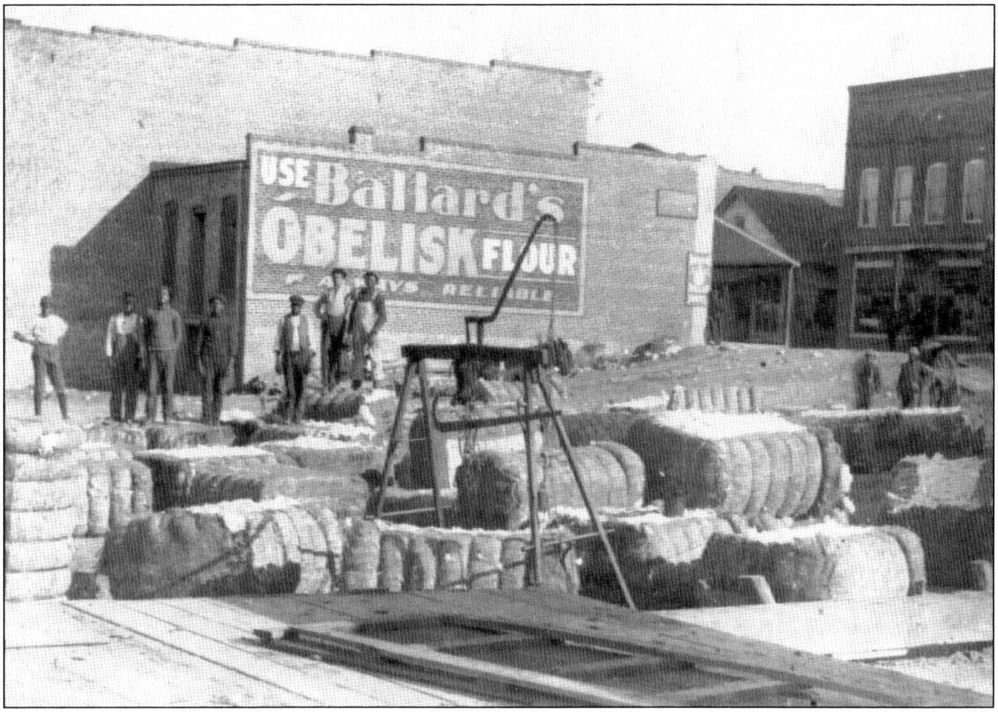

Another view of the Plymouth waterfront, probably taken in the late 19th century, shows men standing near the docks, with bales of cotton in the foreground. The Ballard's Obelisk Flour advertisement on the building indicates the approximate date of the photograph, as the Ballard and Ballard Flour Mills were founded in Louisville, Kentucky, in 1880. (NCMH.)

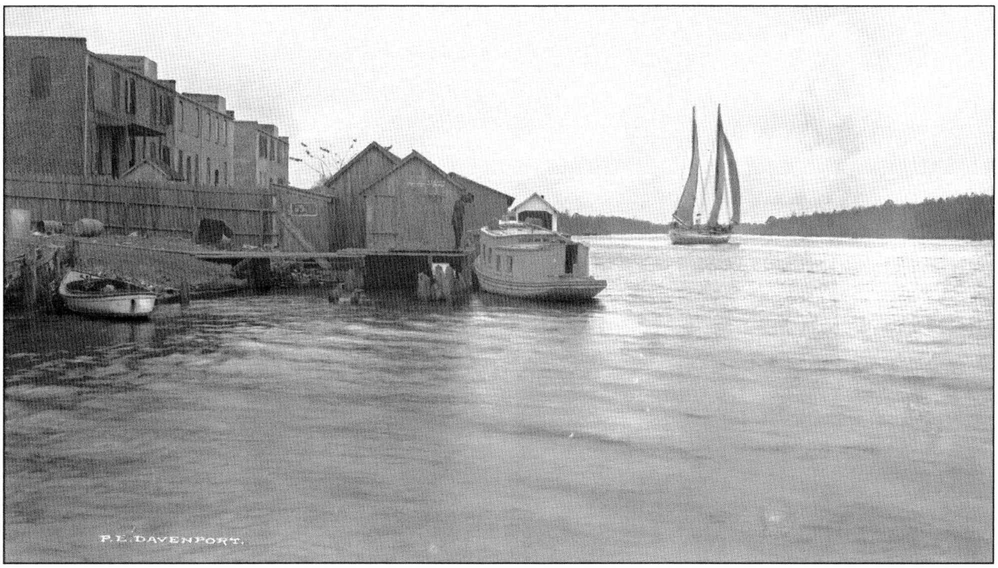

Wind-powered ships were still common in the late 19th and early 20th centuries. In this photograph, a man standing on a dock along the Plymouth waterfront watches a two-masted schooner leaving the port. The advertising signs on the sides of buildings for Sloan's Liniment and Reynold's Sun Cured Tobacco indicate that this photograph is from the early 20th century, perhaps around 1905. (NCC.)

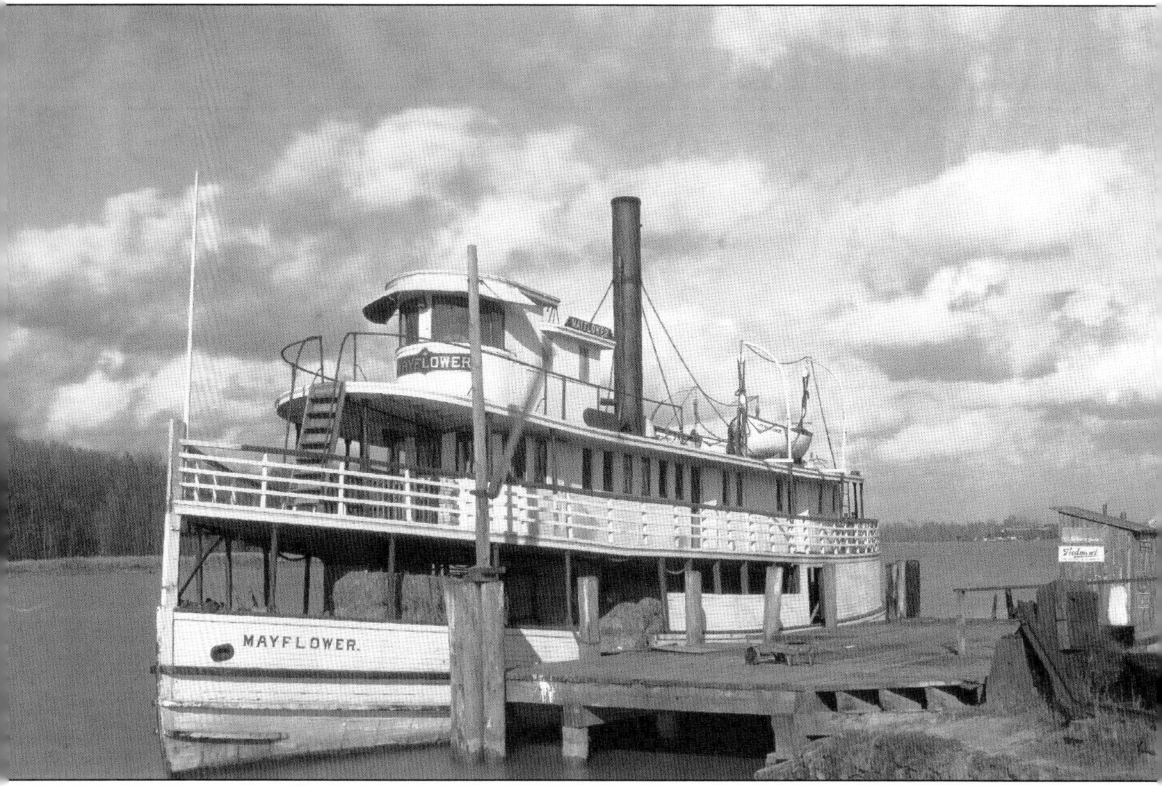

The steamer *Mayflower* was a familiar sight on the Plymouth waterfront in the late 19th and early 20th centuries. On June 30, 1899, the *Mayflower* left Plymouth for its regular run to Windsor. The steamer was hauling plaster and hay bales and carried seven passengers and eight crewmen. About five miles upriver from Plymouth, the captain turned the *Mayflower* into a narrow, twisting creek known as the Thoroughfare. The creek snaked through a mile or so of cypress swamp and connected the Roanoke and the Cashie Rivers. Something happened on the second turn. The top-heavy steamboat suddenly rolled over and sank in 20 feet of water. One passenger—an infant—drowned. The *Mayflower* probably overturned because the plaster in its hold shifted during the turn. The steamer was raised, towed to Edenton, and was back in service on July 21. The captain, H. Davenport, took longer to recover, however. The *Roanoke Beacon* reported on July 7 that Davenport had gone to Norfolk for "medical treatment" and then would spend time in the Virginia mountains. (NCC.)

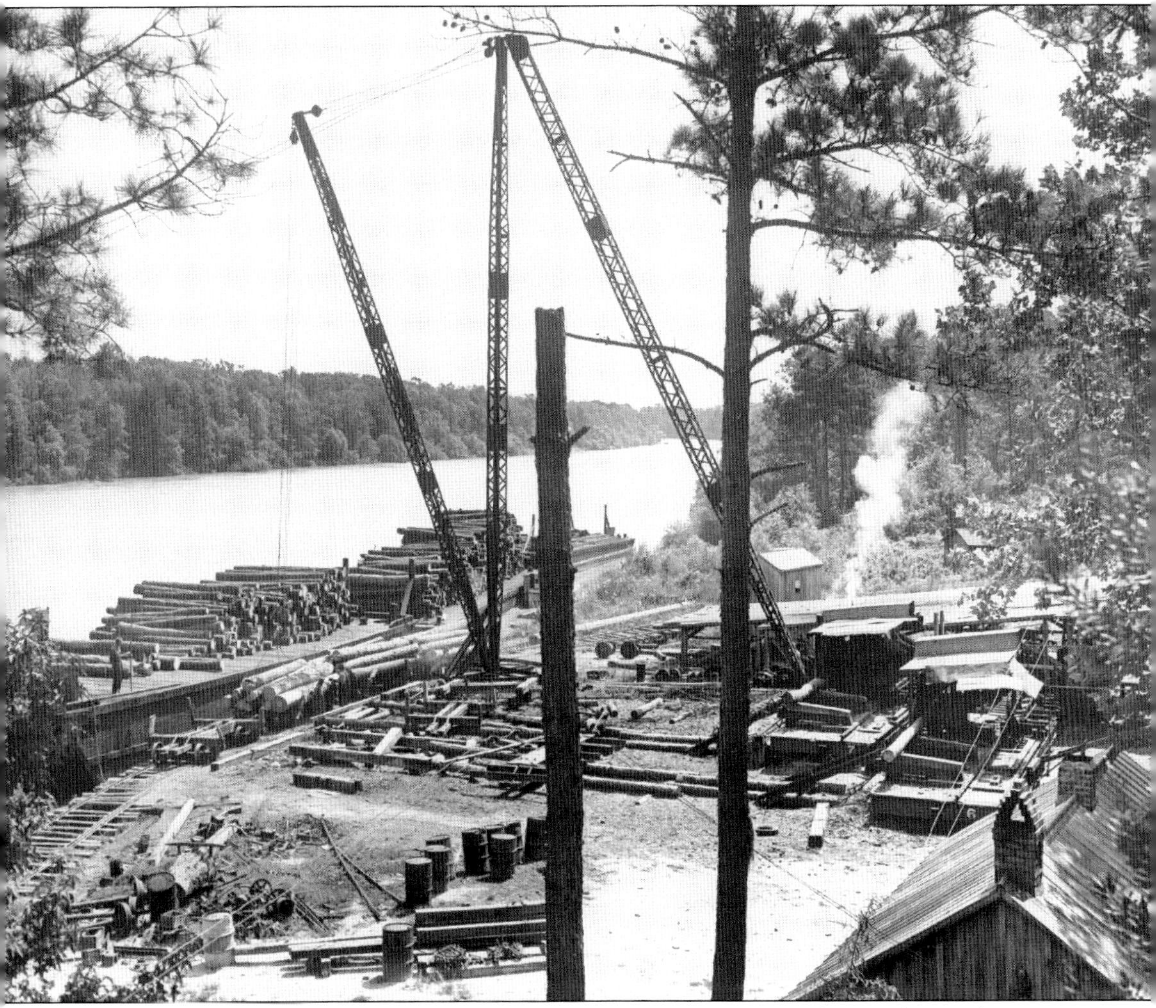

Logging had been an important part of Washington County's economy before the Civil War, but after the war, large-scale mechanized logging began on the Roanoke River. This photograph, taken around 1950, shows a logging operation that included a narrow-gauge railroad to haul logs to barges. A small gasoline-powered locomotive pulled the cars hauling the logs. (SANC.)

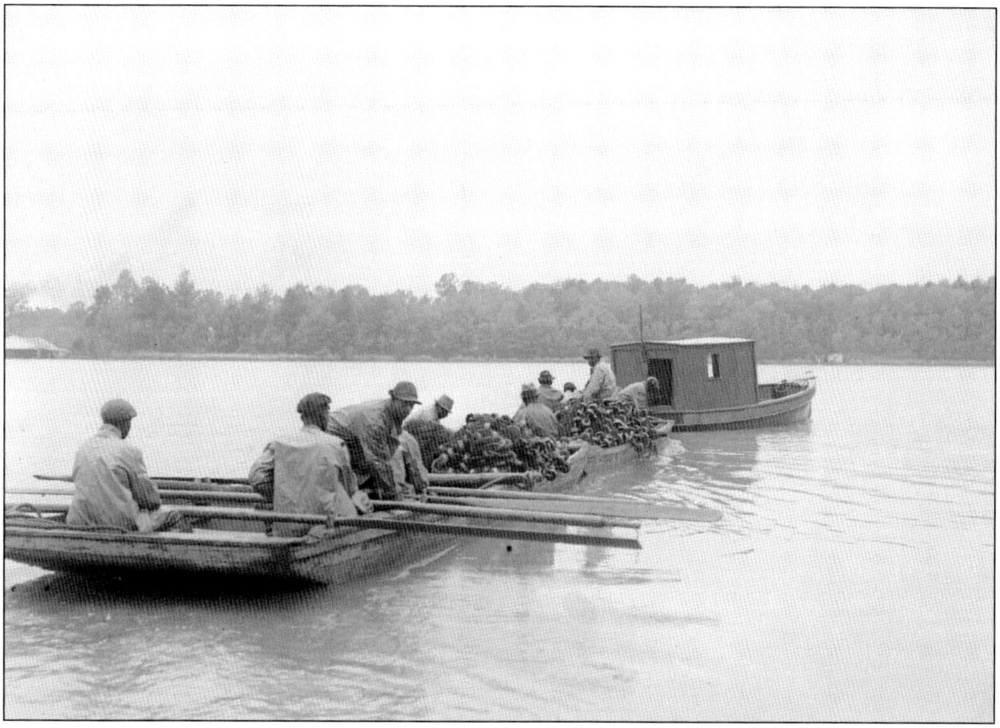

In the mid-19th century, many large seine-fishing concerns operated from the banks of the Roanoke River and the Albemarle Sound. But a century later, only a few of these operations remained. In 1939, the North Carolina Department of Conservation and Development sent a photographer to document seine fishermen on the Roanoke. This photograph shows the fishermen about to deploy their net. (SANC.)

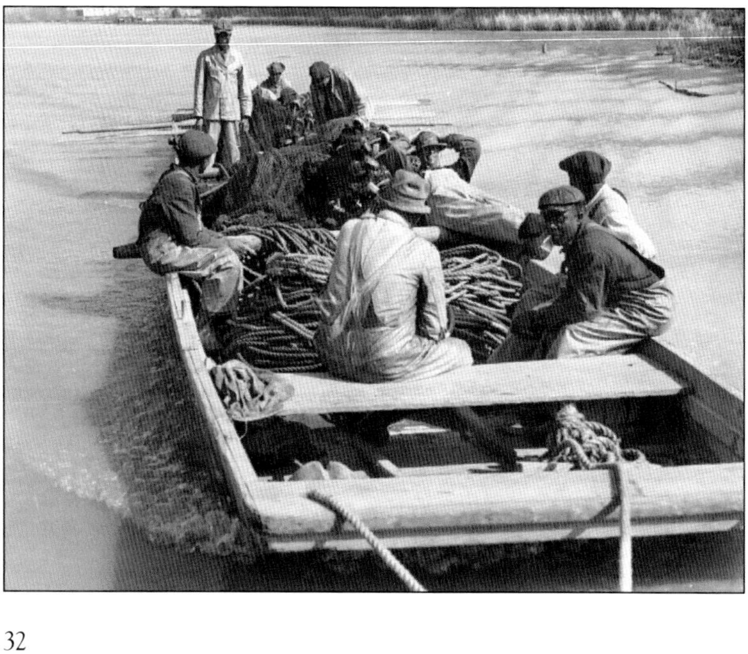

Safety regulations were minimal or nonexistent when this photograph was taken in 1939. Note that the fishermen in these barges are not wearing life jackets. Commercial fishing on the Roanoke River was dangerous work because of the Roanoke's powerful current. If a man fell overboard, the river's current could keep him underwater and drown him. (SANC.)

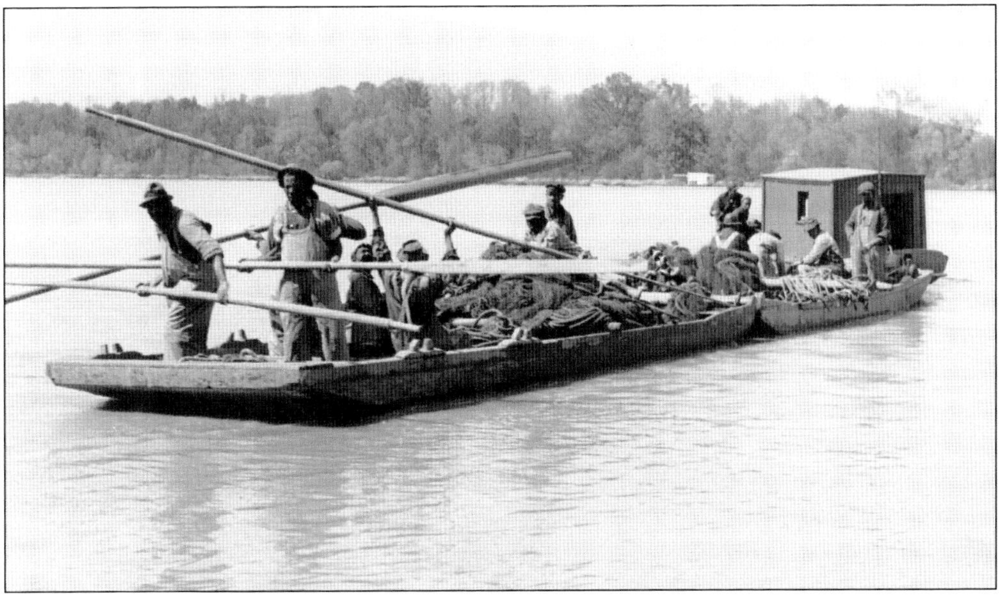

The huge nets used for seine fishing were loaded onto barges and towed out on the river. In this photograph, the barges are about to be detached from the towboat, visible at far right. The fishermen are preparing to use oars to maneuver the barges into position for "shooting," or deploying, the net. (SANC.)

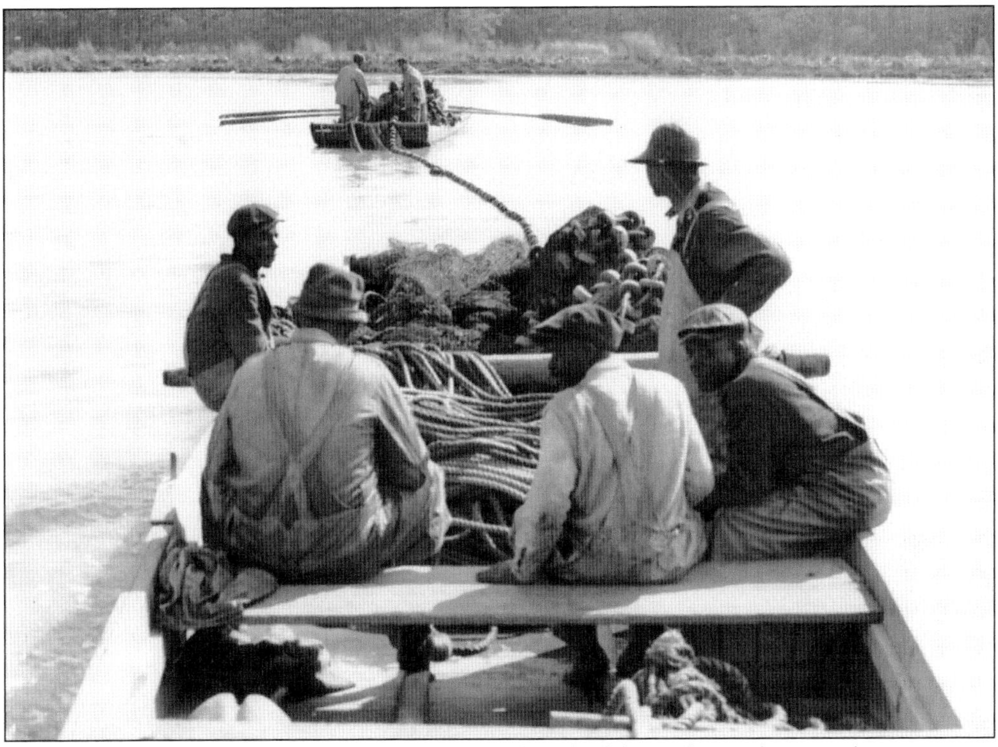

In this 1939 photograph, the barges have been detached from the towboat, and oarsmen are maneuvering the barges into place for shooting the net. Each barge usually had a crew of five men, and two or three barges were used to shoot the net. (SANC.)

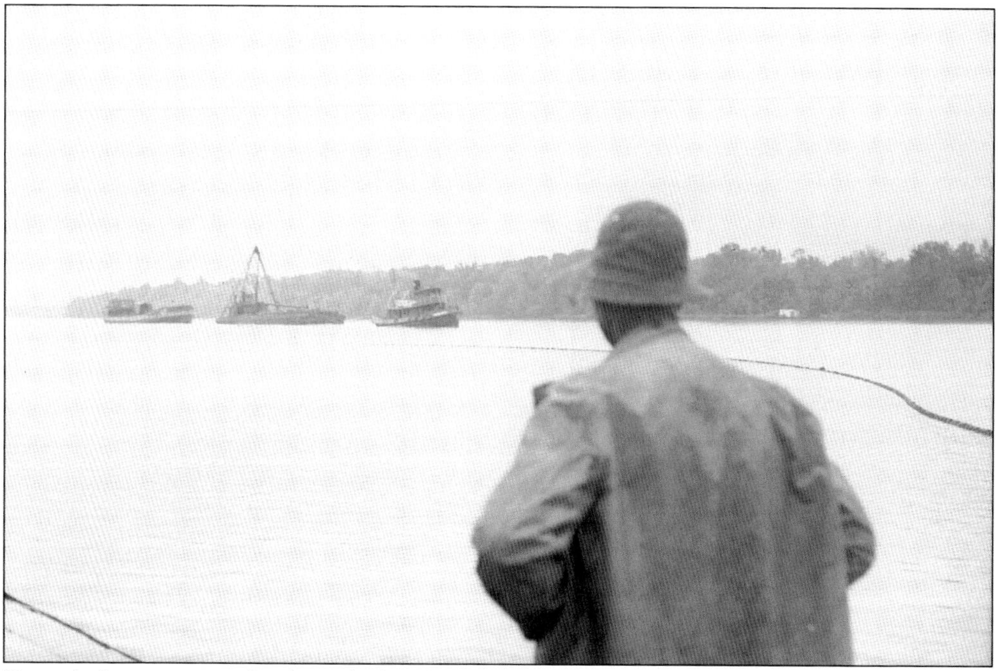

Here, the huge seine net has been deployed, and a fisherman standing on a dock watches a tugboat moving logging equipment past the net. Sometimes the nets were a half mile long. The Roanoke was at a low flood stage when this photograph was taken in 1939. (SANC.)

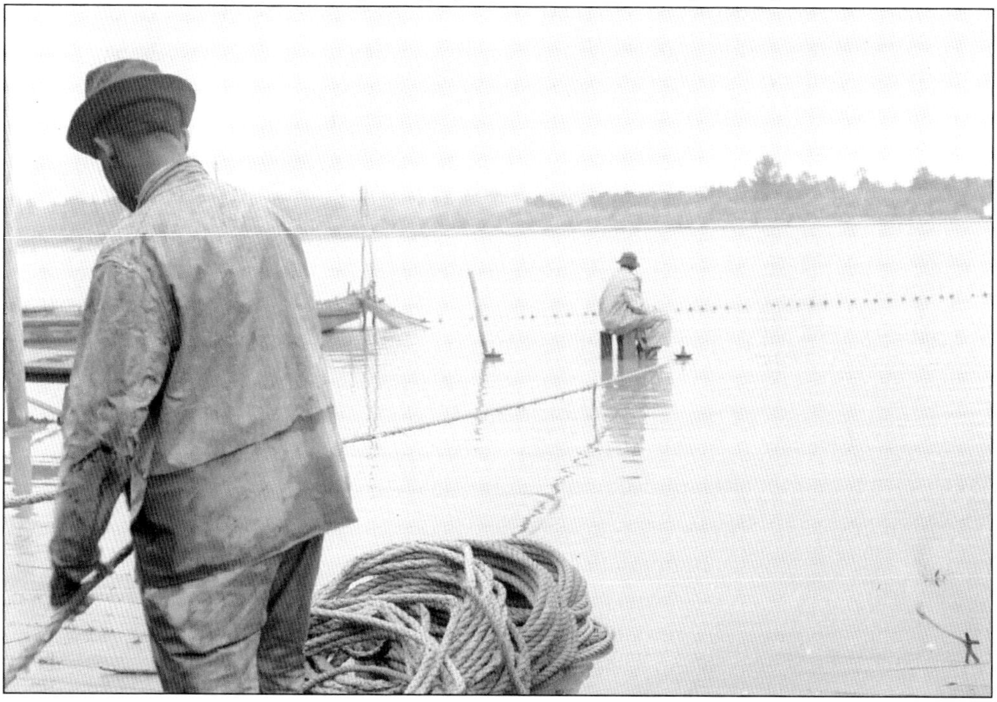

Two fishermen wait until it is time to "bunt," or retrieve, the seine net. It appears that the man on a box is sitting on top of the water; in actuality, he is perched atop a dock that has been submerged in a few inches of water, as the Roanoke River was at a low flood stage at the time. (SANC.)

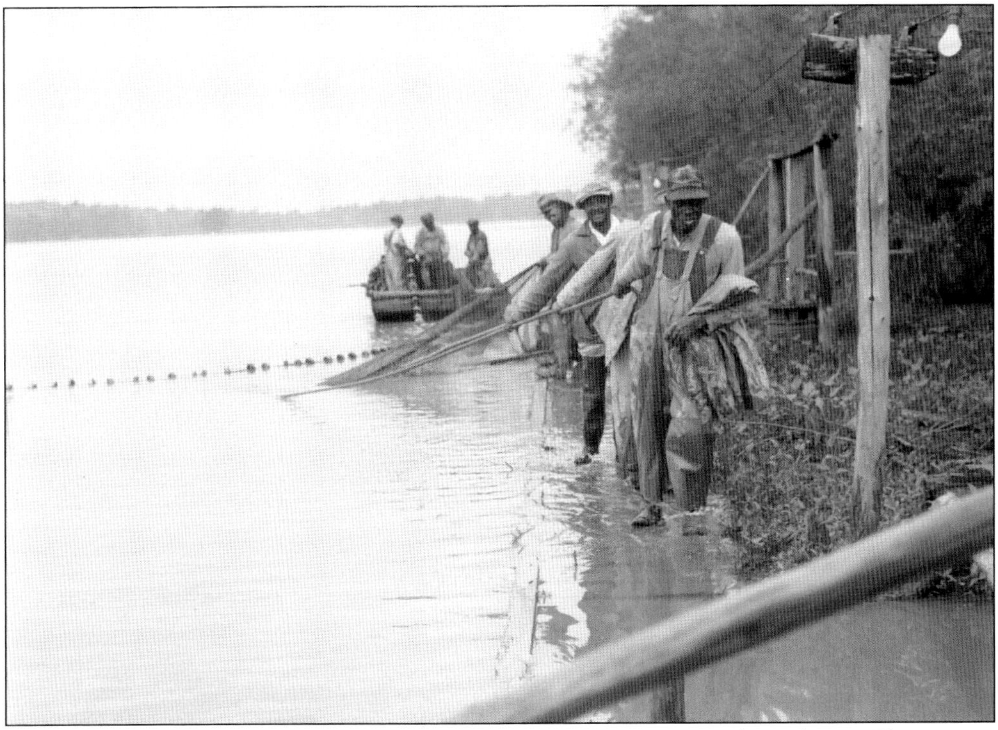

Fishermen drag the lines from the huge seine net to shore in preparation to bunt the net. The men are slogging through water on the docks due to the low flood stage of the Roanoke River. (SANC.)

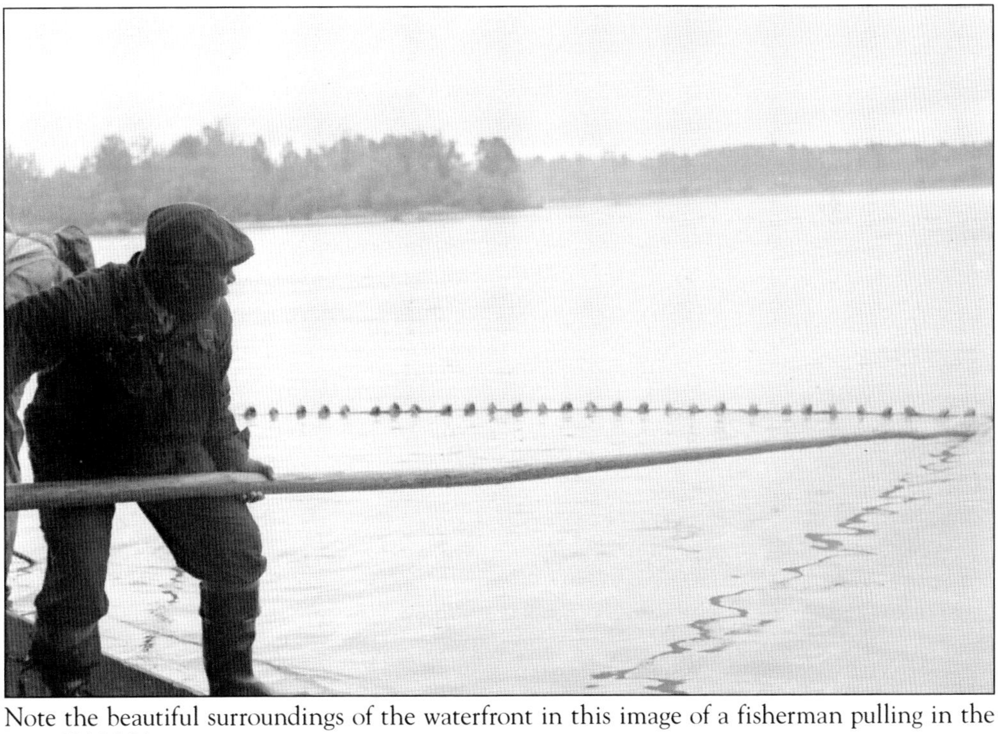

Note the beautiful surroundings of the waterfront in this image of a fisherman pulling in the nets. (SANC.)

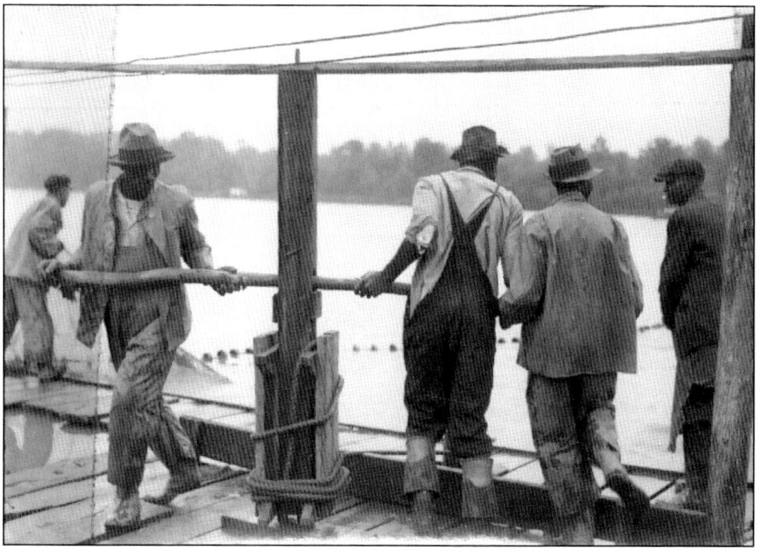

The huge seines used on the Roanoke River were very heavy. Both power tools, such as motor-powered winches, and old-fashioned hand-cranked winches, as seen here, were used to bunt the net. The men working the winch slowly pulled the net toward the dock. (SANC.)

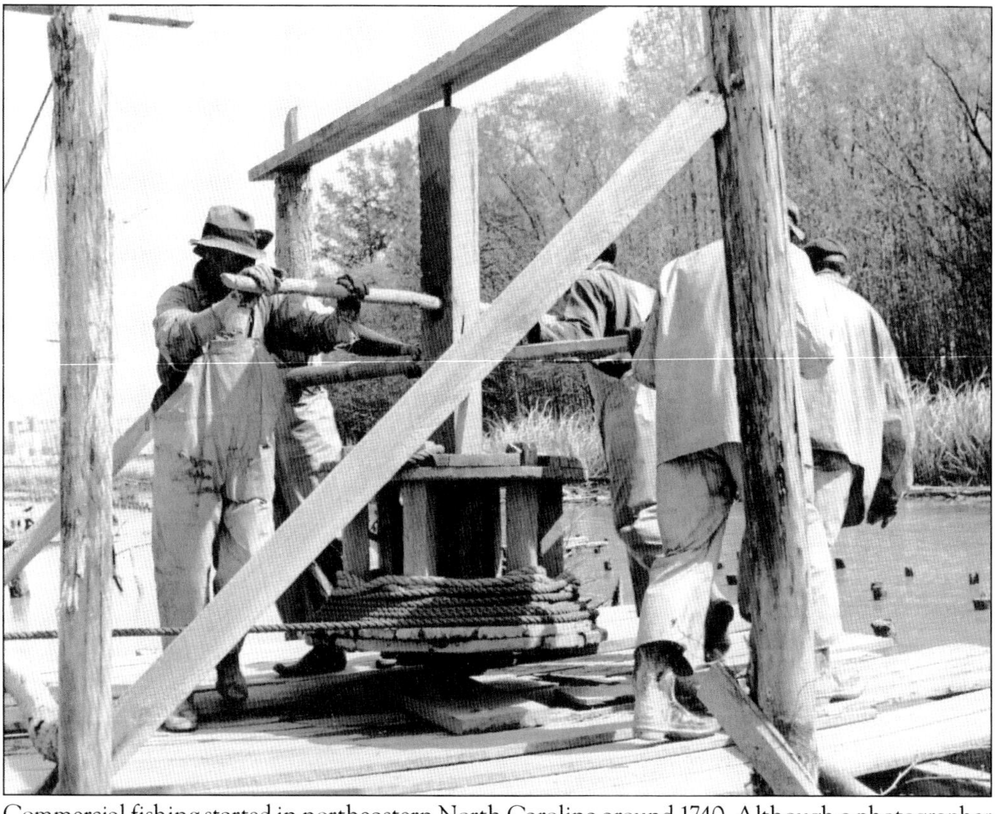

Commercial fishing started in northeastern North Carolina around 1740. Although a photographer captured this image for the North Carolina Department of Conservation and Development in 1939, it shows a tool that, for two centuries, commercial fishermen used on the Roanoke and the Albemarle Sound to retrieve their nets—a hand-cranked winch. (SANC.)

Power winches such as this also were used to retrieve the huge seine nets used for commercial fishing on the Roanoke River. When the seine nets were filled with fish, they could weigh as much as several tons. The winch pulled the net to the dock, where the catch was dumped. (SANC.)

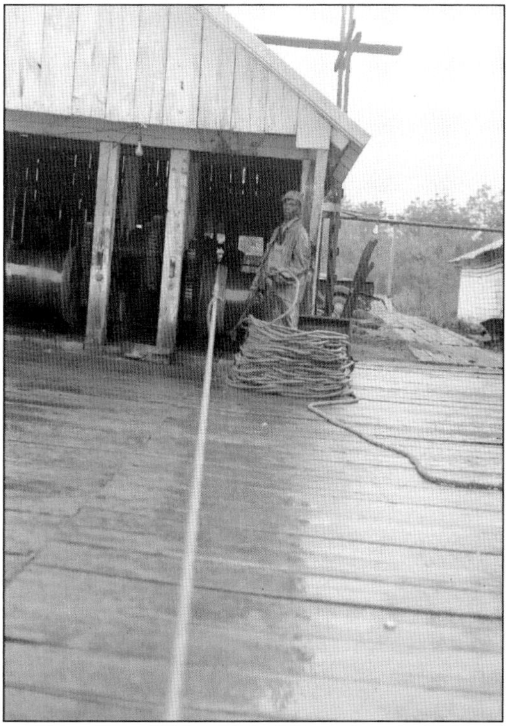

Once the winches and plain old manpower had hauled the seine net to the docks, the fishermen would dump the catch from the nets onto the dock to start processing the fish. Thousands of fish were taken each time the net was deployed. (SANC.)

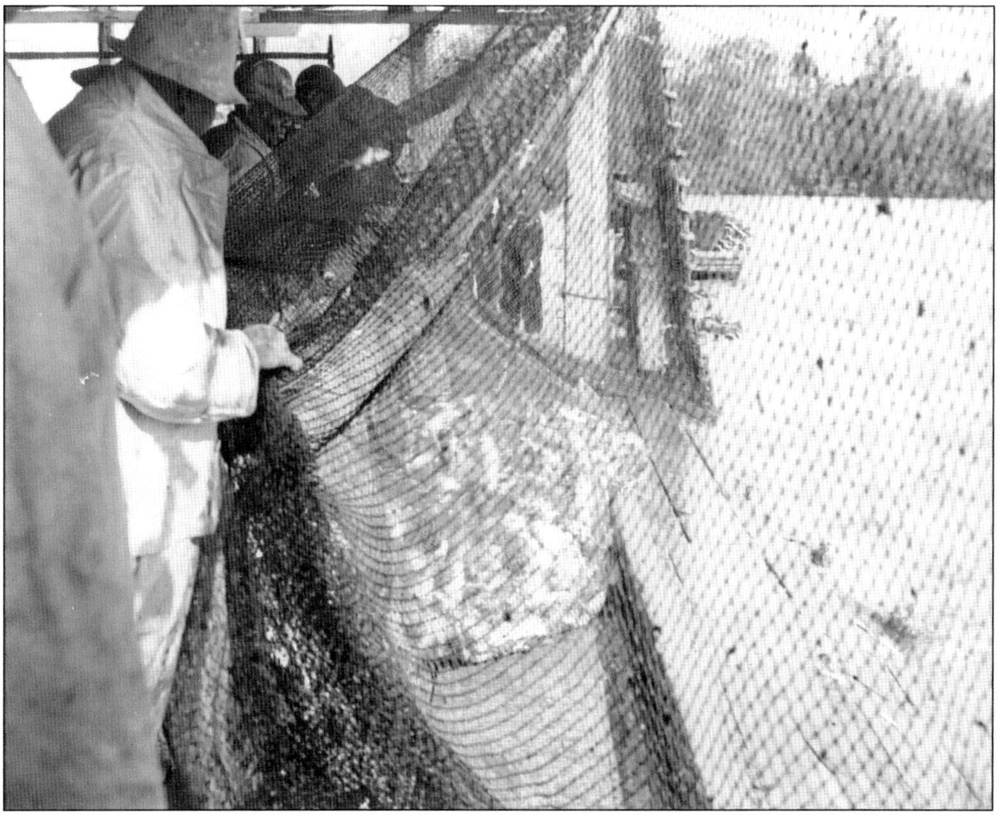

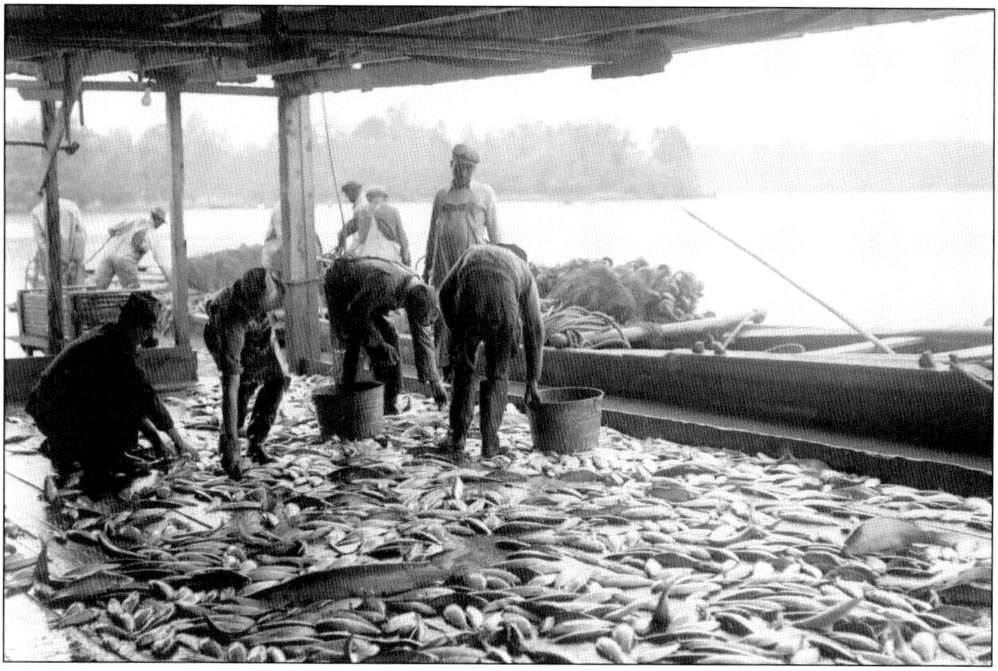

Thousands of fish were hauled onto the docks when the big seine nets were retrieved from the Roanoke River. Rock, shad, perch, and carp were mainly the fish that were taken in the nets; although, in this photograph, a large garfish can be seen in the lower-left foreground. (SANC.)

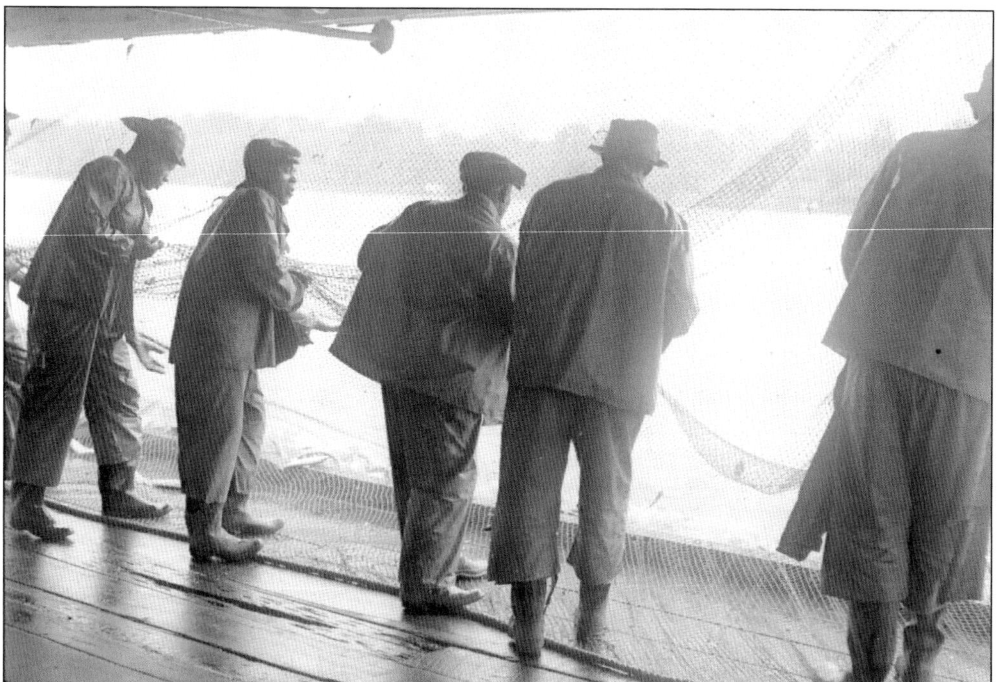

Fishermen clean and inspect the net after the catch has been dumped onto the dock. They are looking for tears or holes in the net that need to be repaired. The inspection and repairs must be done before the net can be reloaded onto the barges and deployed again. (SANC.)

Despite efforts to keep the nets away from snags, sometimes they were torn and needed mending, as seen here with one fisherman holding the net while the other repairs the tear. The mending had to be done before the net could be used again because the tear could worsen if not repaired. (SANC.)

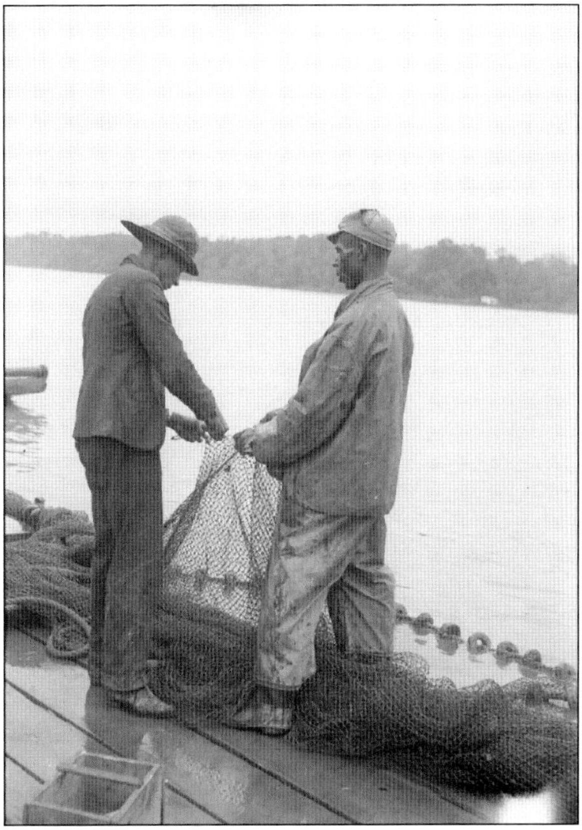

Both men and women worked at the commercial fisheries on the Roanoke River. Men worked the nets, while women were employed in processing the catch. In this photograph, Mary Hester Gaskins cleans the herring to start the process of salting them. The cleaning process included extracting the roe, or eggs, from the fish. (SANC.)

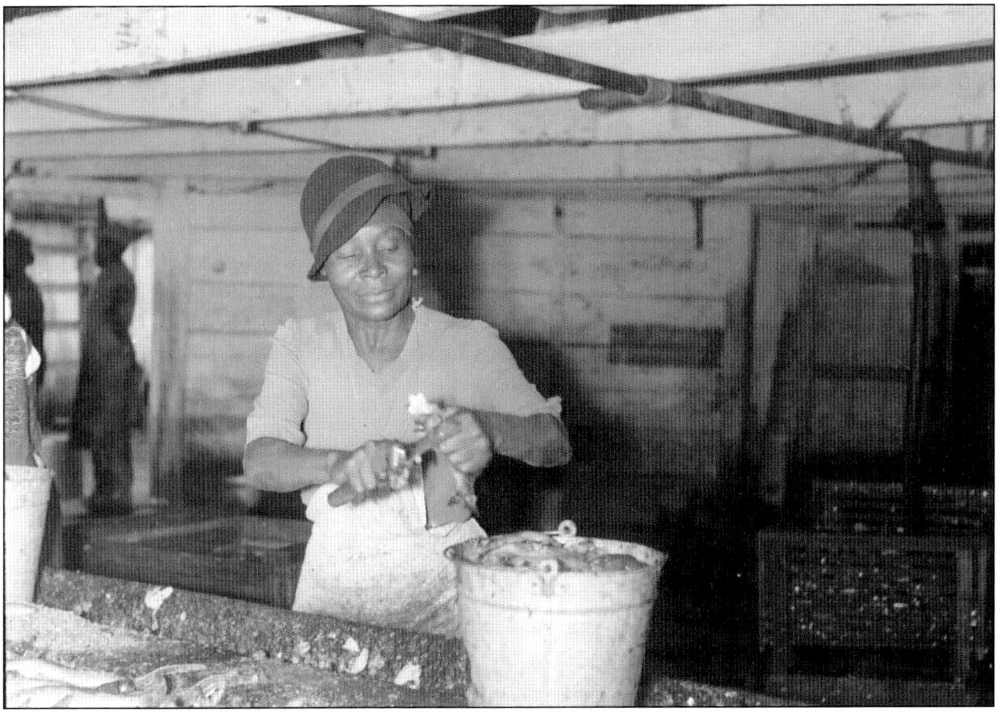

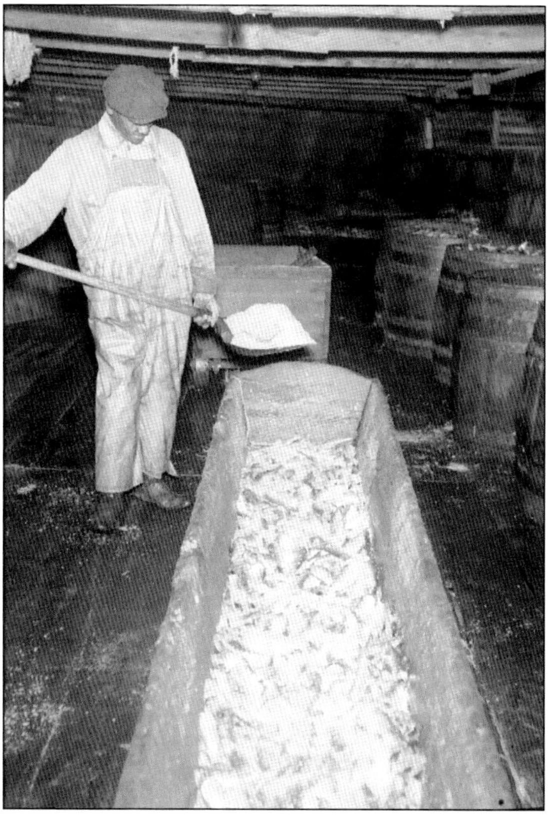

Salted herring was a diet staple in northeastern North Carolina and was shipped from Plymouth up and down the Atlantic coast, to the Caribbean, and elsewhere. The salting process, shown here, preserved the herring. The fish were laid out in the box, then covered with salt. Another layer of fish was covered with salt, and so on, until the box was full. (SANC.)

In this November 1945 photograph, a young man in a homemade wooden skiff is out on the Roanoke River, setting small fishing nets known as perch pots. One of the pots is visible in the front of the boat. The skiff is powered by an early Evinrude outboard motor. (SANC.)

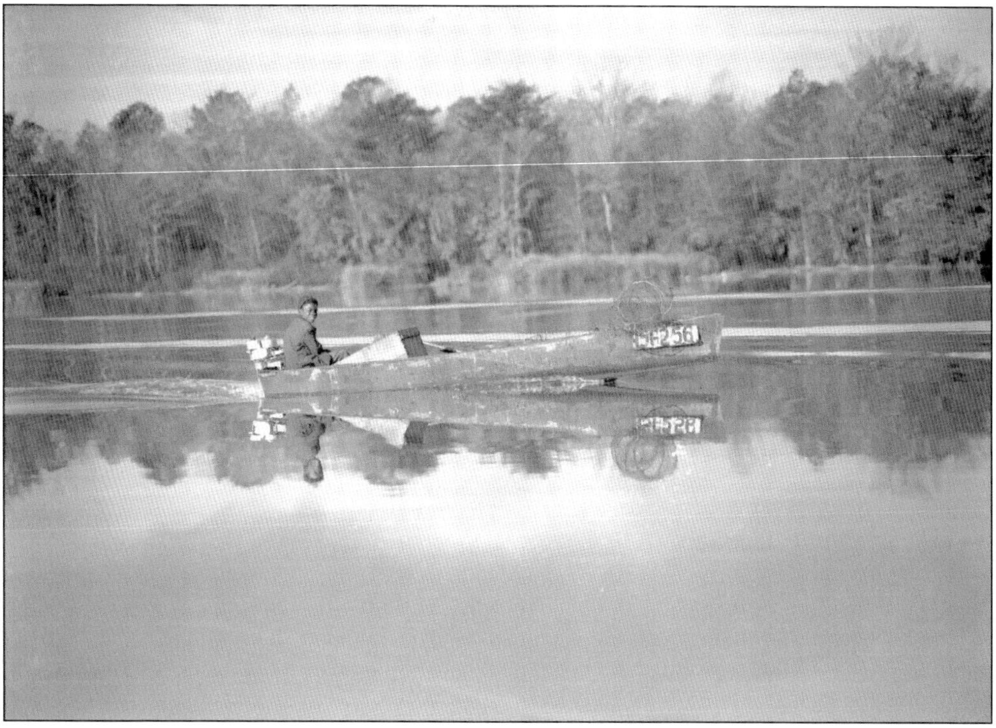

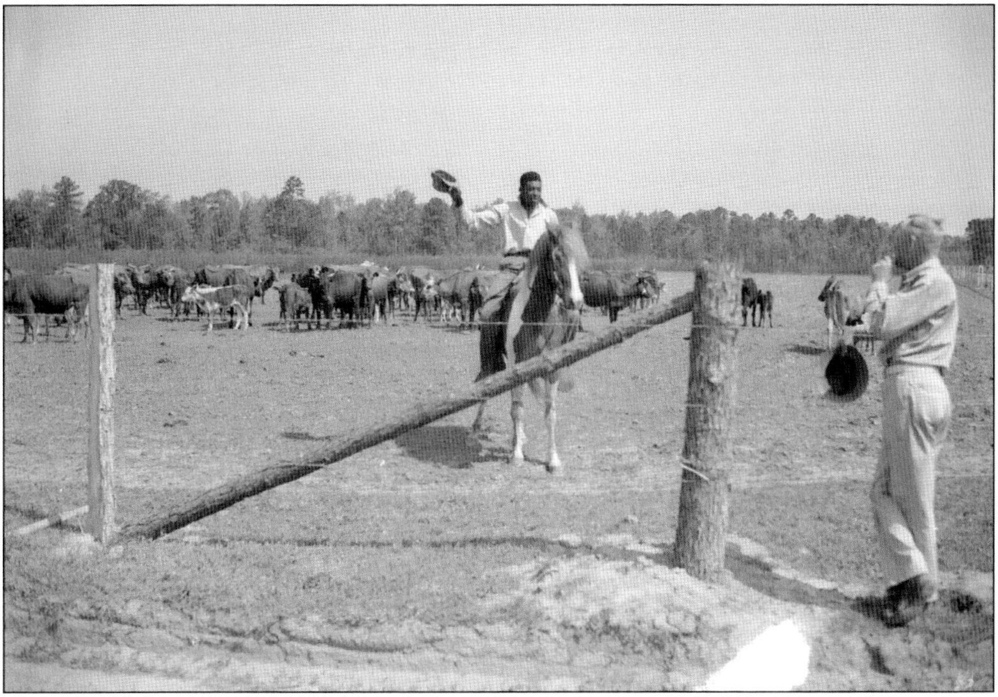

At one time, there were several large cattle ranches in rural Washington County. Though the ranches were fenced in, the cattle were allowed to roam through the woods. The Washington County ranchers often brought in experienced cowboys and their horses from Texas when it was time to round up the cattle. Seen here in 1940 is one such rancher, along with a mounted cowboy. (SANC.)

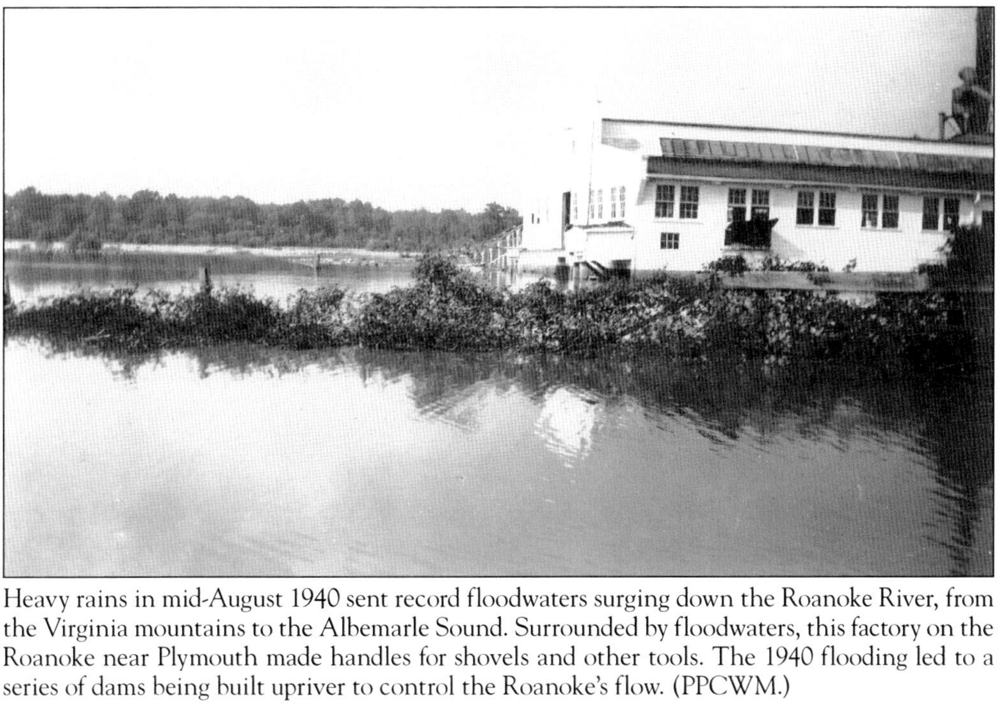

Heavy rains in mid-August 1940 sent record floodwaters surging down the Roanoke River, from the Virginia mountains to the Albemarle Sound. Surrounded by floodwaters, this factory on the Roanoke near Plymouth made handles for shovels and other tools. The 1940 flooding led to a series of dams being built upriver to control the Roanoke's flow. (PPCWM.)

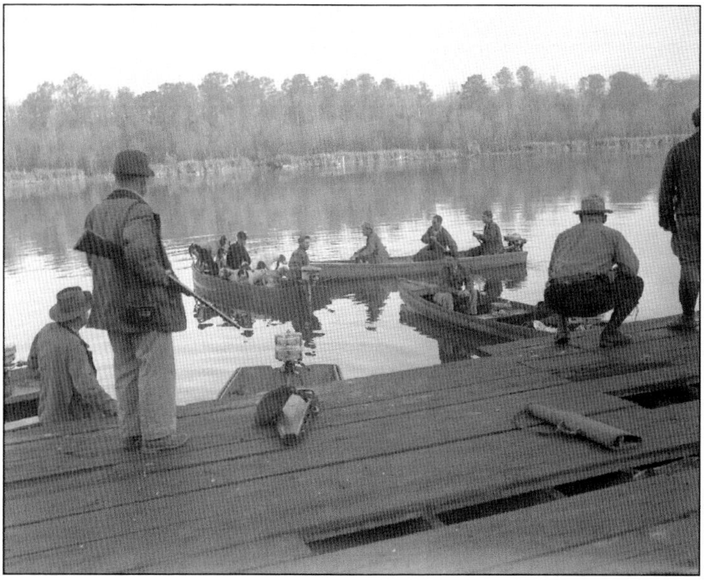

Hunters used a variety of boats, as seen here with small working skiffs at the docks. At the time of this photograph in November 1945, fiberglass boats were not common, and most boats were made of wood. Several of the hunters are standing on docks made of solid planks, the thickness of which indicates that these docks were designed for heavy-duty work. (SANC.)

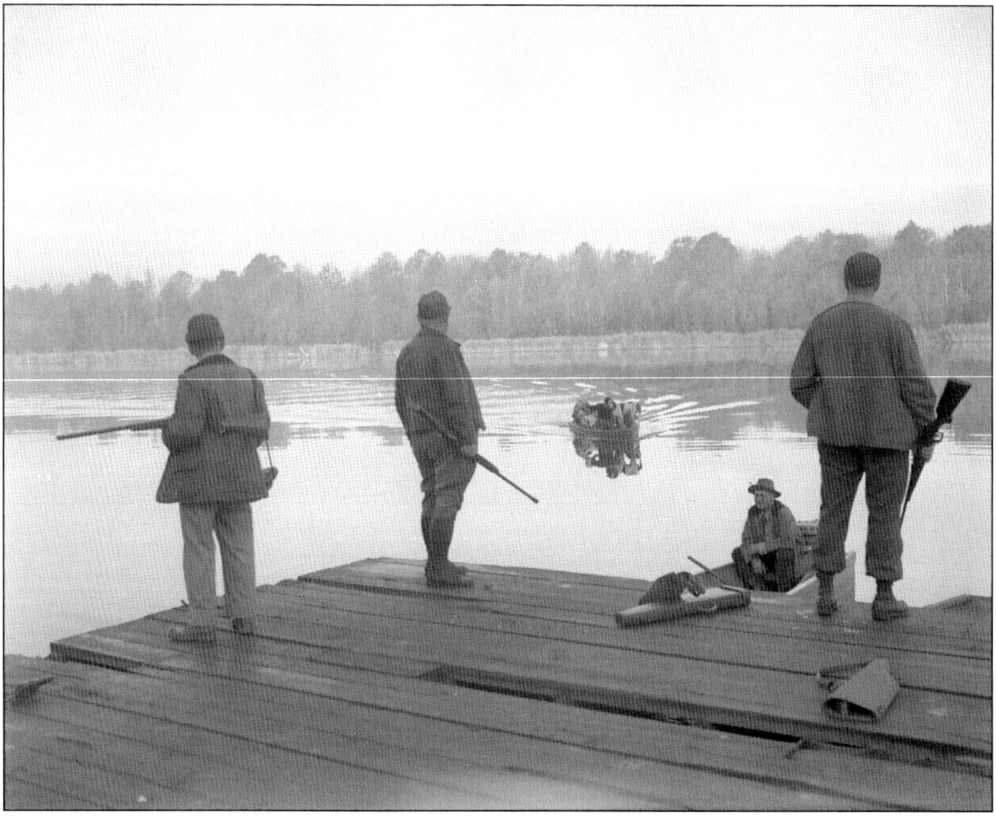

In November 1945, a group of hunters gathered on the Roanoke River docks in downtown Plymouth to head upriver to hunt deer. In this photograph, three such hunters watch as a small boat carrying fellow hunters and their dogs approaches the dock. Two of the hunters are holding shotguns, while the third hunter on the far right is holding a lever-action rifle. (SANC.)

The small, slender Roanoke River flatboat in the foreground is very similar in design to the dugout canoes used by Indians thousands of years earlier. The blunt bow, known as a "pram" bow, allows more of the boat to be used for cargo or seating. This design was easier to build than those with a pointed bow. (SANC.)

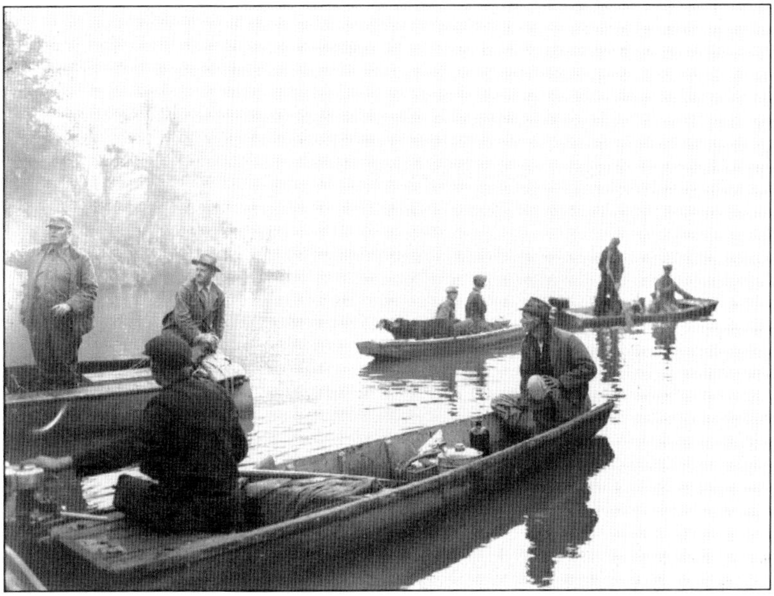

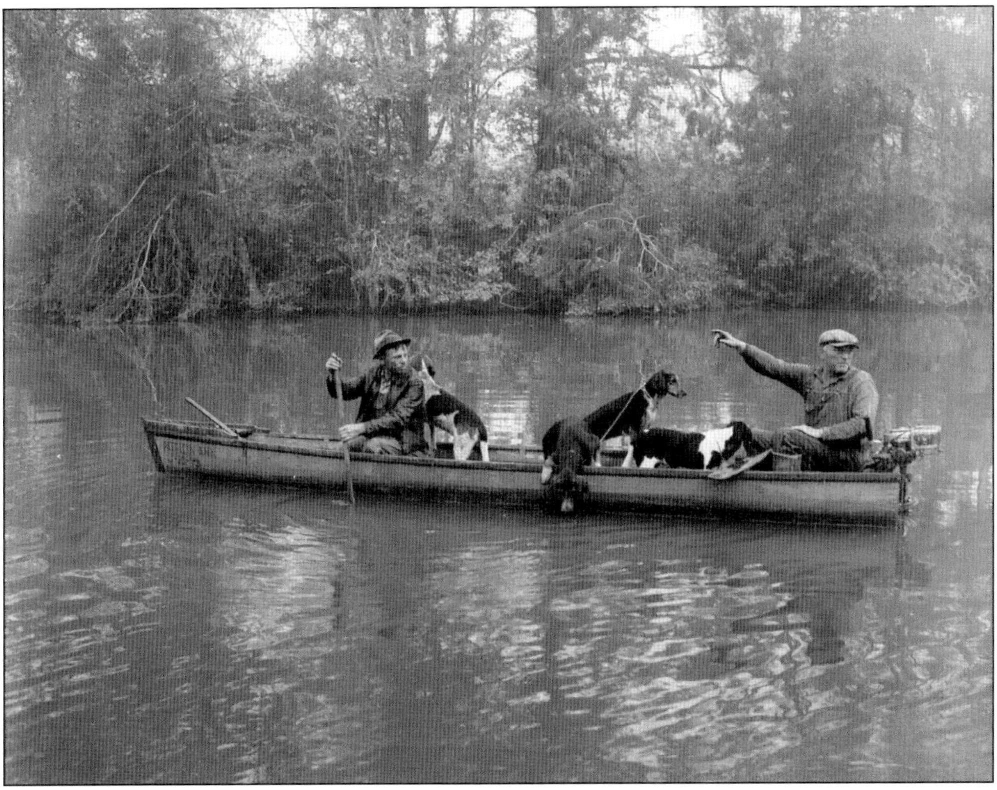

The hunter in the front of this wooden skiff, named the *Patricia Ann*, is using an oar to maneuver the boat on one of the tributaries of the Roanoke River, near Plymouth. The hound near the middle of the boat seems to have found something fascinating in the water. (SANC.)

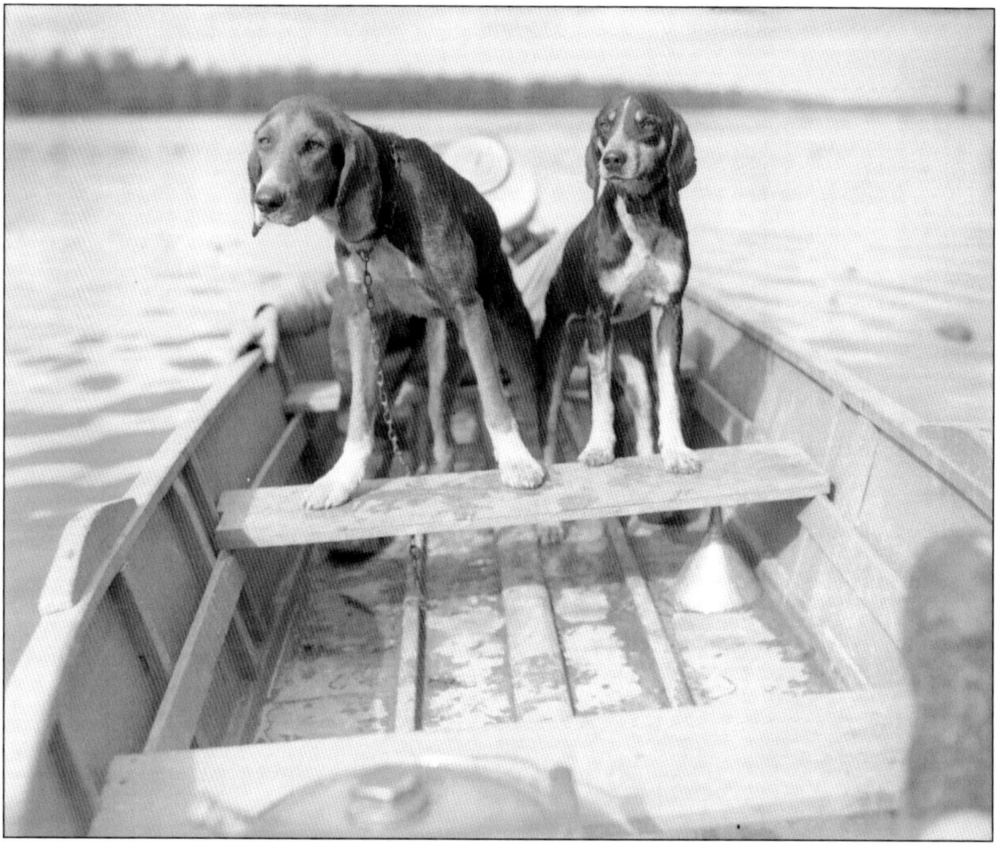

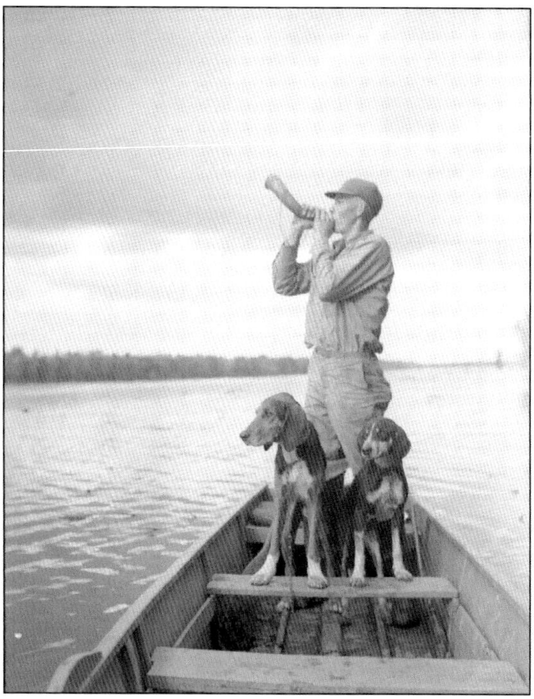

Deer hunters used Walker hounds, such as these two dogs, on their November 1945 hunt on the Roanoke River. George Washington, the first president of the United States, and his close friend John W. Walker developed this breed. Today, hunting deer with dogs is allowed only in certain counties in North Carolina. (SANC.)

As seen here in November 1945, Raymond Ellis called his hounds by blowing into a horn. Two of his hounds are with him in his small wooden skiff. The small strips of wood on the floor of the boat help to strengthen its hull. (SANC.)

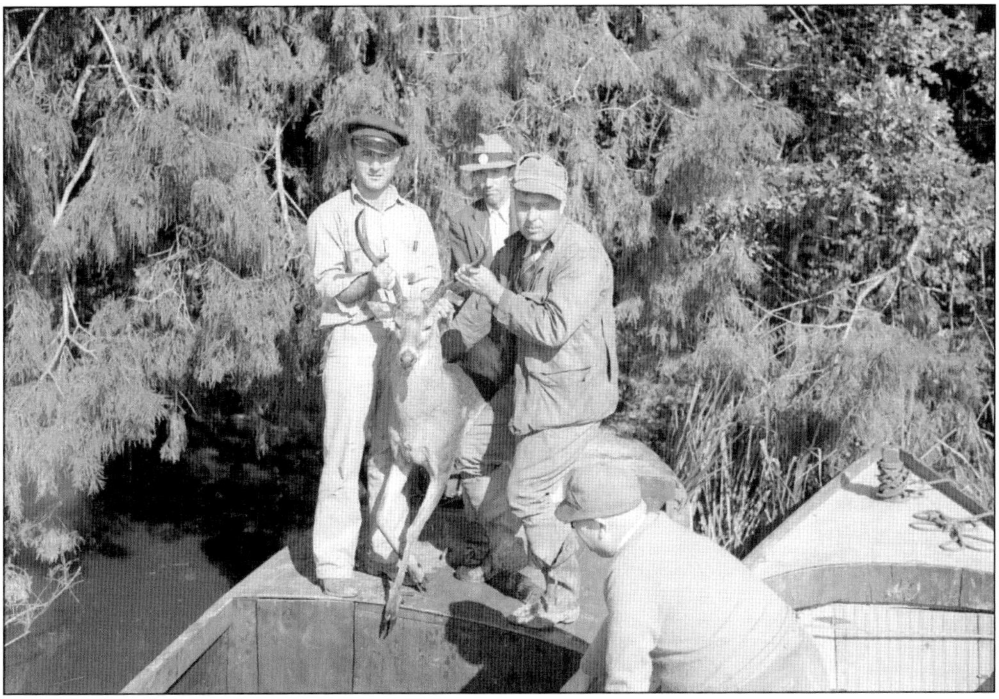

Three hunters display a buck they killed during the November 1945 deer hunt on the Roanoke River. The buck was probably a little over a year old. Female deer, or doe, were protected by law and could not be killed. (SANC.)

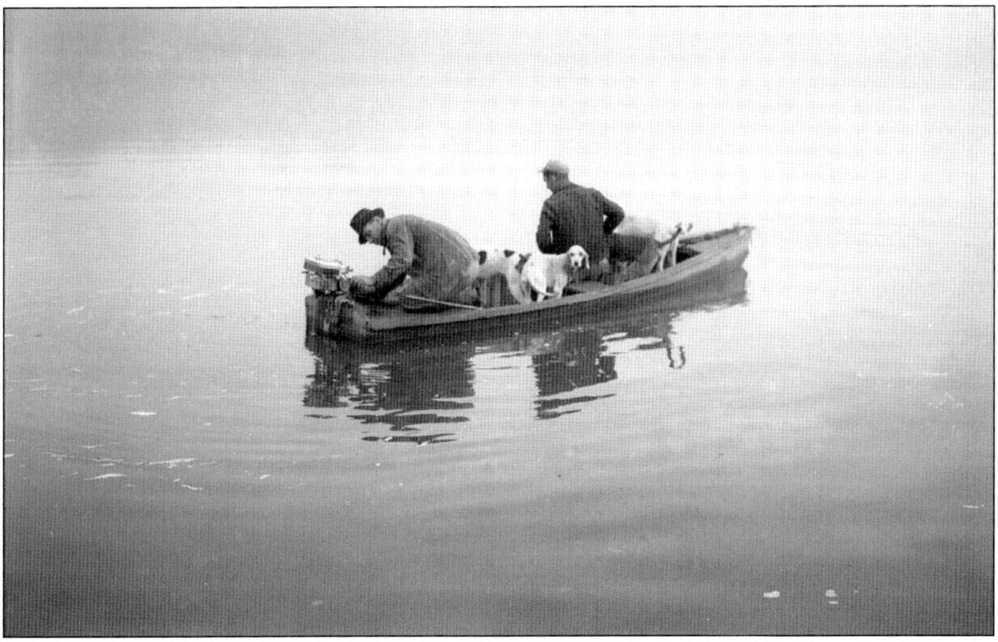

A hunter tinkers with the small outboard motor powering his wooden skiff, perhaps adjusting the mixture of oxygen and fuel to make the engine run more smoothly. Small engines such as these could propel boats through water at a few miles per hour. Usually, they were five horsepower or less. (SANC.)

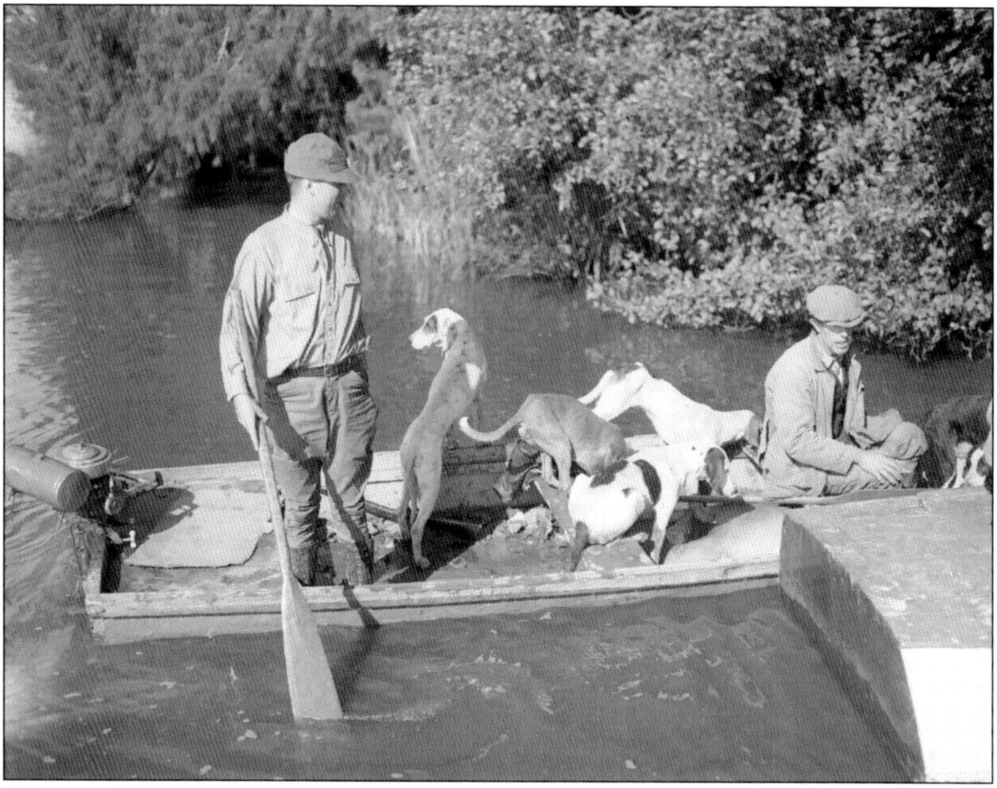

A hunter with a passenger and five dogs in his small wooden skiff uses a paddle to maneuver his boat near the shore of the Roanoke River. Often, the paddles were handmade of ash, the same hardwood used to make baseball bats. Neither of the men is wearing a life jacket, which was not required when this photograph was taken in November 1945. (SANC.)

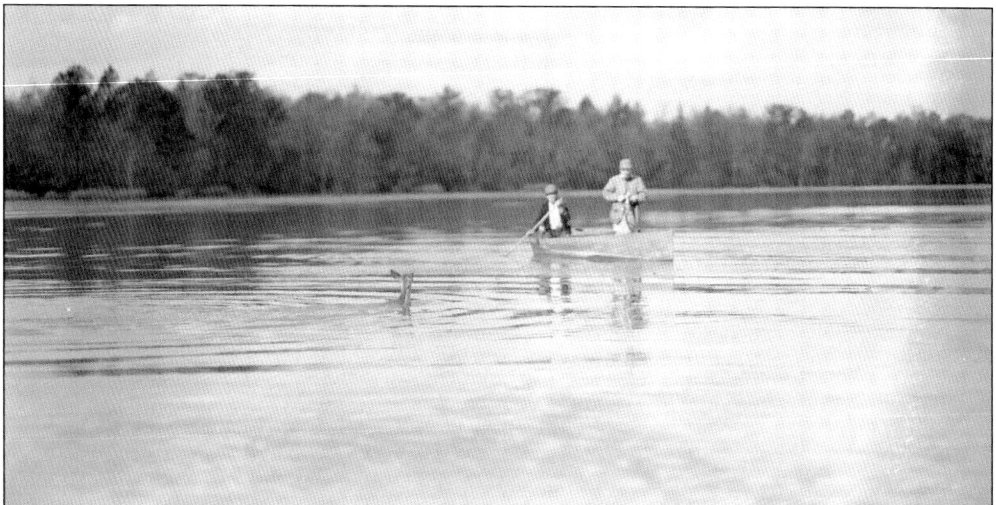

A hunter maneuvers his boat while he and his fellow hunter watch a doe swimming in the Roanoke River in this 1945 photograph. The Roanoke is home to a wide variety of wildlife, including black bears, otters, bald eagles, minks, and beavers. The lower Roanoke's floodplain, near Plymouth, is considered the largest and least disturbed in the Mid-Atlantic region. (SANC.)

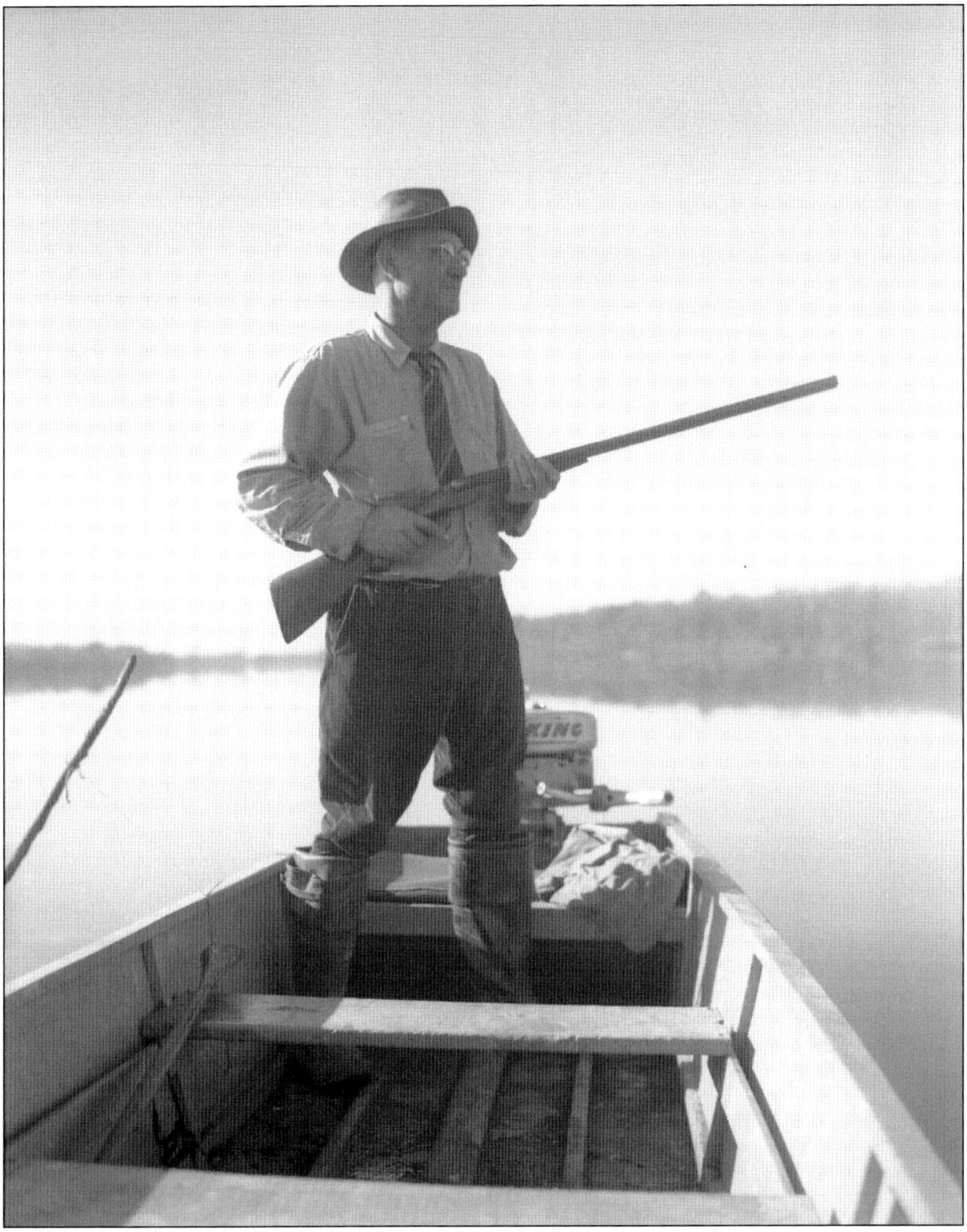

Dress codes were drastically different in 1945. Holding a double-barreled shotgun, this hunter wears a tie to go deer hunting on the Roanoke River in November 1945. His boat was powered by a Sea King outboard motor, probably about five horsepower. The retailer Montgomery Ward manufactured these small engines. (SANC.)

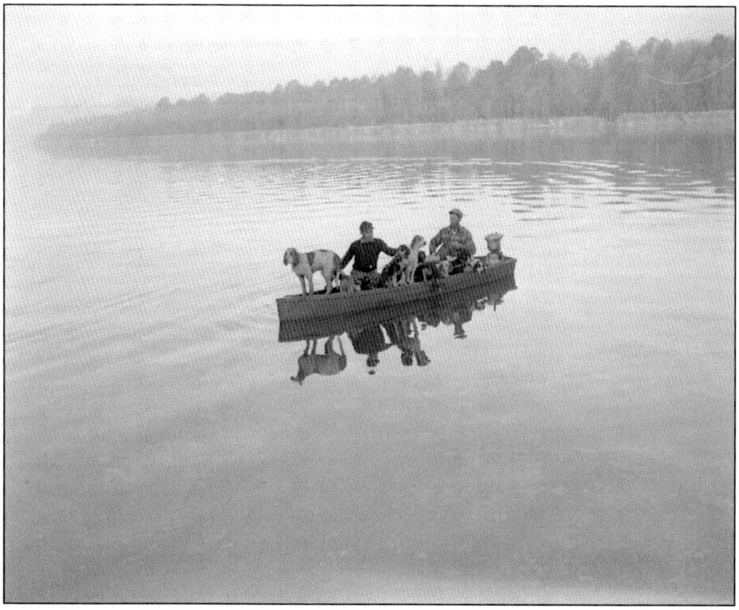

Boaters in a small skiff are transporting six Walker hounds on the Roanoke River. Walker hounds do not tree their quarry, but chase it. They also are used for fox hunting, but hounds used for deer hunting are trained differently. Deer hunters do not want hounds that will be distracted by a fox. (SANC.)

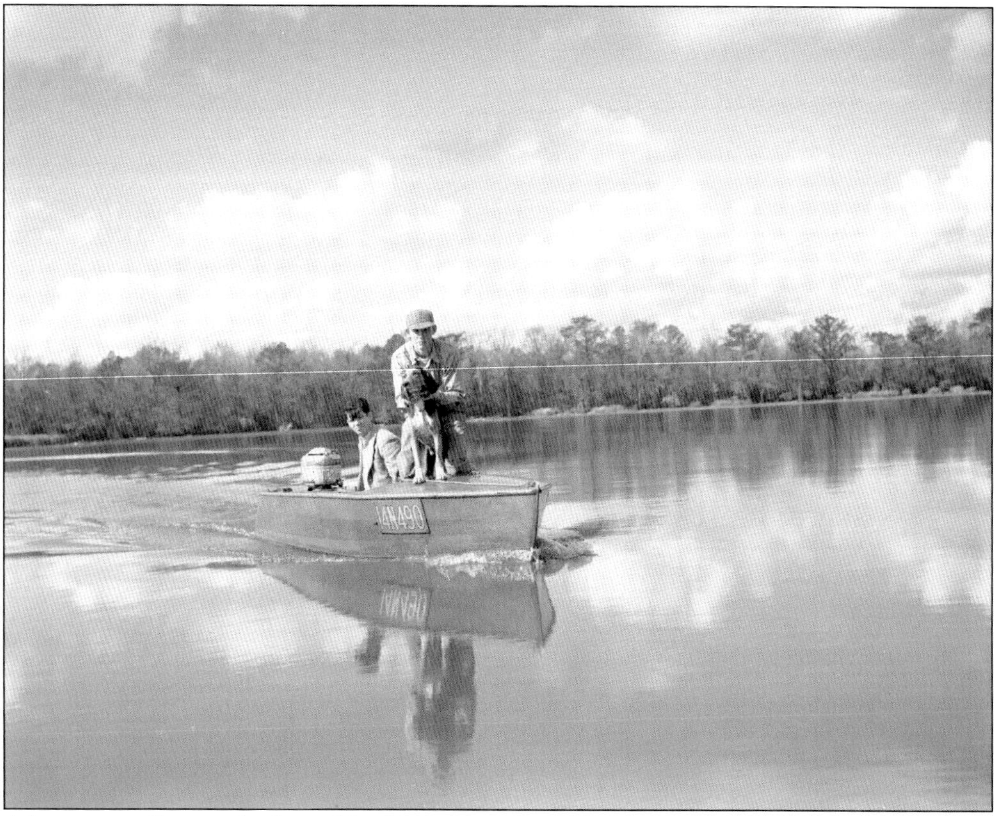

A hunter proudly poses his hound for the cameraman. Walker hounds are known for their friendly, playful disposition. But their lean bodies and quickness also make them excellent deer hunters. Today, Washington County is one of the counties in North Carolina where deer hunting with dogs is allowed. (SANC.)

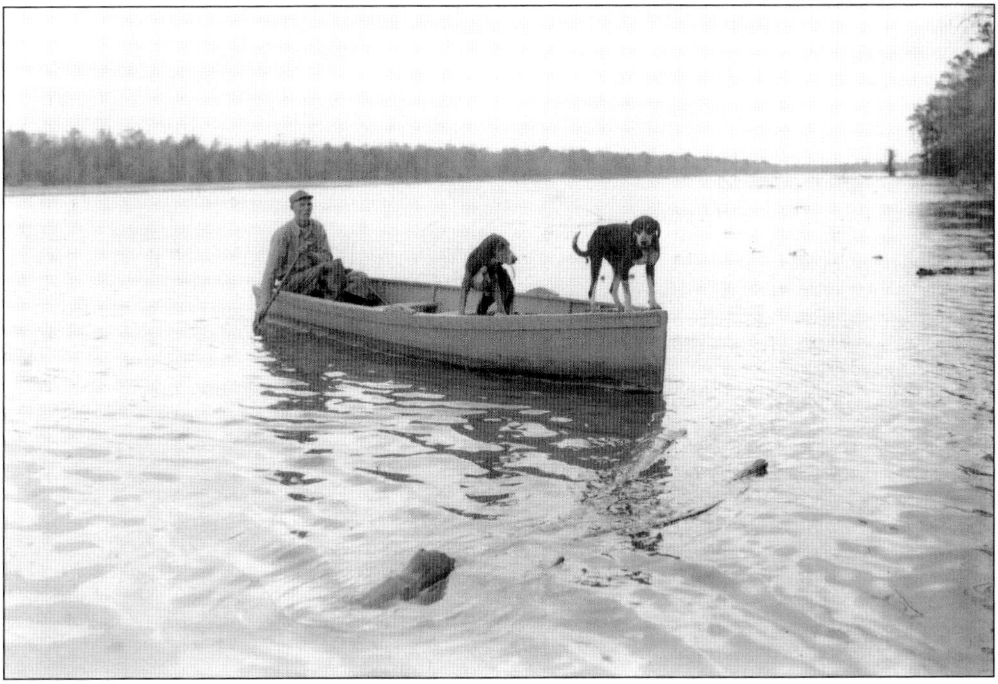

Deer hunter Raymond Ellis, with his Walker hounds, uses an oar to maneuver his boat toward the shore of the Roanoke River. A photograph of Ellis and his hounds appeared in the *State* magazine shortly after this one was taken in November 1945. (SANC.)

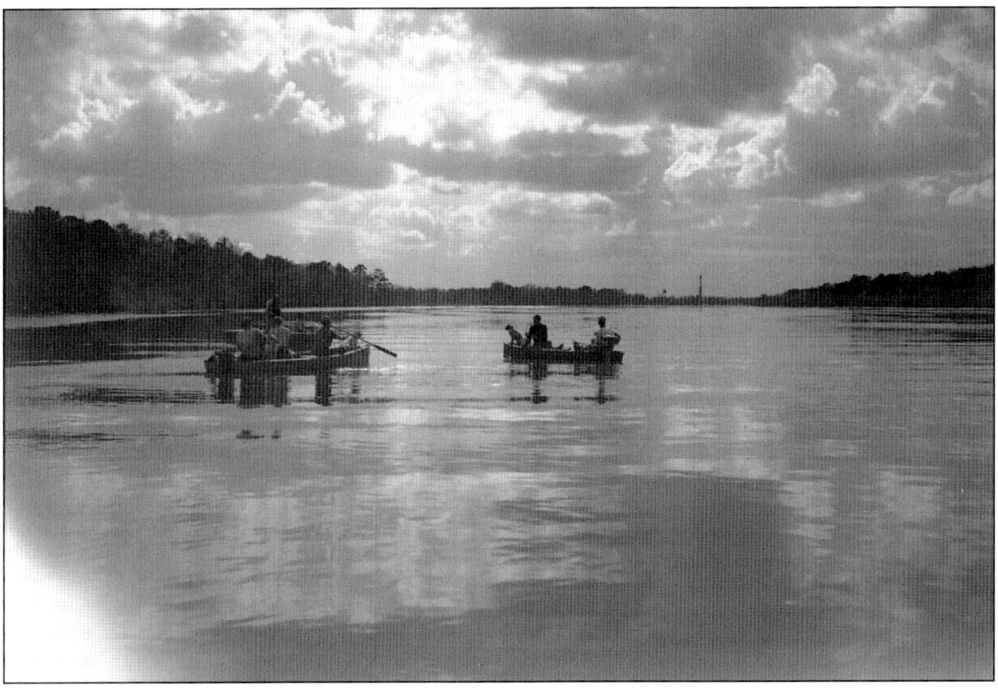

Hunters head down the Roanoke River toward Plymouth at the end of a day of deer hunting. They were several miles upriver and the sun was starting to set when this photograph was taken. In the distance, an industrial smokestack and a water tower in Plymouth are visible. (SANC.)

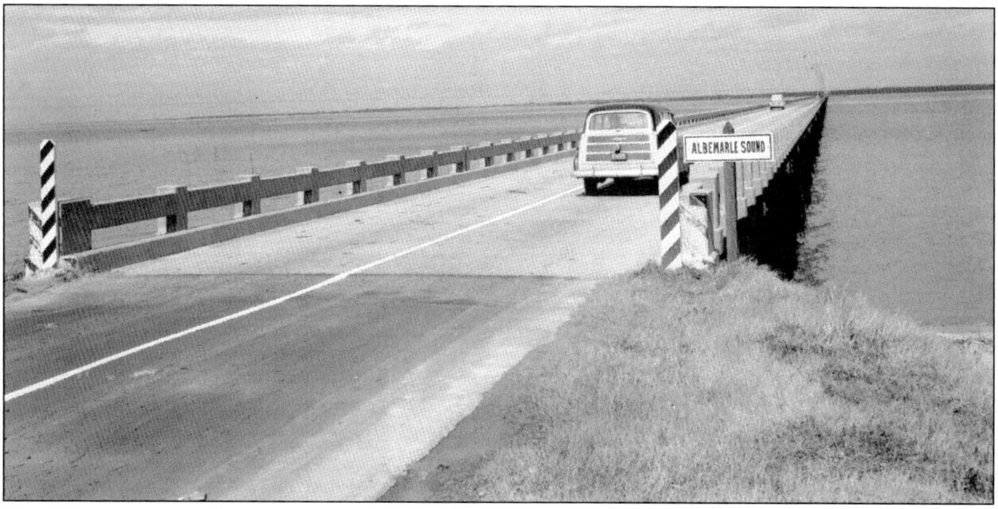

For 200 years, travelers wanting to cross the Albemarle Sound had to ride a ferry between Washington and Chowan Counties, but in August 1938, a new drawbridge more than three miles long opened. At the time, it was the largest construction project ever attempted by the state highway commission. This photograph shows traffic crossing the bridge in March 1950. (SANC.)

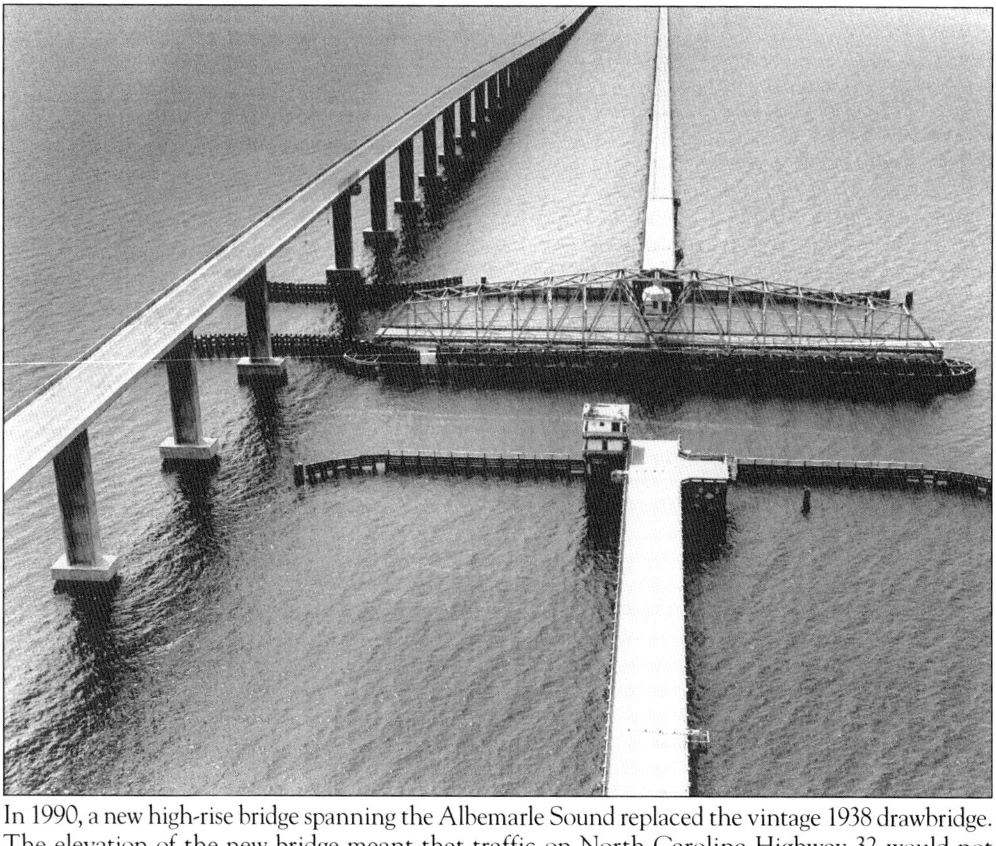

In 1990, a new high-rise bridge spanning the Albemarle Sound replaced the vintage 1938 drawbridge. The elevation of the new bridge meant that traffic on North Carolina Highway 32 would not have to be halted to open the drawbridge to allow boats to pass. This photograph shows the old and new bridges before the old bridge was taken down. (Doward Jones Jr.)

Two

Plymouth, Mackeys, Roper, and Creswell

Plymouth is one of North Carolina's most historic towns, and it retains much of its character from the late 19th and early 20th centuries.

But several other communities in Washington County have their own deep, rich, and colorful histories.

Originally known as Mackey's Ferry, Mackeys formed around an early-18th-century ferry that ran from the southern shore of the Albemarle Sound to Edenton on the north shore. The ferry operated in various forms for almost two centuries, until a bridge replaced it in 1938.

The arrival of the John L. Roper Lumber Company in the late 19th century transformed the town of Lee's Mill, established in the early 18th century, and residents changed its name to Roper in gratitude for the improvements that the lumber company had made to their community. For many years thereafter, Roper vied with Plymouth for the distinction of being the Washington County seat.

Creswell's growth was tied to the nearby Somerset Plantation, one of the largest in North Carolina when the Civil War erupted in 1861. Today, Creswell's small business district closely resembles its appearance of a century ago.

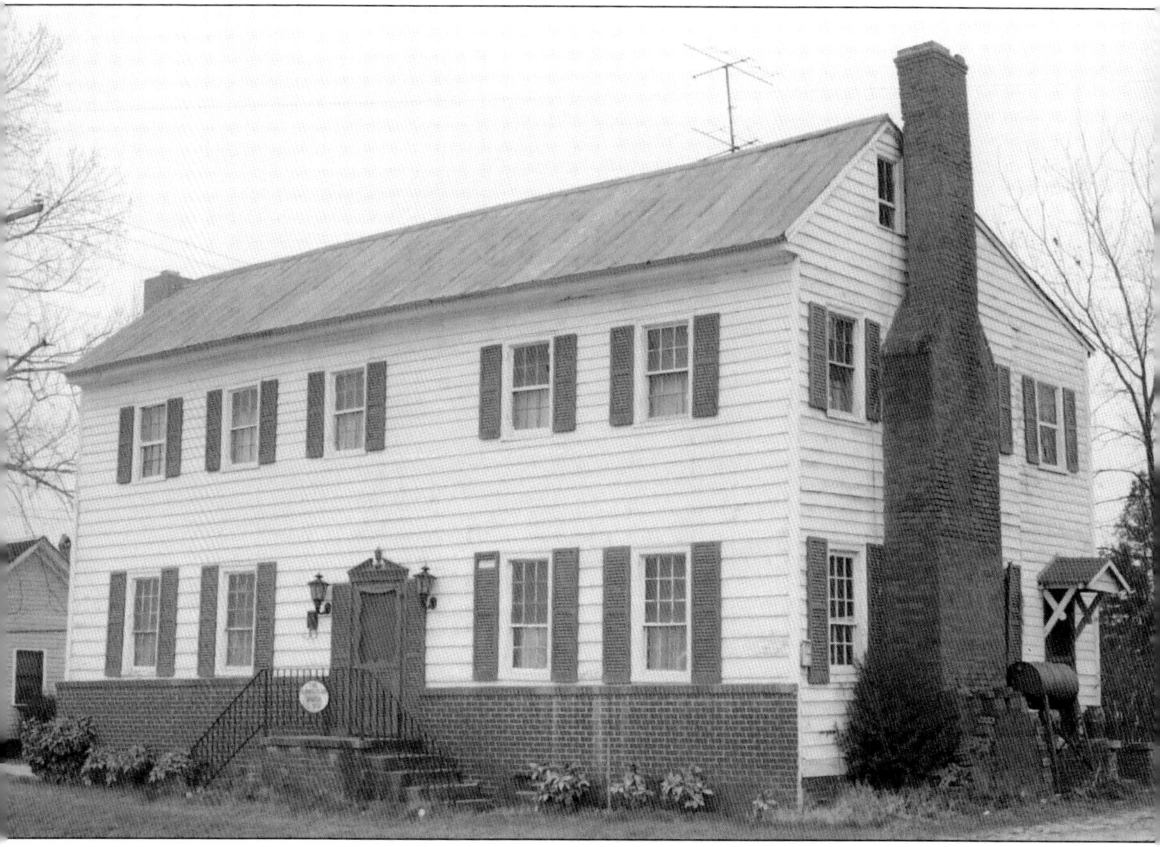

In 1814, Dr. Julian Picot, probably Plymouth's first medical doctor, bought a lot at the corner of West Main and Monroe Streets. A Frenchman thought to have been a friend of King Louis XVI, Picot came to Plymouth around 1780. In 1832, he sold his lot to his son Peter Picot, who built a house there. (SANC.)

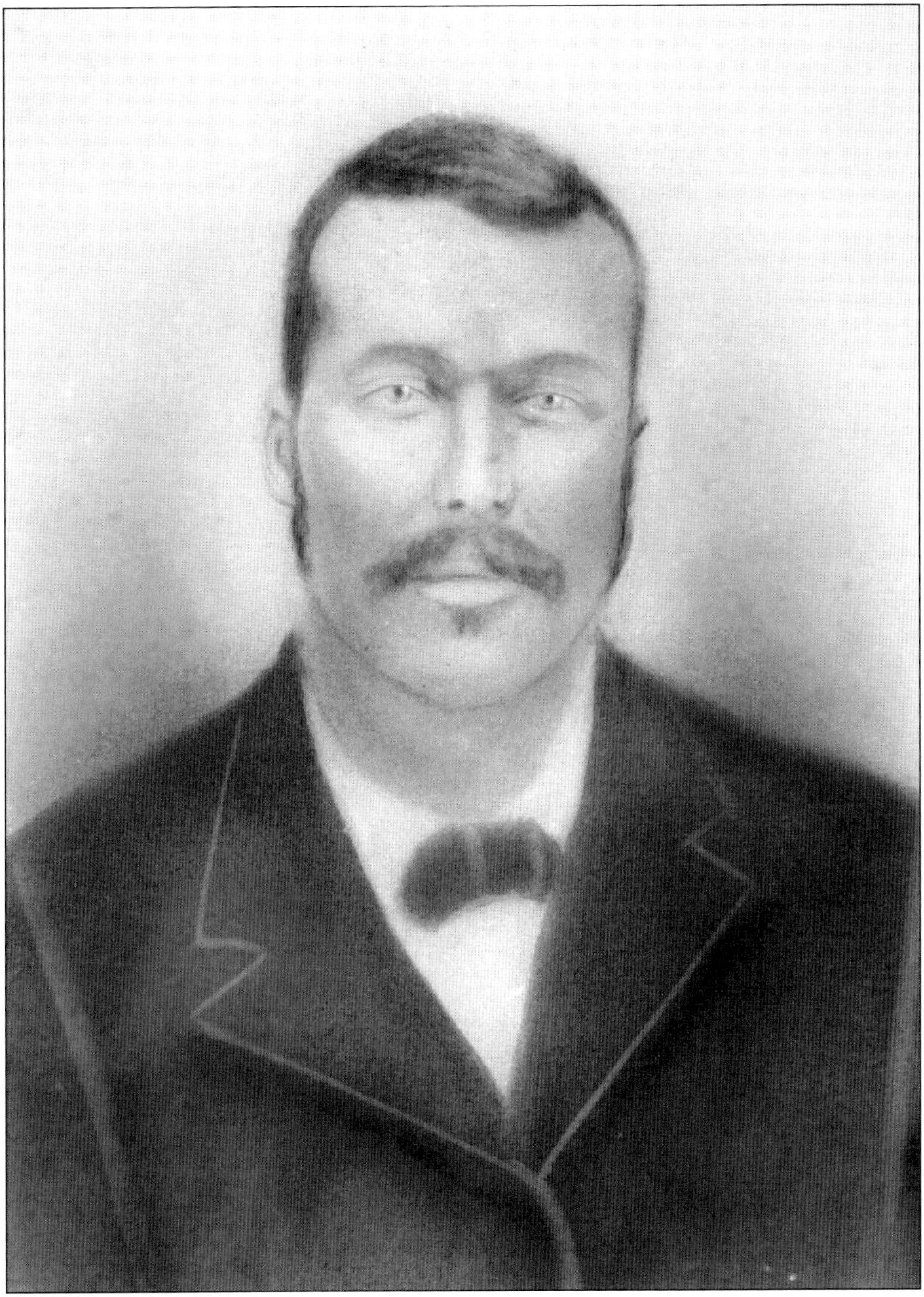

During the so-called "Jim Crow" era of segregation after the Civil War, the Picot-Armistead-Pettiford House served as a hotel and boardinghouse for African Americans in Plymouth. Roofers working on the house in 2012 found this photograph in the attic. Experts at the North Carolina State Archives in Raleigh believe it dates to around 1910, but the identity of the man is unknown. (Velma Braye.)

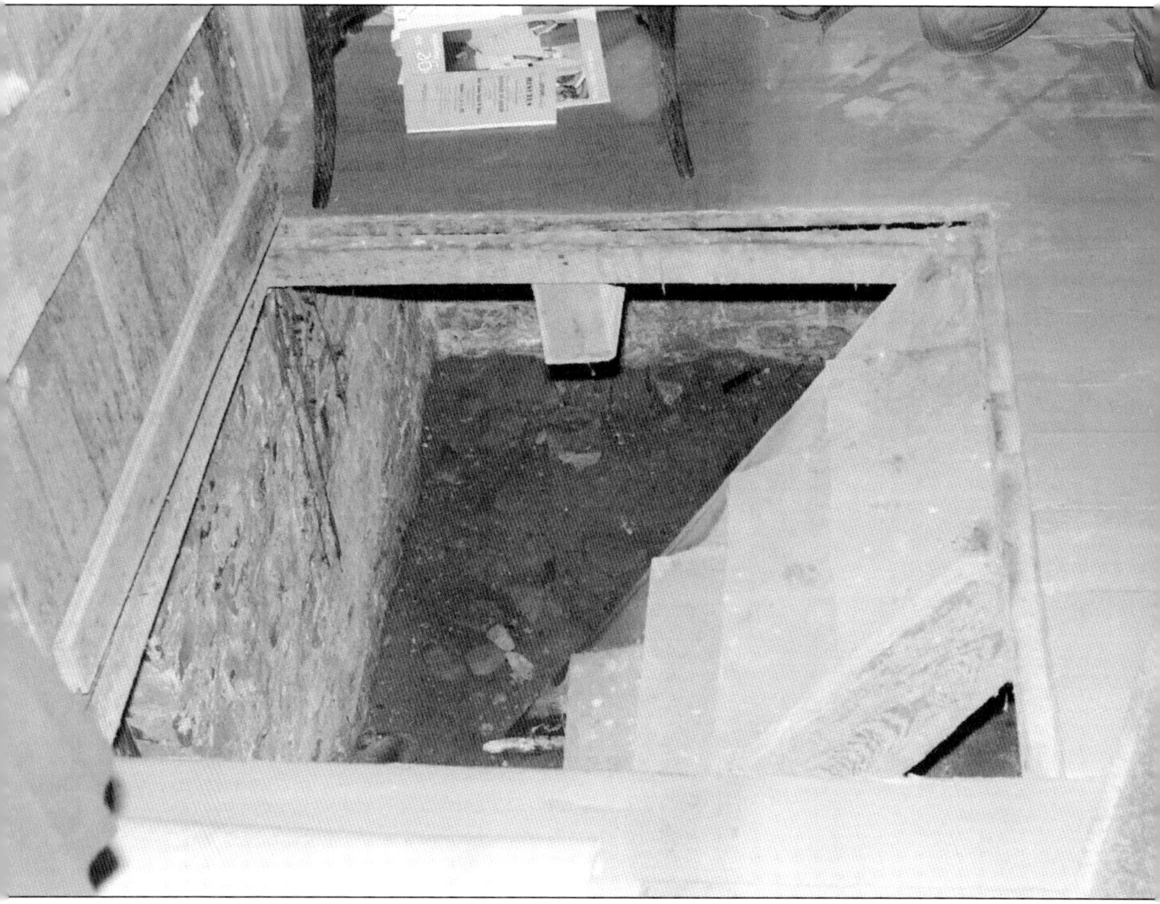

According to local oral history, before the Civil War, this trapdoor in the Picot-Armistead-Pettiford House led to a cellar where fugitive slaves hid until they could board a departing ship to begin their journey to freedom. But the owners of the house were slaveholders, and some historians doubt they would have harbored fugitives. The cellar was filled in around 1960. (SANC.)

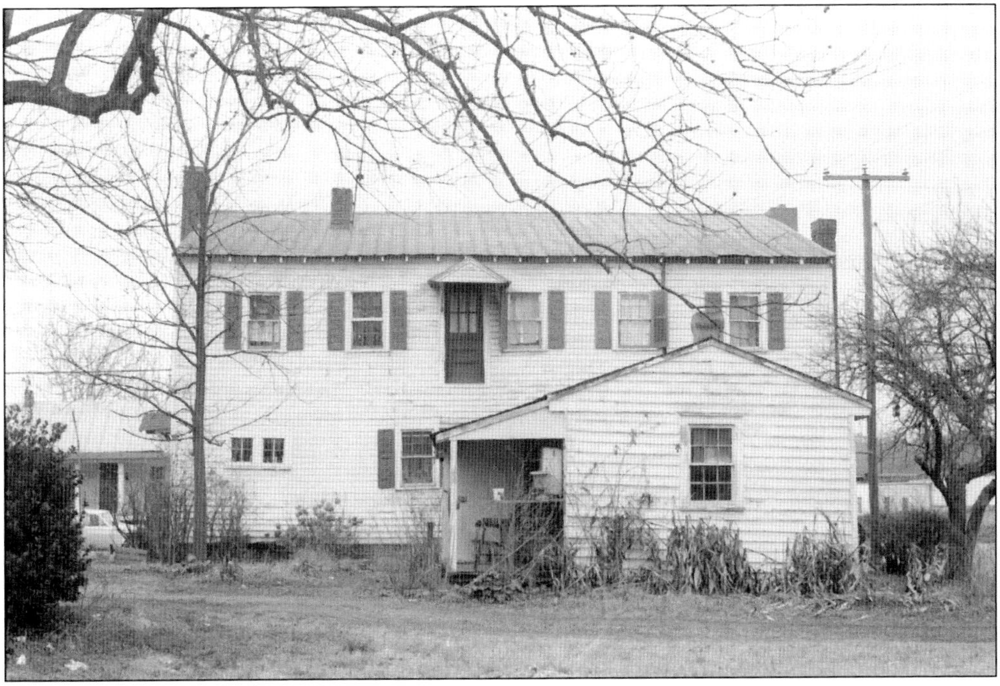

This 1974 photograph shows the rear of the Picot-Armistead-Pettiford House. The Picot family sold the house to Robert Armistead, a Plymouth merchant, in 1847. Reuben Pettiford, a brick mason in Plymouth, bought the house in 1914. It was an unusual transaction for the time because Pettiford, an African American, bought the house from a white owner. (SANC.)

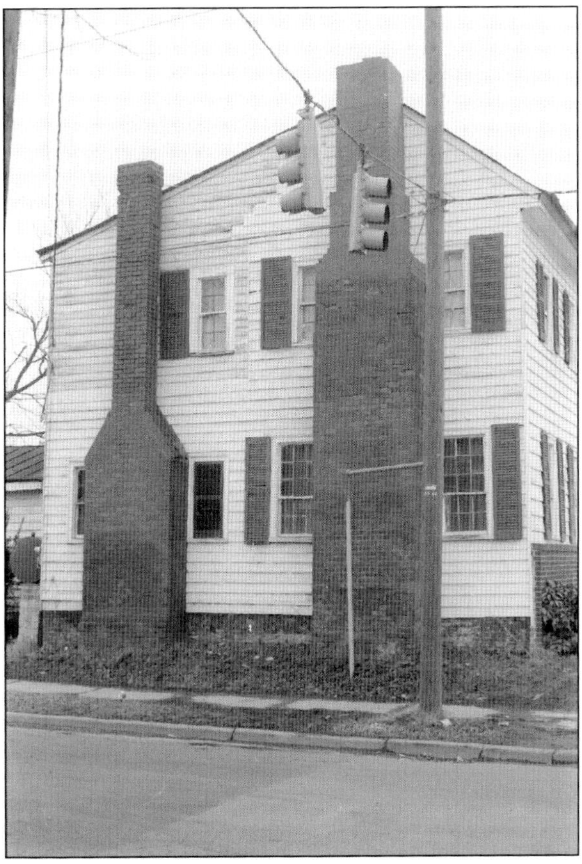

The Picot-Armistead-Pettiford House overlooks the Roanoke River in downtown Plymouth. It was one of the few buildings in Plymouth to escape damage during the Civil War. The chimney on the right was damaged at some point after the war, possibly by a hurricane. The original 19th-century bricks make up about two-thirds of the chimney, but newer bricks were added on top of that. (SANC.)

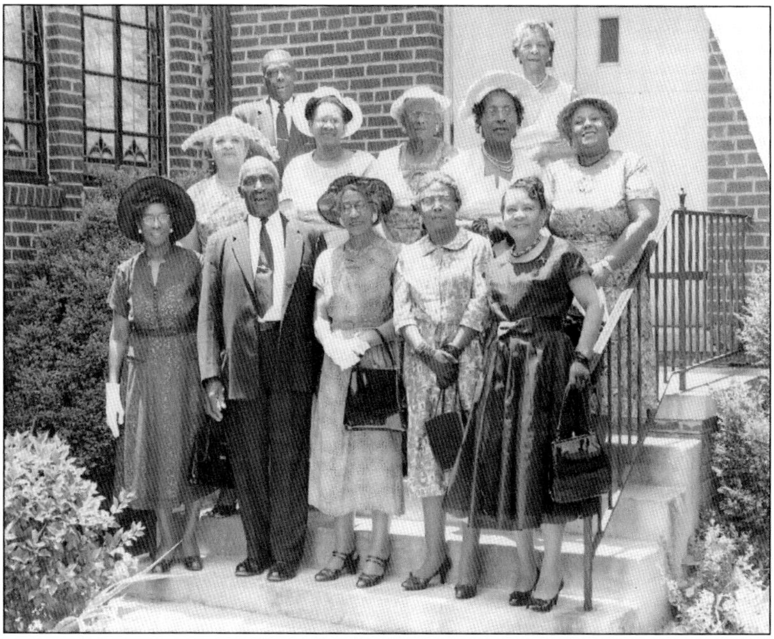

Seen here in a 1950s photograph of a church group, Gladys Stapelfoote (first from left, second row) was the last heir of Reuben Pettiford to live in the historic Picot-Armistead-Pettiford House in Plymouth. Her husband, Harvey Stapelfoote, is also pictured (second from left, first row). (Velma Braye.)

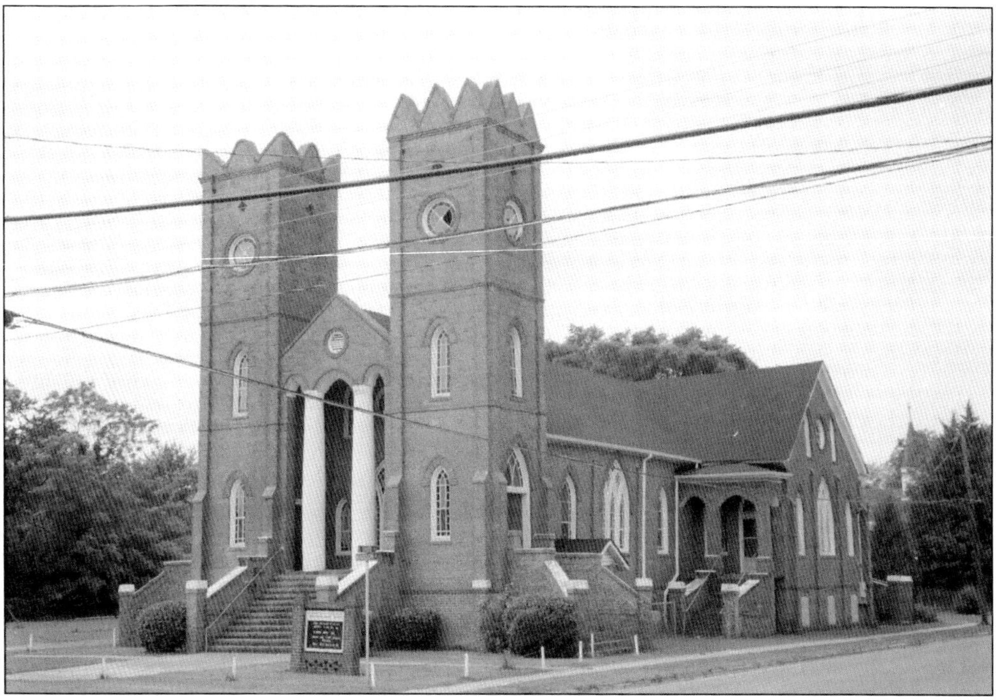

The New Chapel Baptist Church congregation was organized in 1867. Rev. S.C. Copeland, who was pastor at the time, designed a new building, which was completed in 1924. Copeland is said to have based his striking Gothic Revival design on a biblical description of Solomon's temple. The handsome brick building, still in use, is considered an architectural landmark. (NCSHPO.)

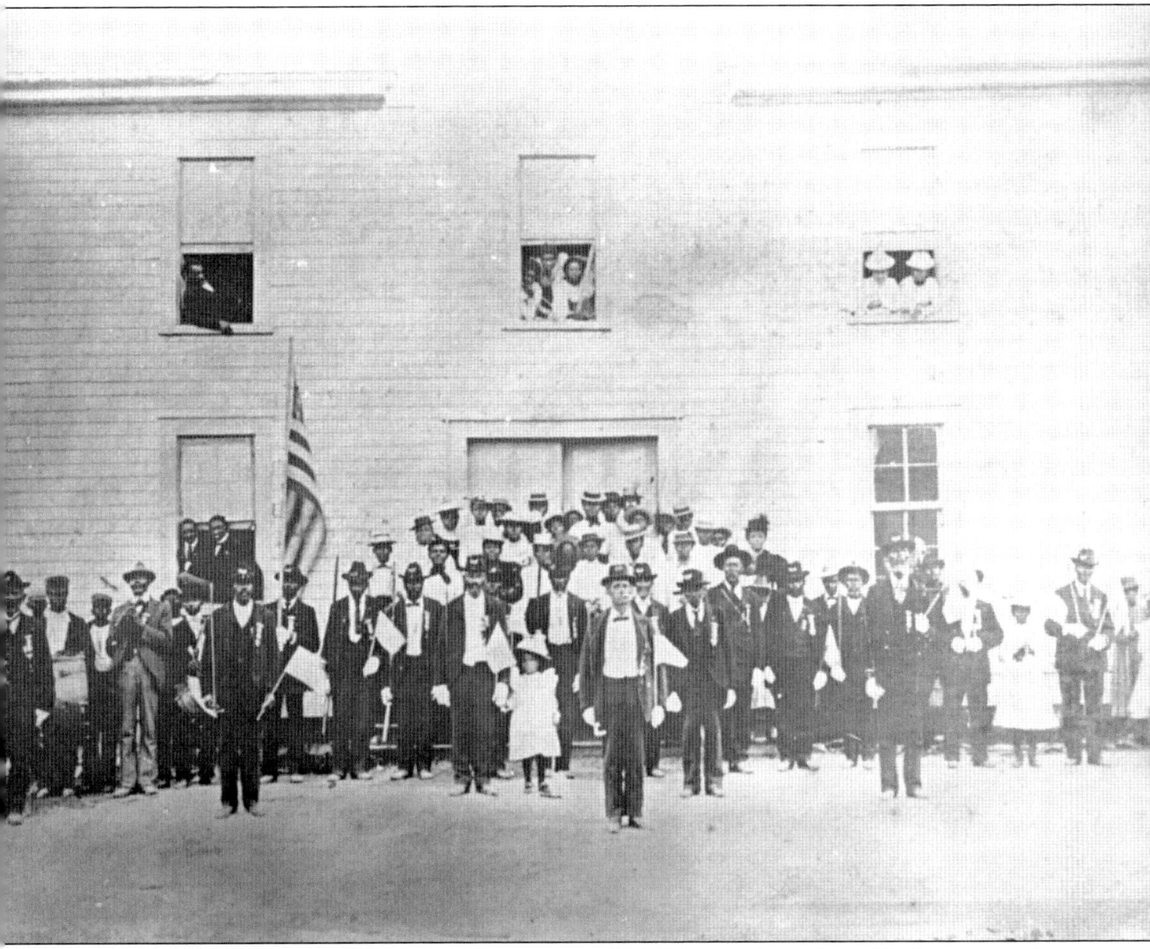

The 35th US Colored Infantry, organized in 1864, included former slaves from Washington and nearby counties. The unit spent most of the Civil War in Florida and took part in the Battle of Olustee, the largest battle in that state. This c. 1905 photograph shows a reunion of the 35th in Plymouth at the Prince Hill Masonic Lodge. (SANC.)

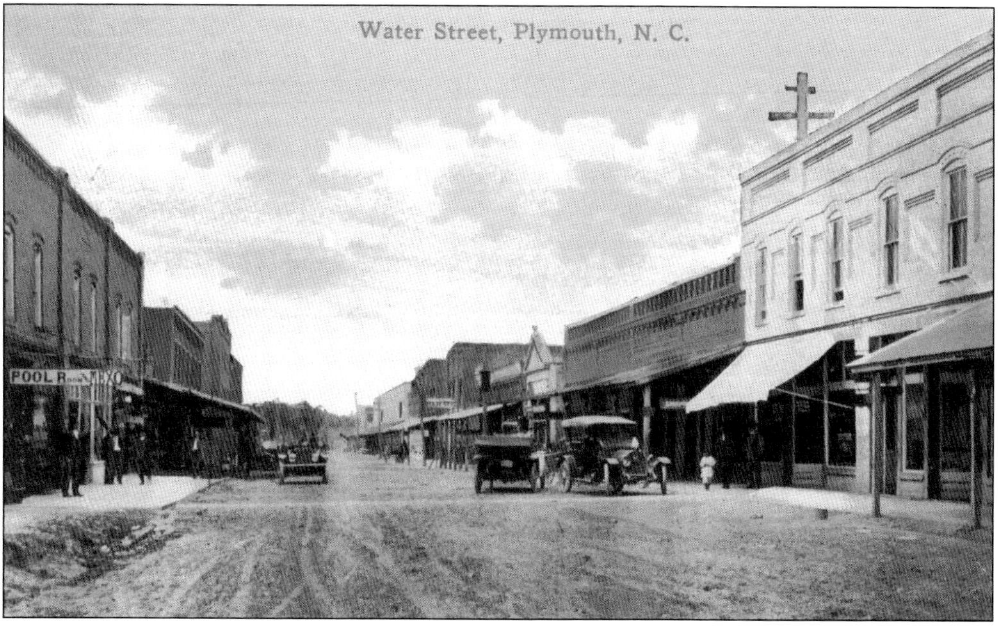

Early-20th-century automobiles had started appearing on Water Street when this real-photo postcard was made around 1915, but Plymouth's main commercial street still had not been paved. This view shows East Water Street, looking west toward a pool hall on the left and the Majestic Theater farther down the street, near the center of the photograph. (NCC.)

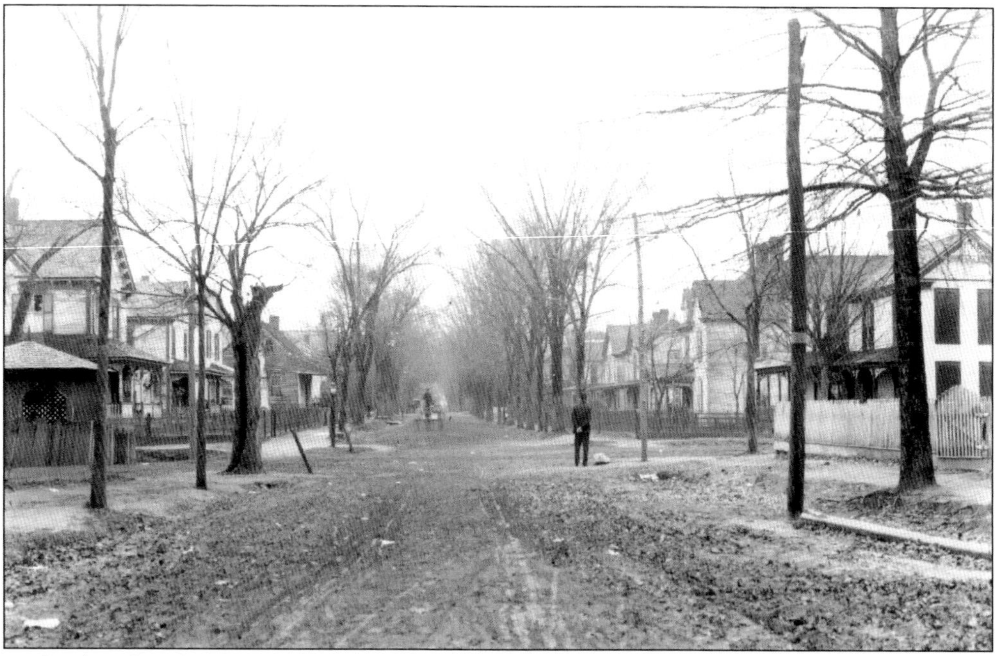

In the first decade of the 20th century, Plymouth's population more than doubled, increasing from 1,011 in 1900 to 2,165 in 1910. A man standing at the corner of the unpaved Main and Washington Streets, a main intersection in the town during its growth, watches a horse-drawn wagon as it travels down Main Street. Diagonally across the street from the man is an original gaslight streetlamp. (NCC.)

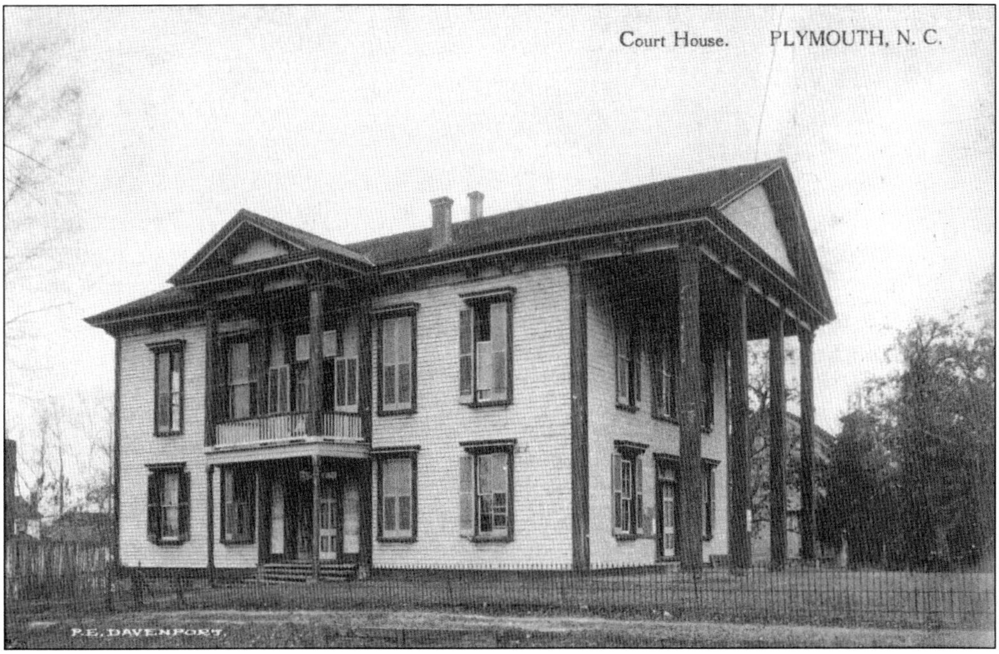

Washington County's courthouses burned regularly in the 19th century, including one destroyed during the Civil War. In 1873, a defendant in a trial supposedly set fire to the courthouse to destroy evidence against him. A massive fire in downtown Plymouth destroyed another in 1881. This photograph shows the Washington County Courthouse at the corner of Main and Adams Streets in 1911. (NCC.)

Around 1917, Washington County officials hired Benton & Benton Architects of Wilson, North Carolina, to draw up plans for a new courthouse. This drawing is an architect's rendering, which suggests replacing the wooden building at the corner of Main and Adams Streets. In 1918, the wooden courthouse was torn down, and this building was constructed on the same site in 1920. (NCC.)

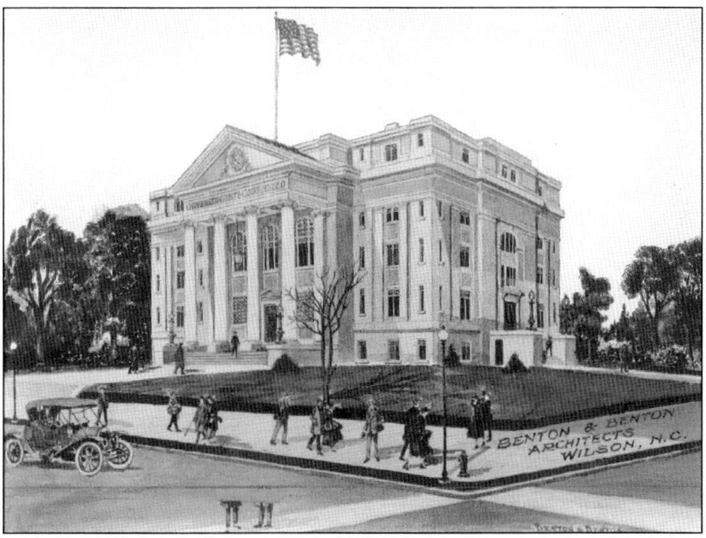

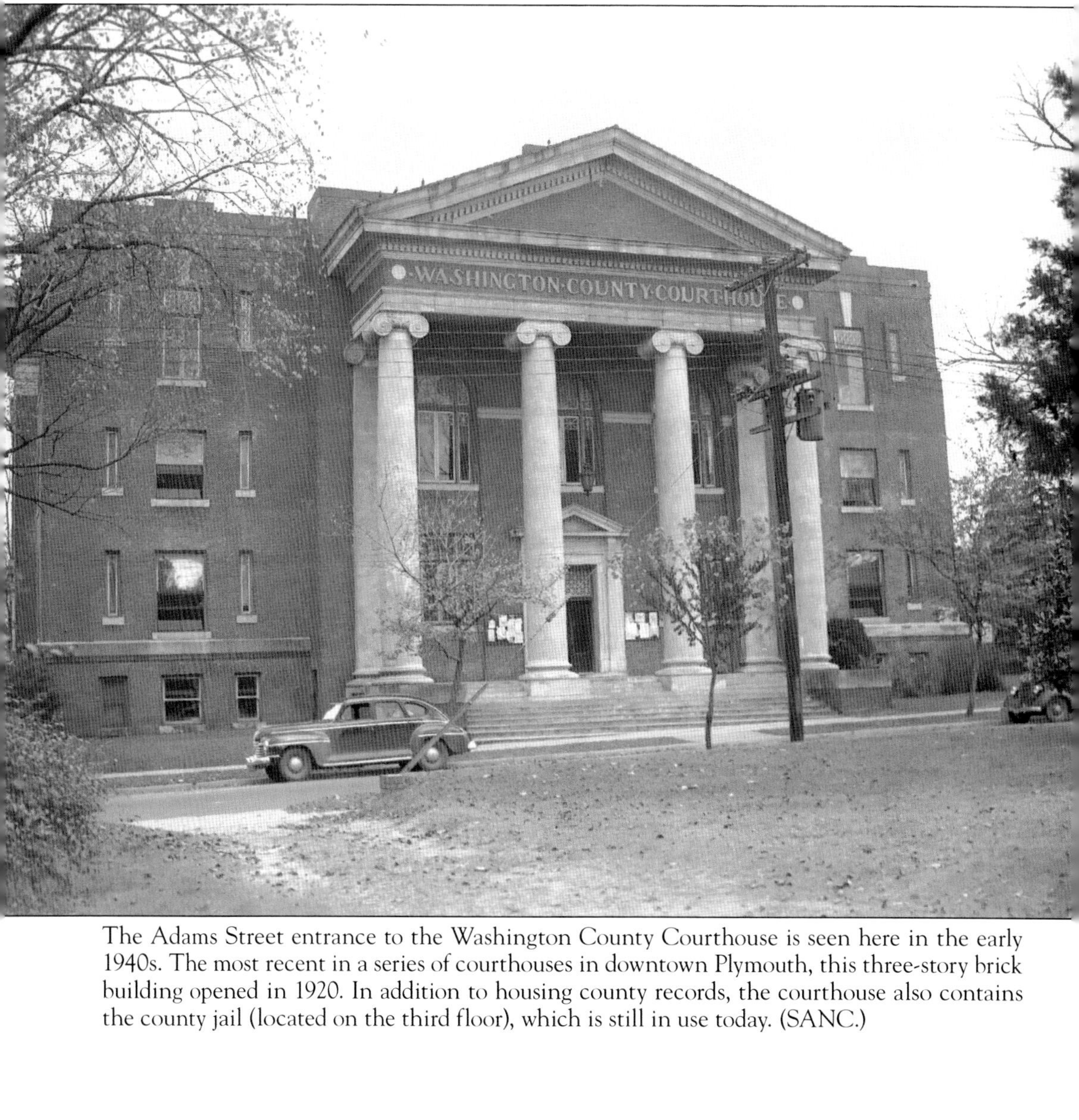

The Adams Street entrance to the Washington County Courthouse is seen here in the early 1940s. The most recent in a series of courthouses in downtown Plymouth, this three-story brick building opened in 1920. In addition to housing county records, the courthouse also contains the county jail (located on the third floor), which is still in use today. (SANC.)

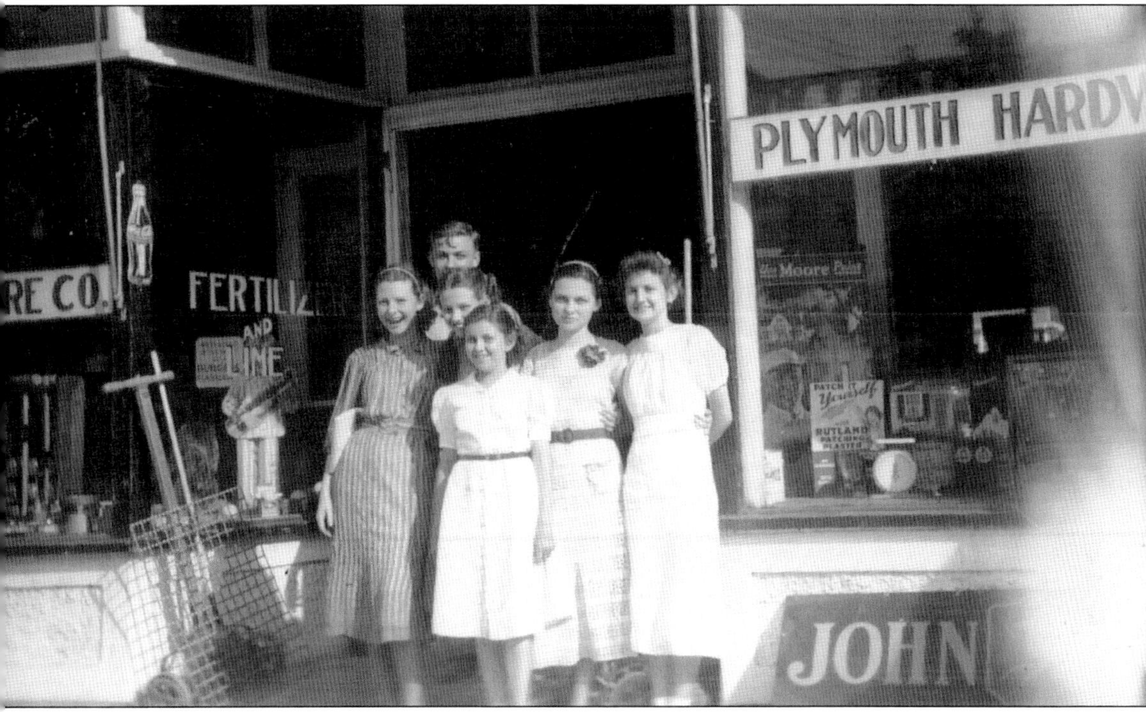

A group of pals pose in front of Plymouth Hardware Company on Water Street in downtown Plymouth in this World War II–era photograph. Among those identified are Margie White, far left; Hallett Everett, in the rear; Virginia Ward, second from right; and Mary Cotten Davenport, far right. (Mary Cotten Davenport.)

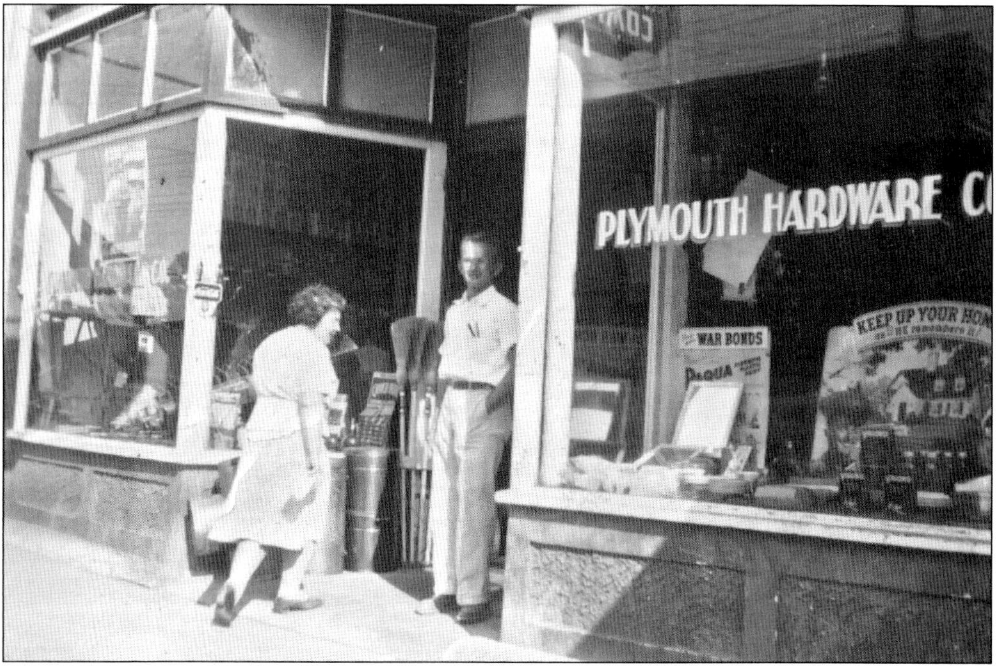

A customer enters the Plymouth Hardware Company on Water Street, owned by Alva Edison Davenport, while another stands in the doorway. The sign in the window, urging customers to "Buy More War Bonds," indicates that the photograph was taken during World War II. (Mary Cotten Davenport.)

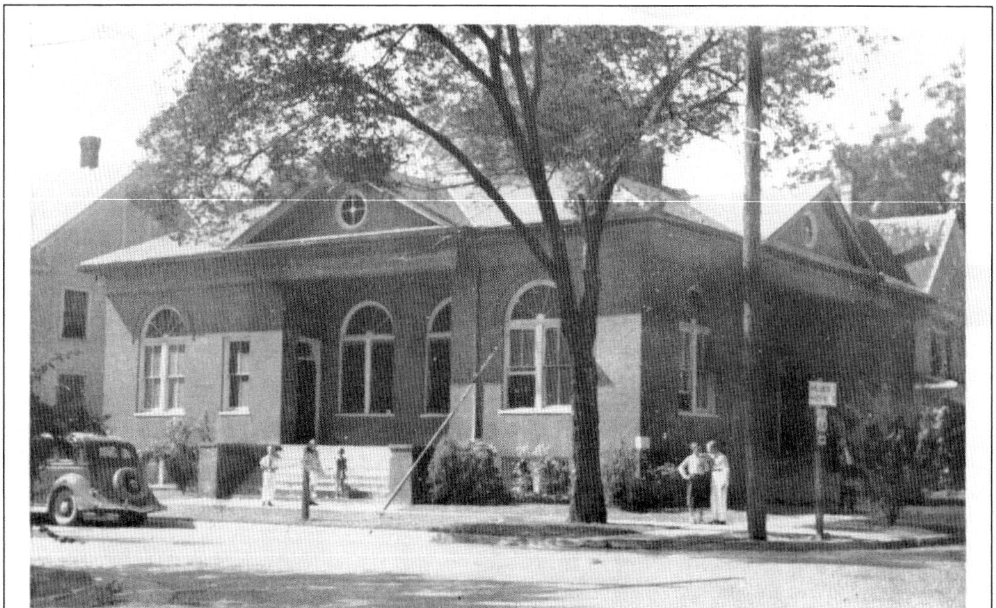

BAPTIST CHURCH, PLYMOUTH, NORTH CAROLINA

In 1866, a dozen people gathered in a private home in Plymouth to establish a Missionary Baptist church. The congregation built a church at Fifth and Madison Streets in 1868 and used the building until 1915, when they built a new building at the corner of Washington and Third Streets. This postcard shows the church in the 1930s. (NCC.)

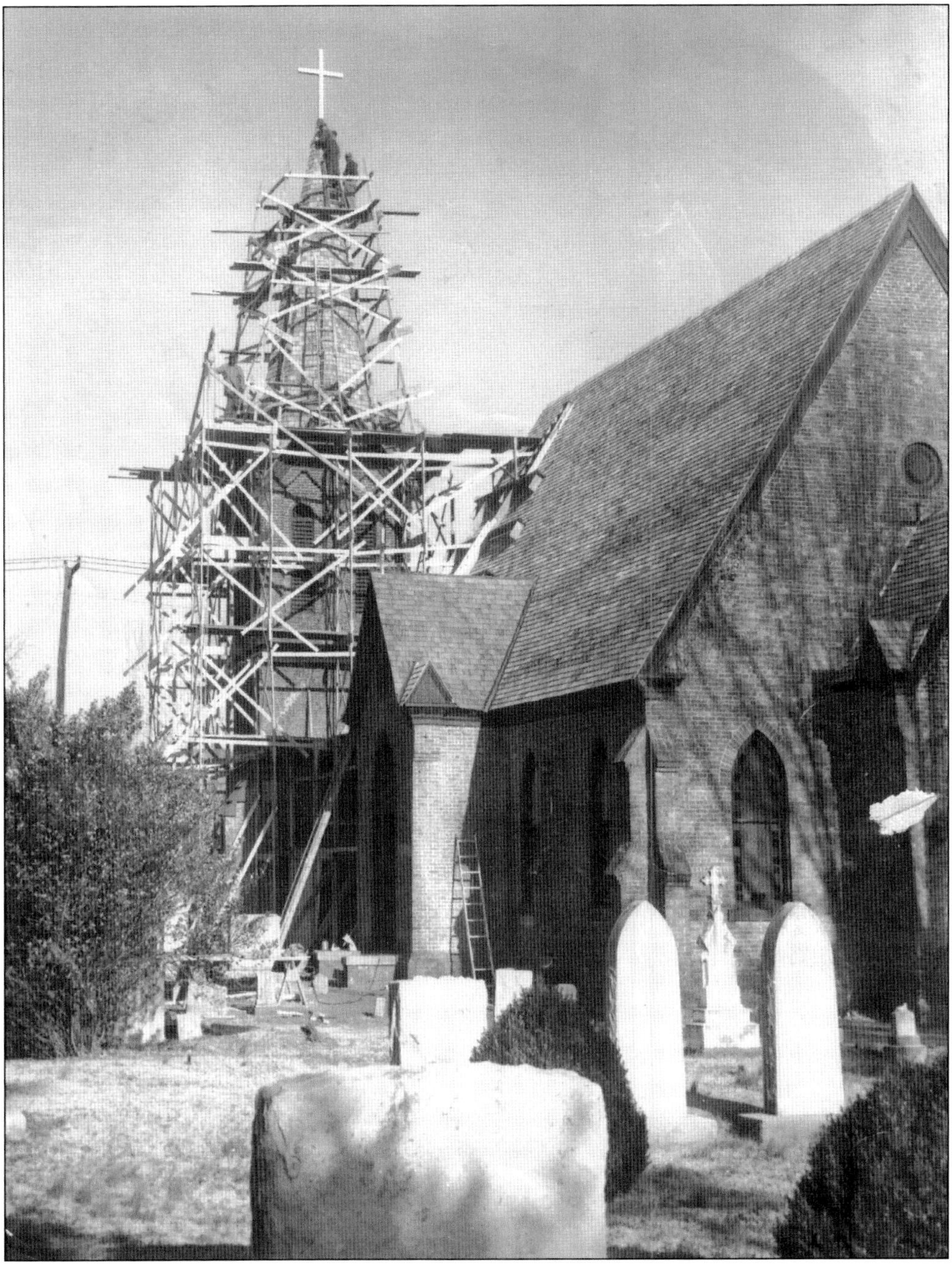

Plymouth's Grace Episcopal Church was organized in 1837. The church's distinctive steeple can be seen in engravings of battles published in *Harper's Weekly* during the Civil War. The church was damaged during the war, and Union soldiers returned to Plymouth after the war to make repairs. This photograph, taken in 1970, shows workers repairing the steeple. (Grace Episcopal Church.)

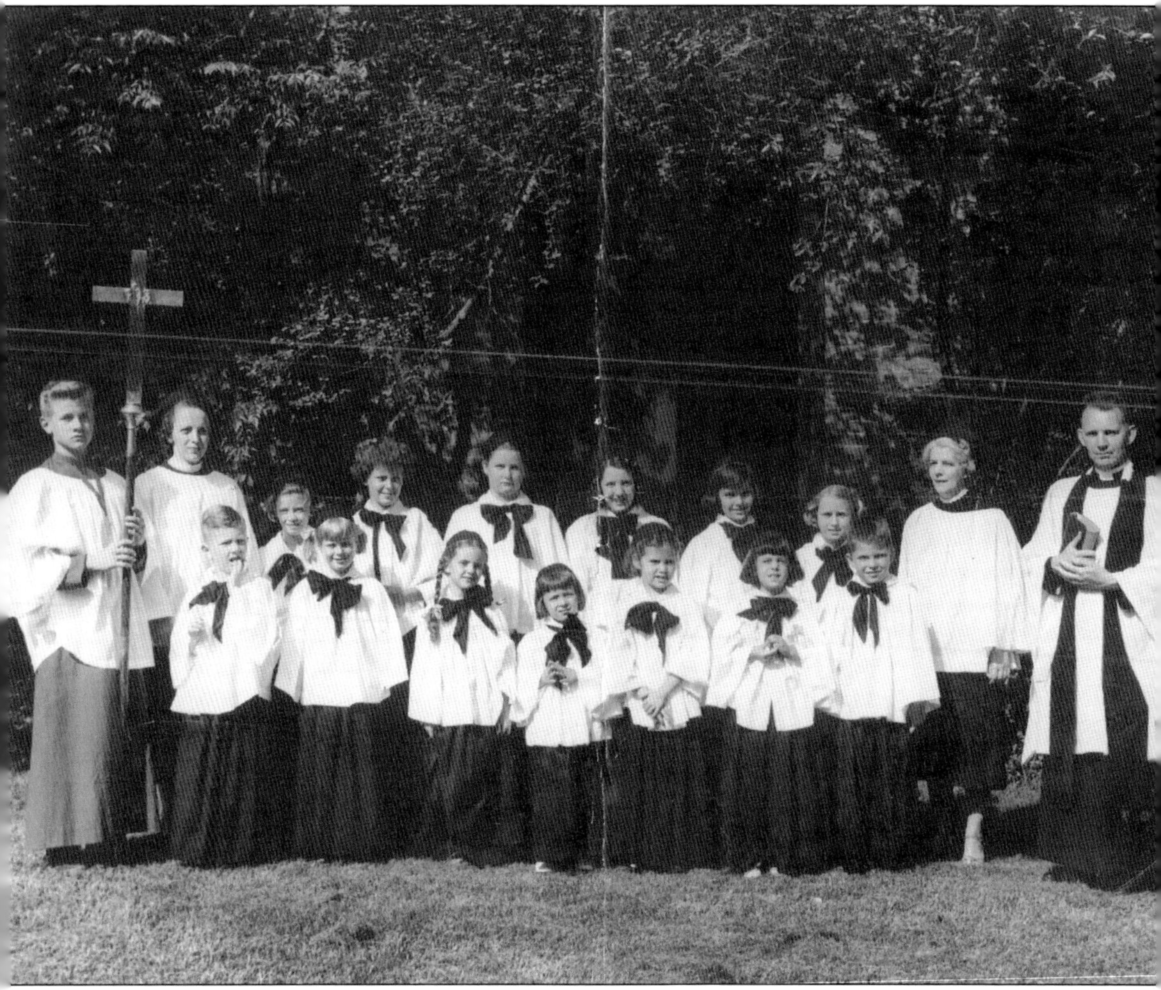

Pictured in this 1950s photograph of the Grace Episcopal Church children's choir are, from left to right, (first row) Lloyd Horton, Jimmy Ashby, Jeannie Popenieu, Judy Frank, Janie Williford, Diane Weaver, Janet Bruce, and Lim Doxey; (second row) Meredith ?, Martha Simpson, Judy Evans, Sue Knowles, two unidentified, Linda Popenieu, Isabelle Read, and Ed Spruill. (Grace Episcopal Church.)

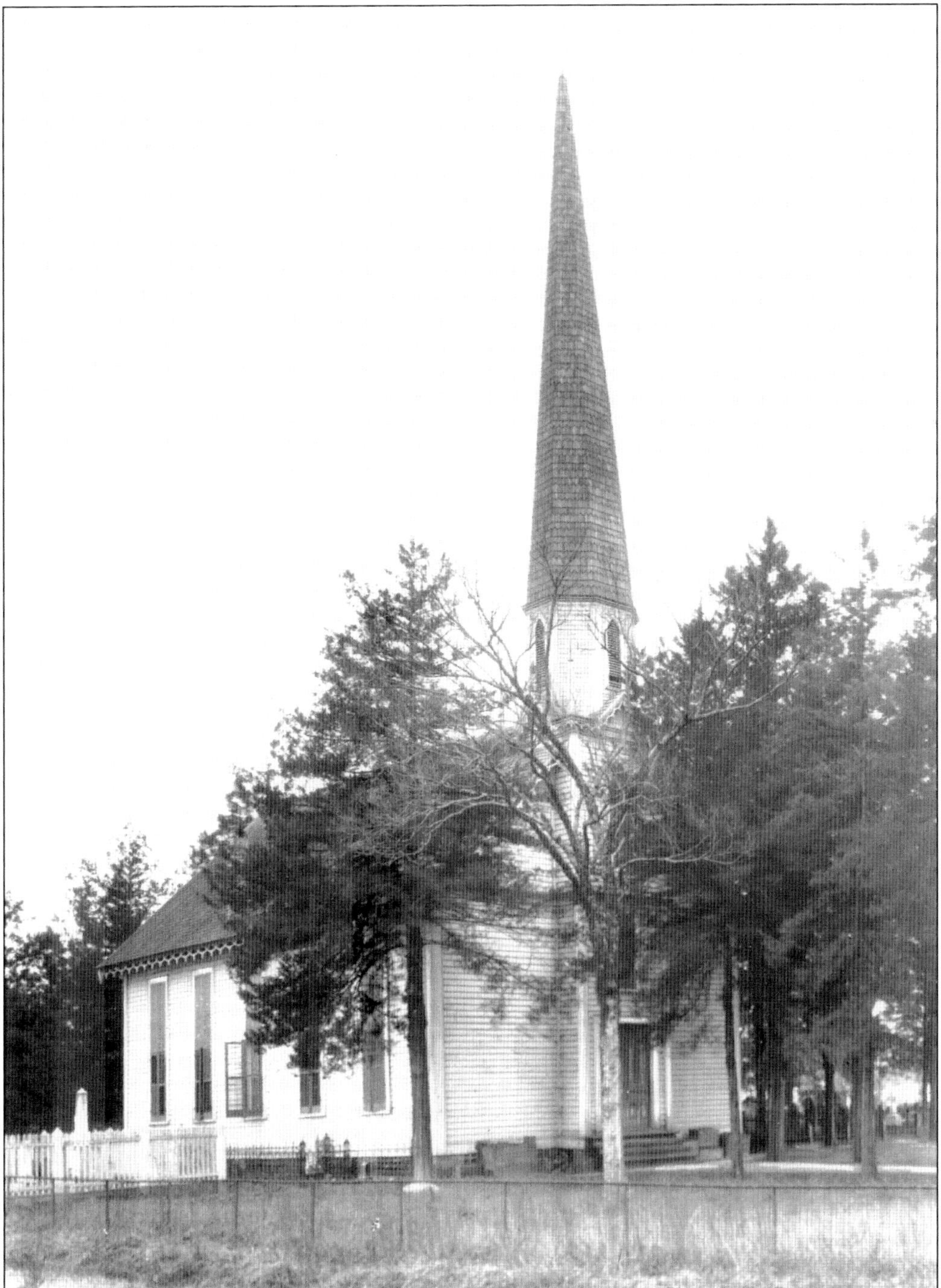

On January 29, 1862, two Union officers were attending a concert at the Plymouth Methodist Church when word that Confederate troops were approaching reached them. The officers could not get through the crowd to a door, so they climbed through a window and hurried to their troops. The church, shown in this c. 1909 photograph, was heavily damaged during the war and later rebuilt with a brick facade. (Plymouth United Methodist Church.)

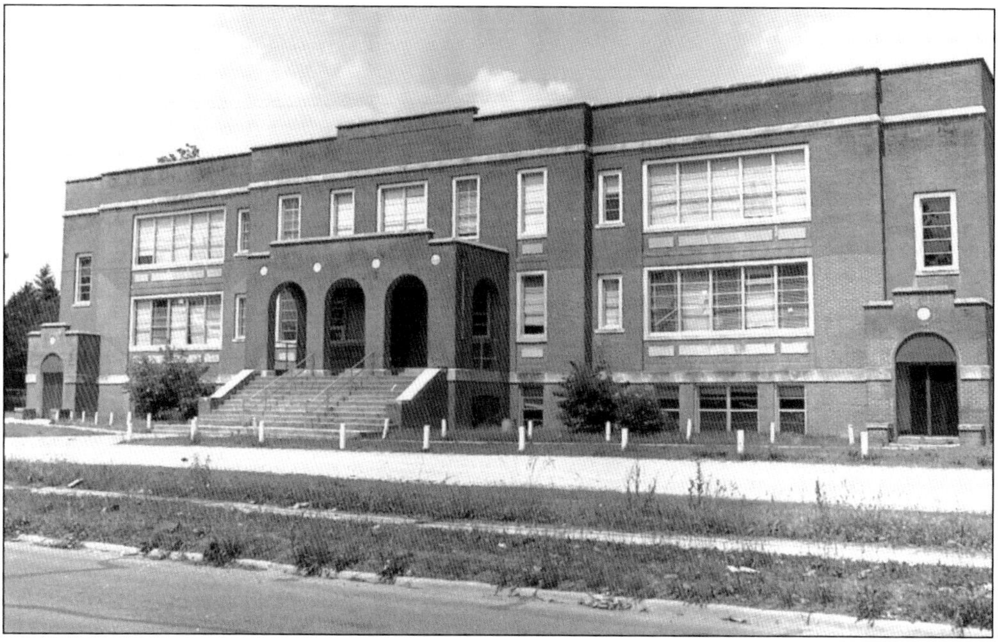

During the days of segregated public schools, this building on Washington Street housed the Plymouth High School for white students. When a new high school for whites was built in 1959, the building became an elementary school. Plymouth's public schools were fully integrated by the late 1960s. (Doward Jones Jr.)

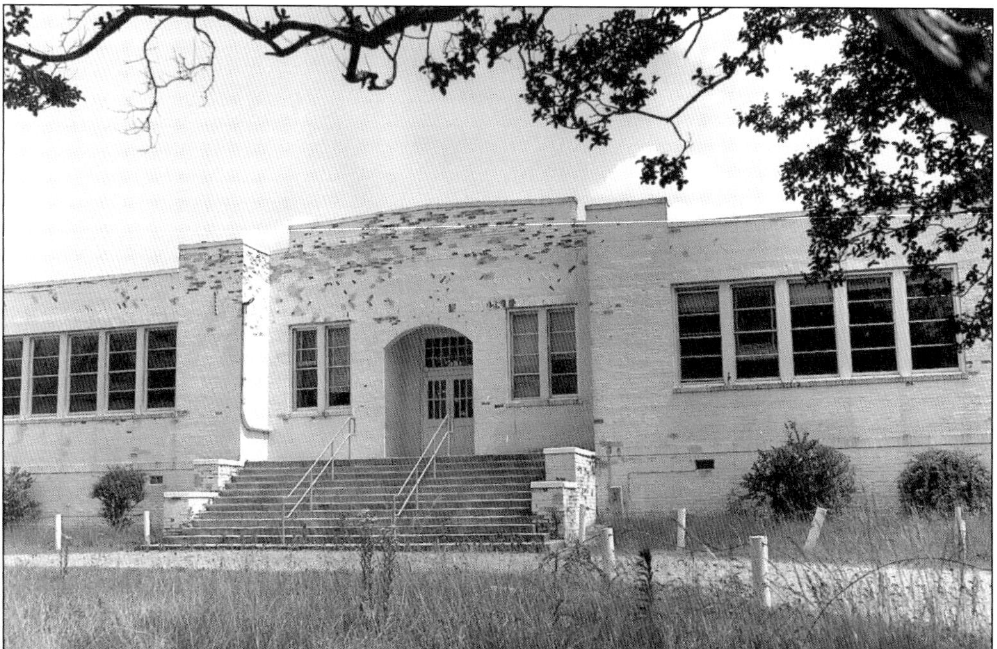

Before public schools were integrated, the Fourth Street School housed a high school and grade school for African American students in Plymouth. The school burned in 1999, but the iconic entrance survived. Plymouth residents are converting the entrance and lot into a memorial park for teachers. (Doward Jones Jr.)

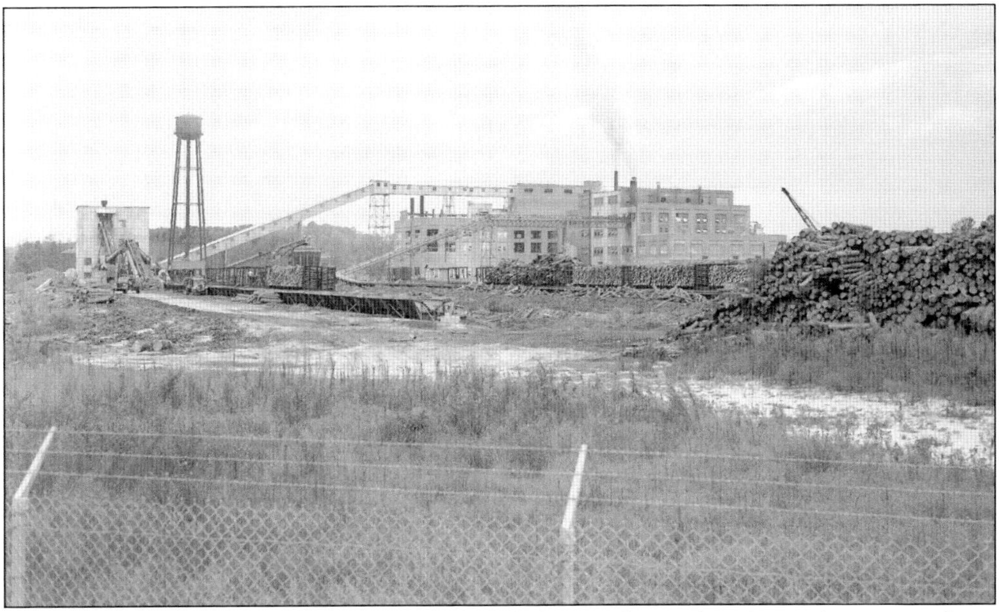

In 1937, Kieckhefer Container Company opened the North Carolina Paper Company, a large pulp mill on the Roanoke River, just upstream from Plymouth. The mill is shown here in August 1938, shortly after it opened. In 1957, Kieckefer merged with Weyerhauser Timber Company. Despite cutbacks in operation, the mill has been a backbone of the regional economy since it opened. (SANC.)

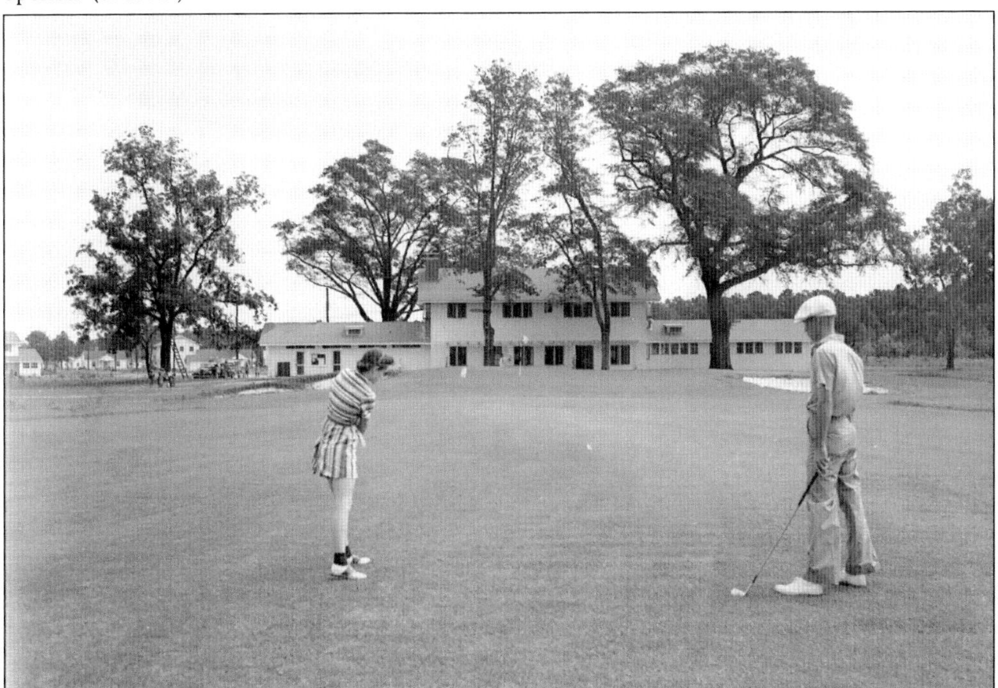

North Carolina Paper Company built a subdivision in Plymouth to house its workers, including a nine-hole golf course and country club. In August 1938, two golfers are seen making their approach to the ninth hole, with the country club in the background. (SANC.)

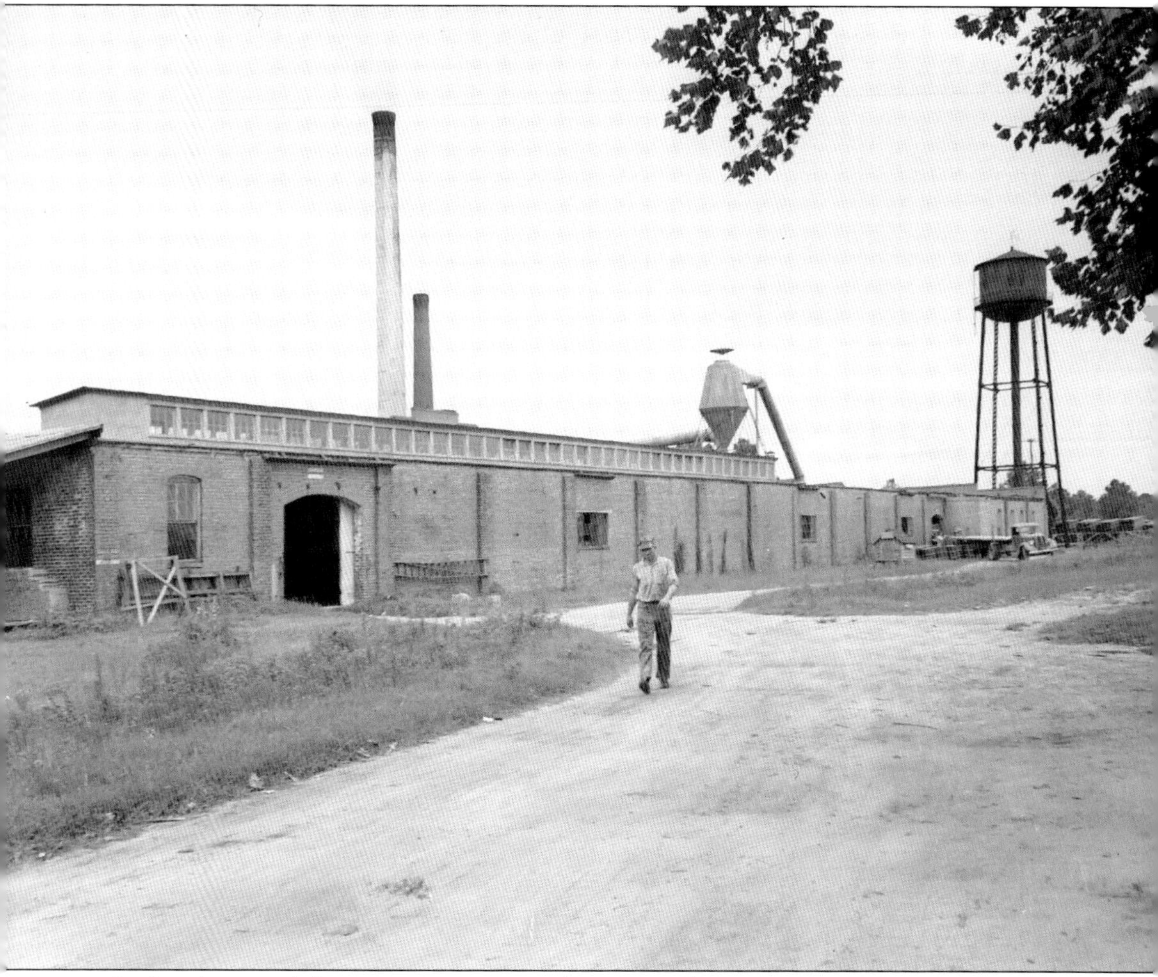

In this photograph from August 1938, a worker crosses the yard at the Atlas Plywood Company, formerly Wilt's Veneer Company. The company was located on the Roanoke River, just below downtown Plymouth. The Georgia Pacific Company later purchased the site. (SANC.)

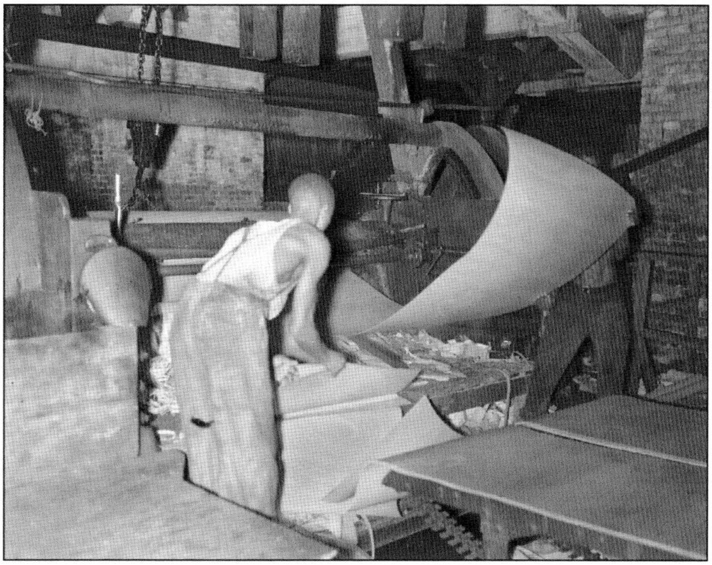

Workers at Atlas Plywood Company monitor a "peeler" machine. Logs were inserted into the machine, and as the log was rolled around on a spindle, it was peeled into the long, thin sheets used to make plywood. Workers were careful to keep their hands away from the large knife that peeled the logs. (SANC.)

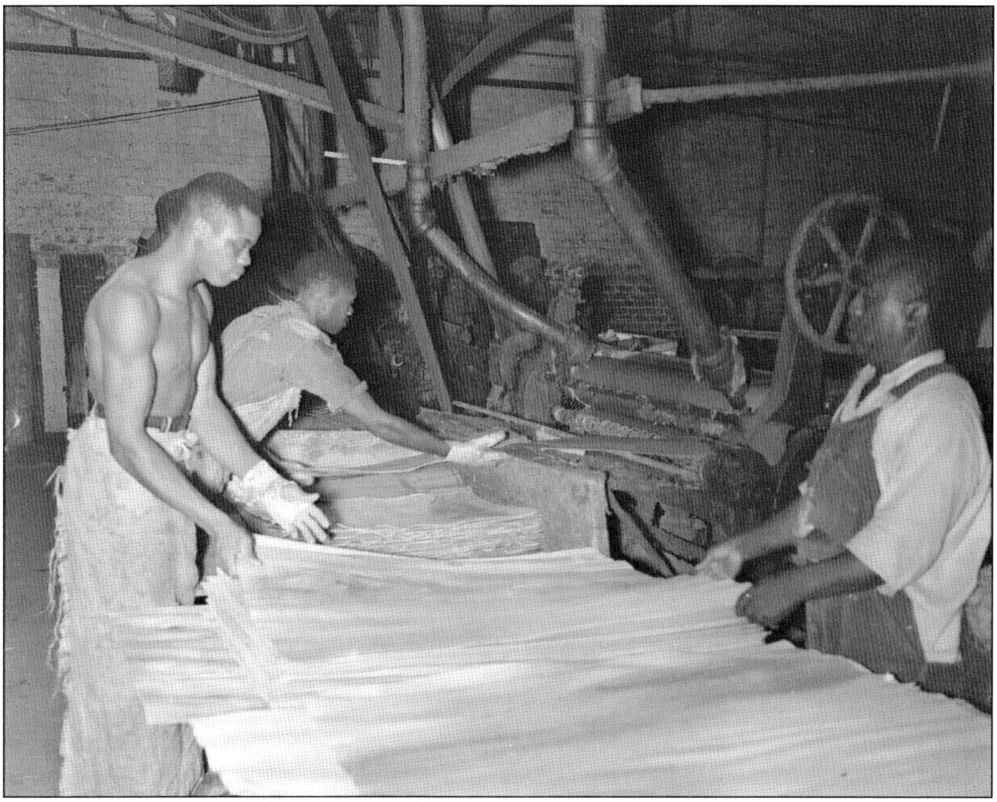

Seen in August 1938, workers at the Atlas Plywood Company handle the peeled sheets of wood that were used to make plywood. The sheets were dried, then glue was spread between the sheets, and finally, they were pressed together to make plywood. Gum, pine, and walnut were among the woods used in this process. (SANC.)

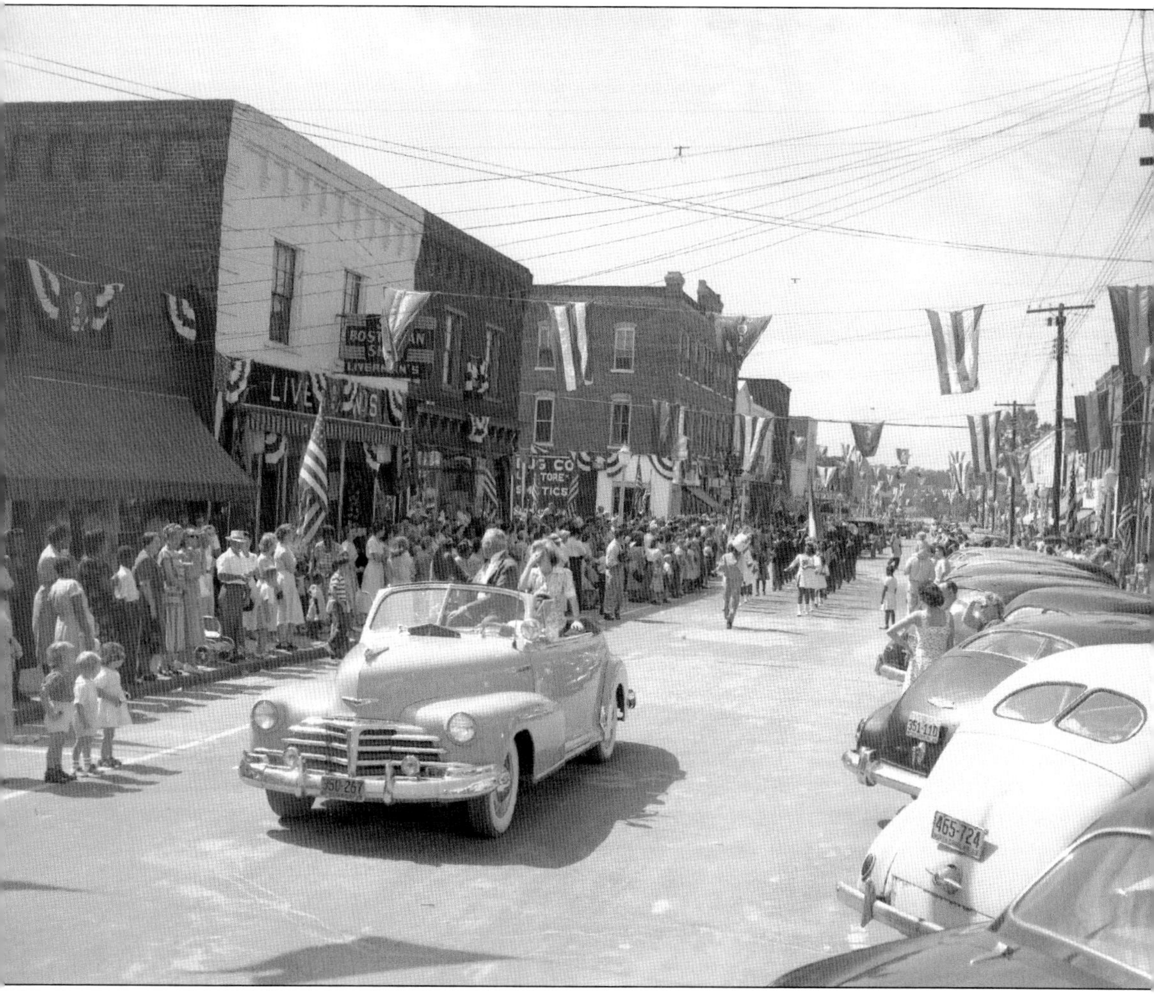

In September 1949, Plymouth mayor Archie J. Riddle Sr., riding in a shiny 1948 Chevrolet convertible, spots a friend on the sidewalk of Water Street during one of the daily parades celebrating Washington County's 150th anniversary. Special VIP guests during the five-day event included two US senators, members of the state legislature, journalists, and high-ranking officers from military bases in North Carolina. (SANC.)

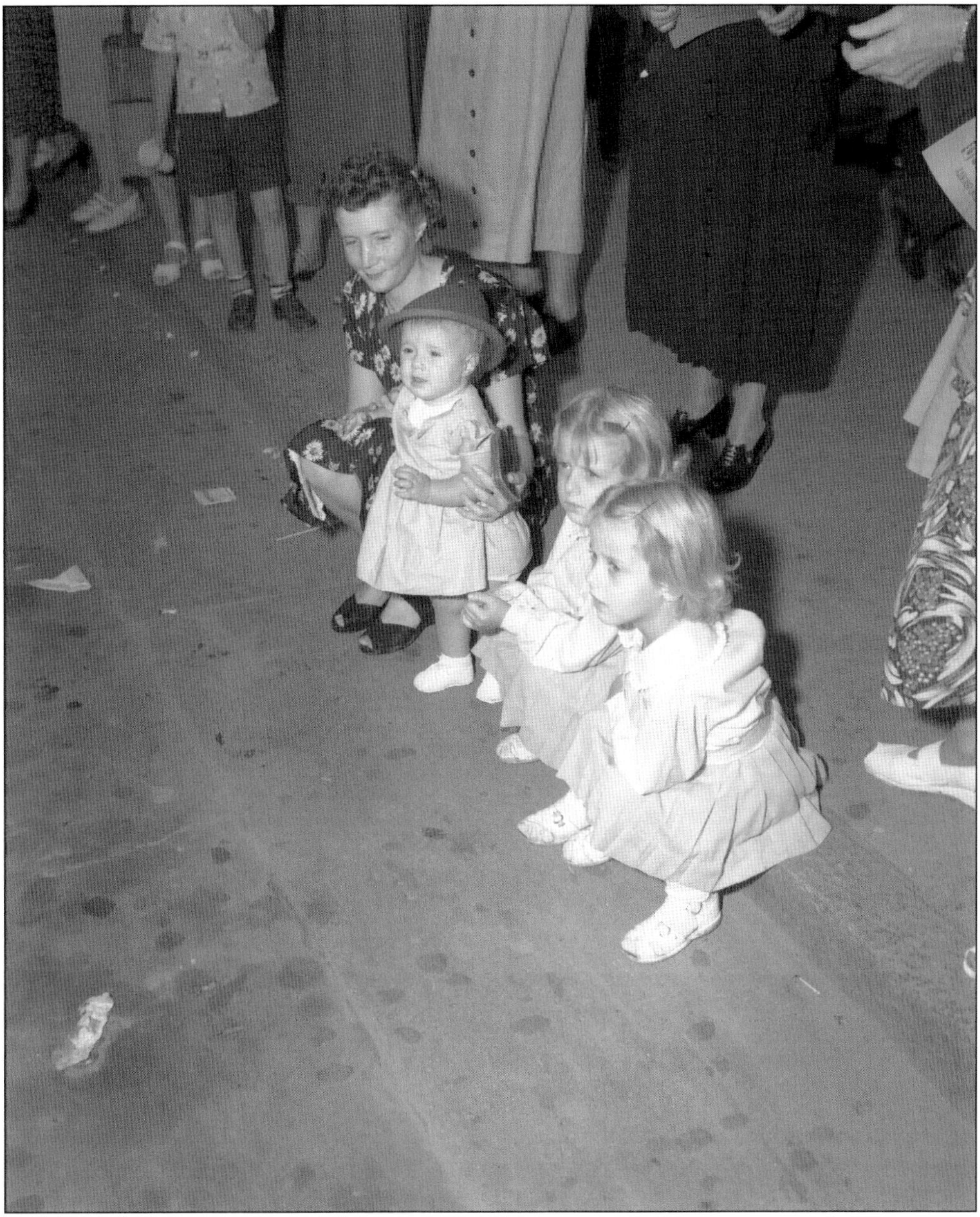

Among the five days of festivities during Washington County's 150th anniversary were activities geared toward kids, including these young blond twins who are watching one of the parades. The clowns featured in the parades, as well as nightly fireworks displays at the local baseball park, also got the kids' attention. (SANC.)

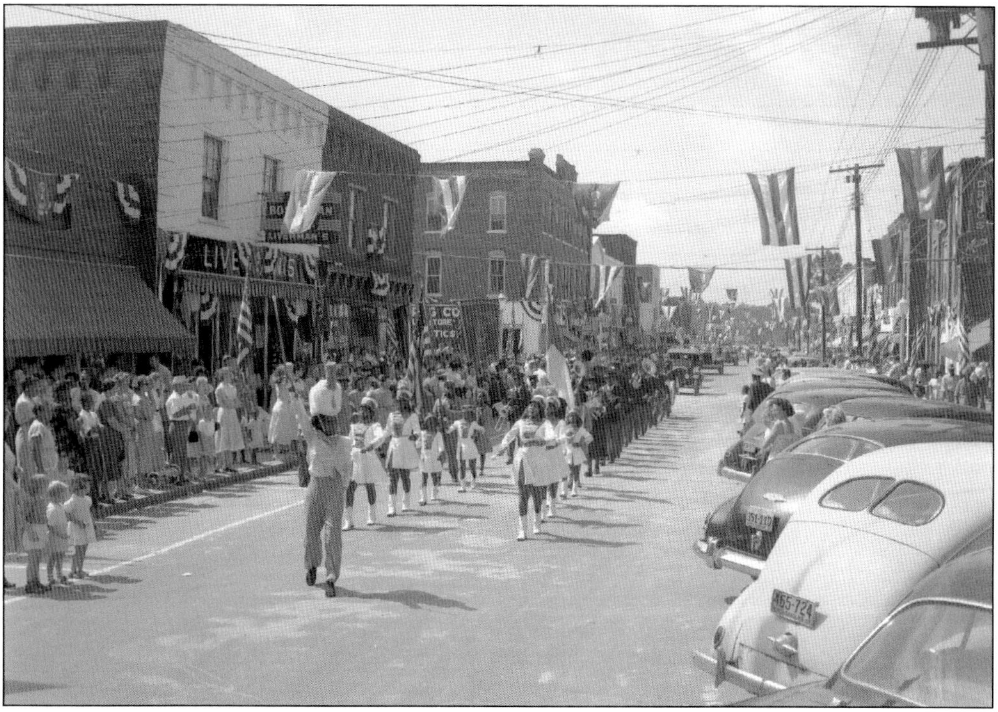

Marching bands from local high schools set the pace for the series of parades. Here, a large crowd watches as the J.J. Clemons High School band from Roper marches down Water Street, Plymouth's main commercial thoroughfare. Below, a banner carried by the color guard announces the approach of the Plymouth High School marching band. Parades were held daily for four days during the celebration and included military units. The Plymouth Jaycee Club sponsored the sesquicentennial celebration, and while planning the event, a consultant warned them that their plans were too ambitious and that they would not be able to stage so grand a celebration. But the Jaycees proved the consultant wrong. (SANC.)

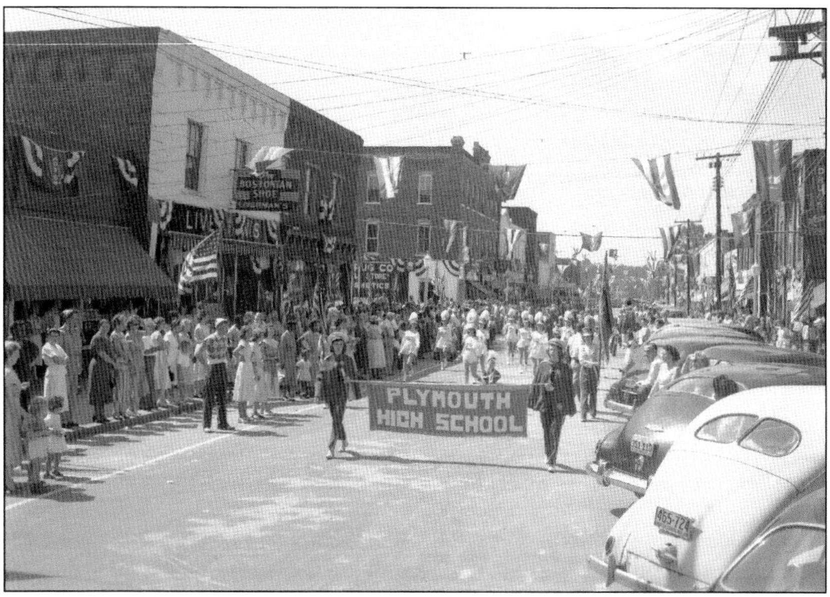

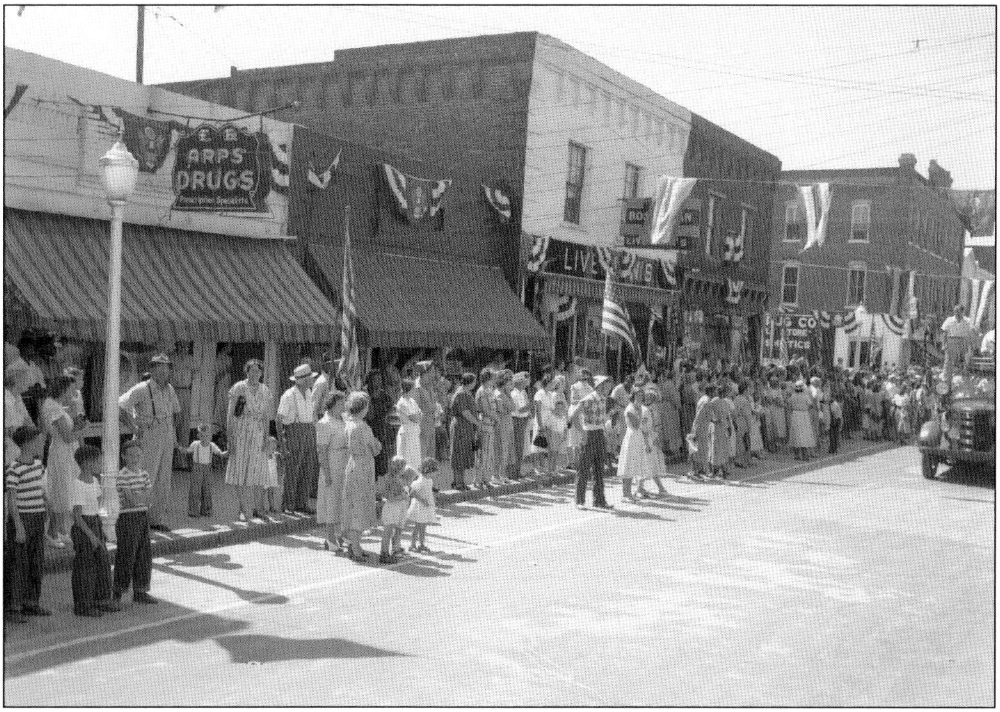

When Plymouth hosted its 150th-anniversary celebration, town officials received letters of congratulations from Pres. Harry Truman as well as leaders in both Plymouth, England, and Plymouth, Massachusetts. In addition to the many parades, the celebration included special church services and singing hymns at the local baseball park, firefighting demonstrations and water fights by local firemen, visits by VIPs, a beauty contest, and other events. The photograph above shows part of the large crowd that gathered on Water Street for one of the parades, all of which featured marching bands, clowns, beauty queens, and fire trucks. The photograph below shows young students watching the parade, with one man holding an American flag. (SANC.)

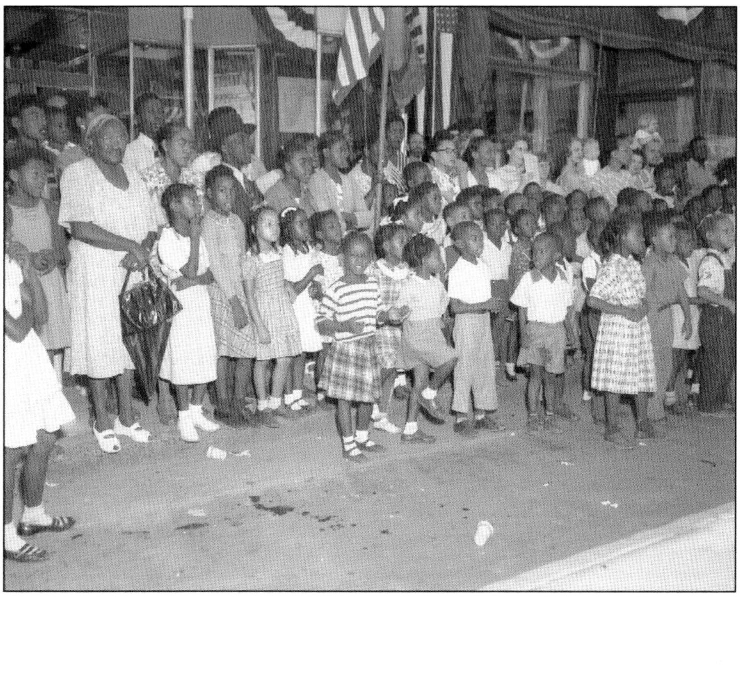

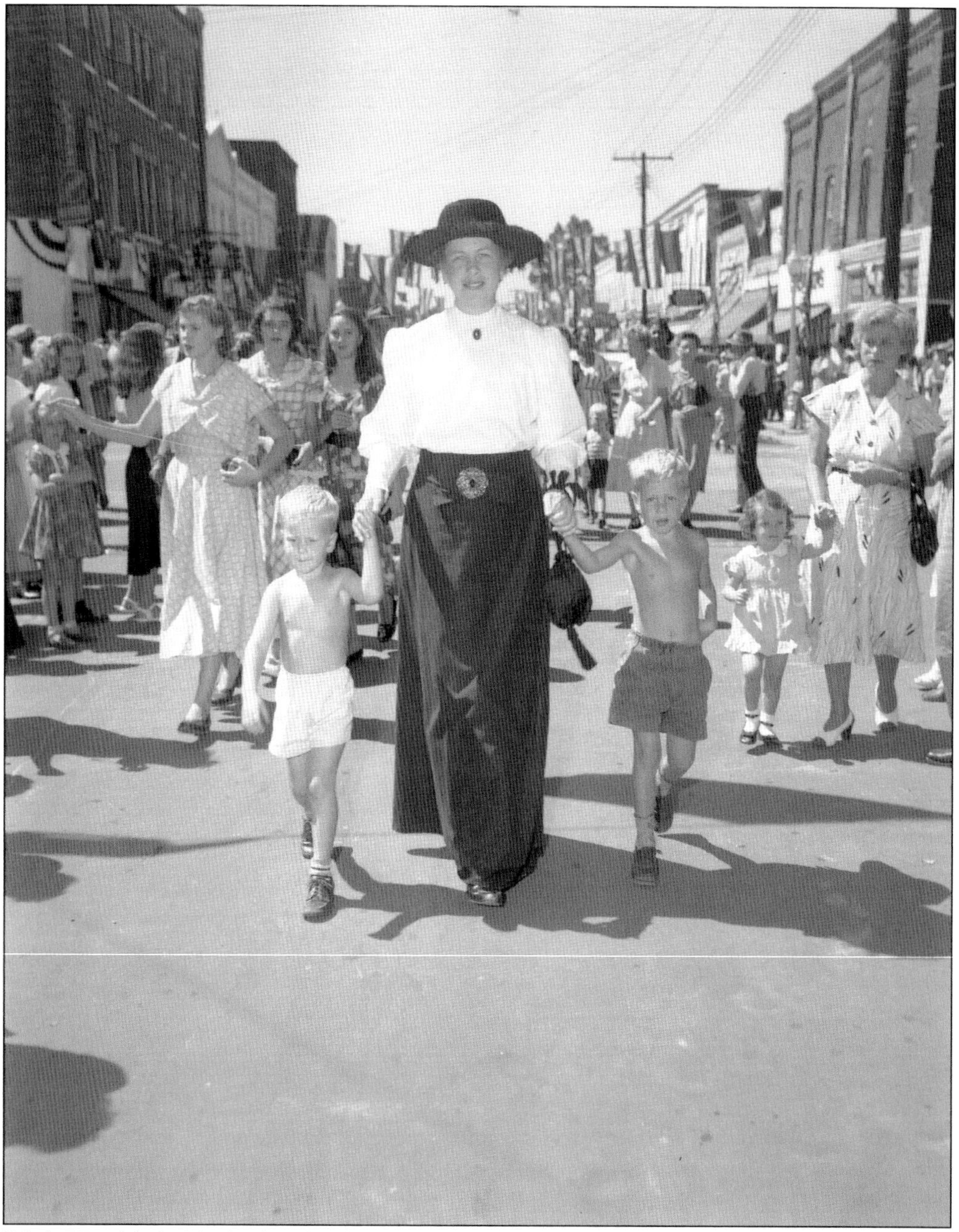

Edith Womble holds the hands of her two sons—Ed and Logan—as she marches with other mothers. Behind Womble, near the left edge of the photograph, Barbara McCombs is holding what appears to be a yo-yo. (SANC.)

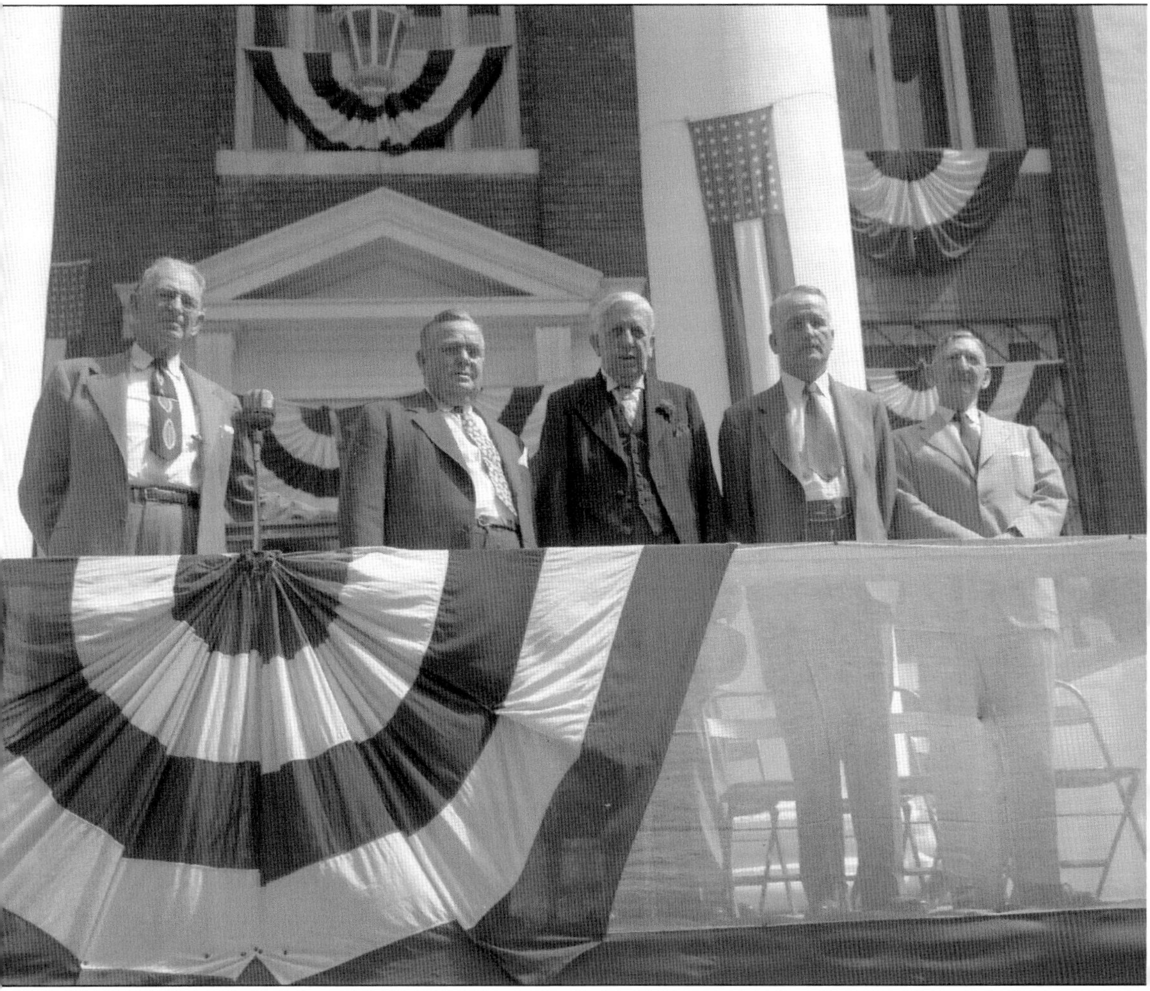

Both of North Carolina's US senators were among the dignitaries who came to Plymouth for Washington County's 150th birthday party in September 1949. From left to right are US senator Frank P. Graham, Plymouth businessman Roy Hampton, US senator Clyde Hoey, Plymouth attorney W.O. Whitley, and Plymouth attorney and former member of the North Carolina legislature Zeb Vance Norman. (SANC.)

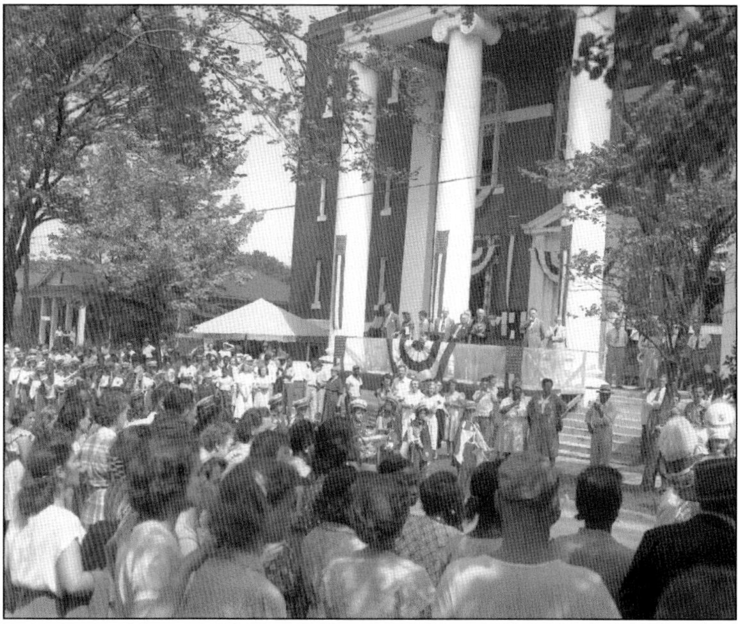

Here, the dignitaries watch one of the parades from a viewing stand on Adams Street, where the Plymouth High School marching band passes the Washington County Courthouse. (SANC.)

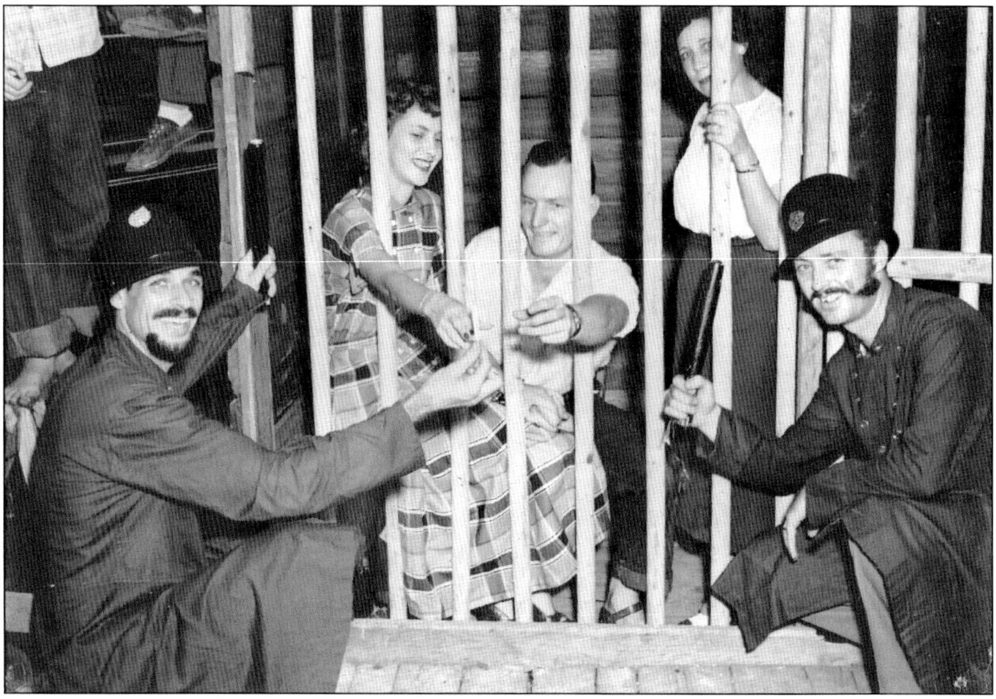

As part of a fundraising effort during the Washington County sesquicentennial in 1949, prominent Plymouth citizens were "arrested" and held for "bail," which consisted of a voluntary contribution. In this photograph, Paul Hardison (far let) hands a cigarette to his "prisoners," and Omega Rogers (far right) brandishes a nightstick. (RRMM.)

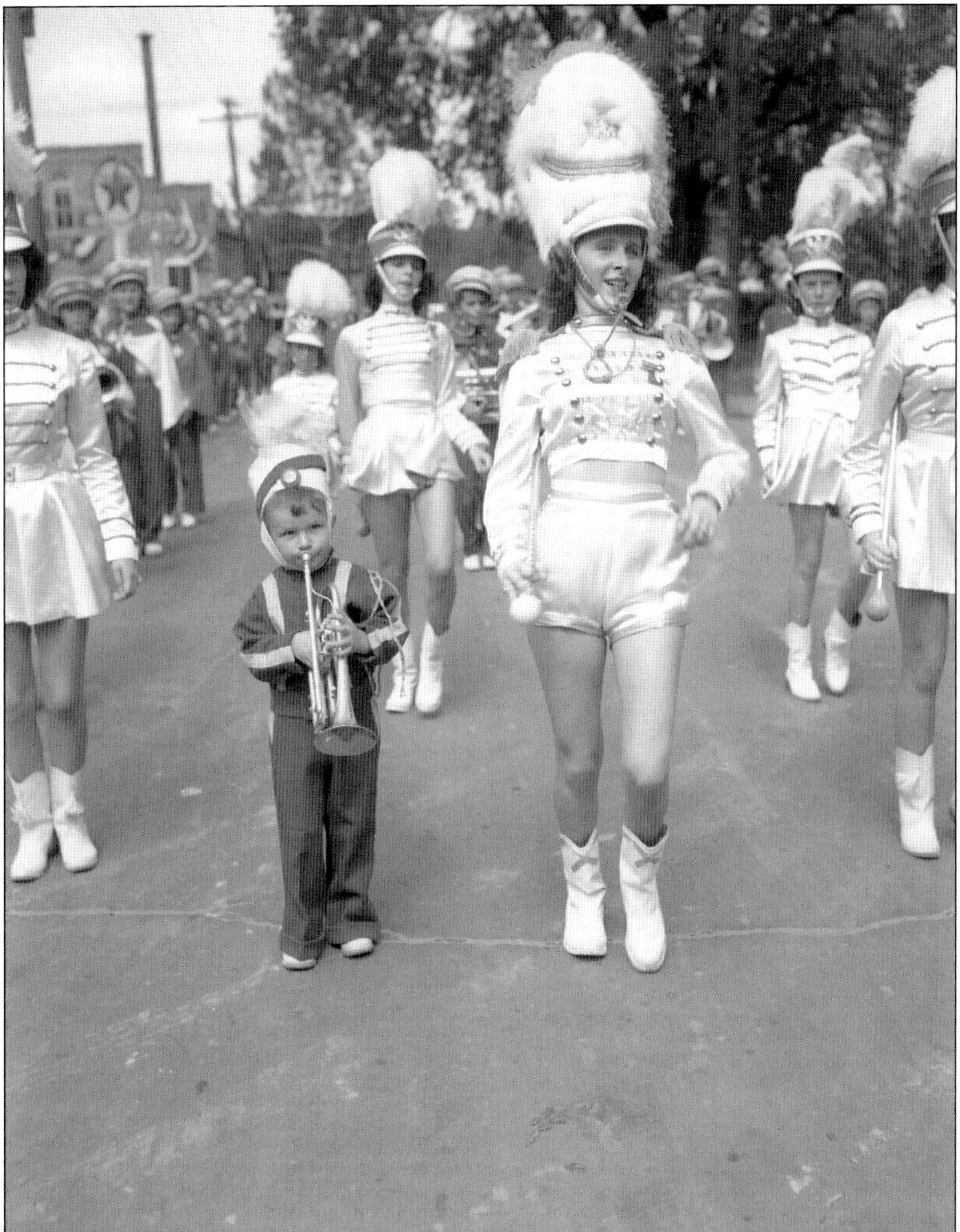

Accompanied by a young trumpet-blowing friend, chief drum majorette Betty Jean "B.J." Jackson leads the Plymouth High School marching band down Adams Street, where the band was about to pass before a viewing stand of dignitaries set up at the Washington County Courthouse. (SANC.)

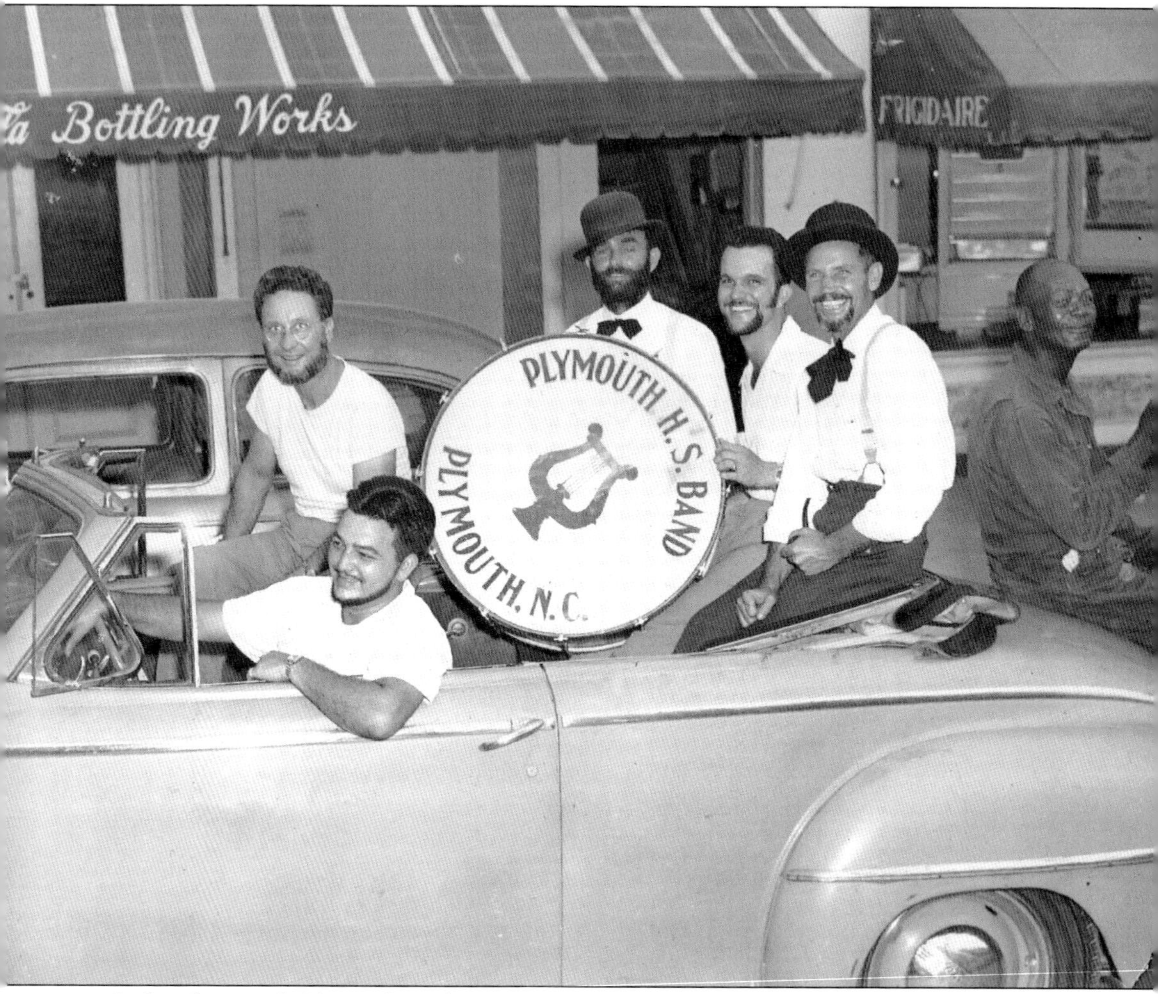

In this photograph, Plymouth residents pose in a convertible on Water Street during the Washington County sesquicentennial in September 1949. The driver is Ivan Atamanchuk. With him in the front seat is Ludford McNair. In the back seat are, from left to right, Perry Turner, Gilbert Mobley, and Floyd Asby. "Happy" Horton is sitting on the trunk. (RRMM.)

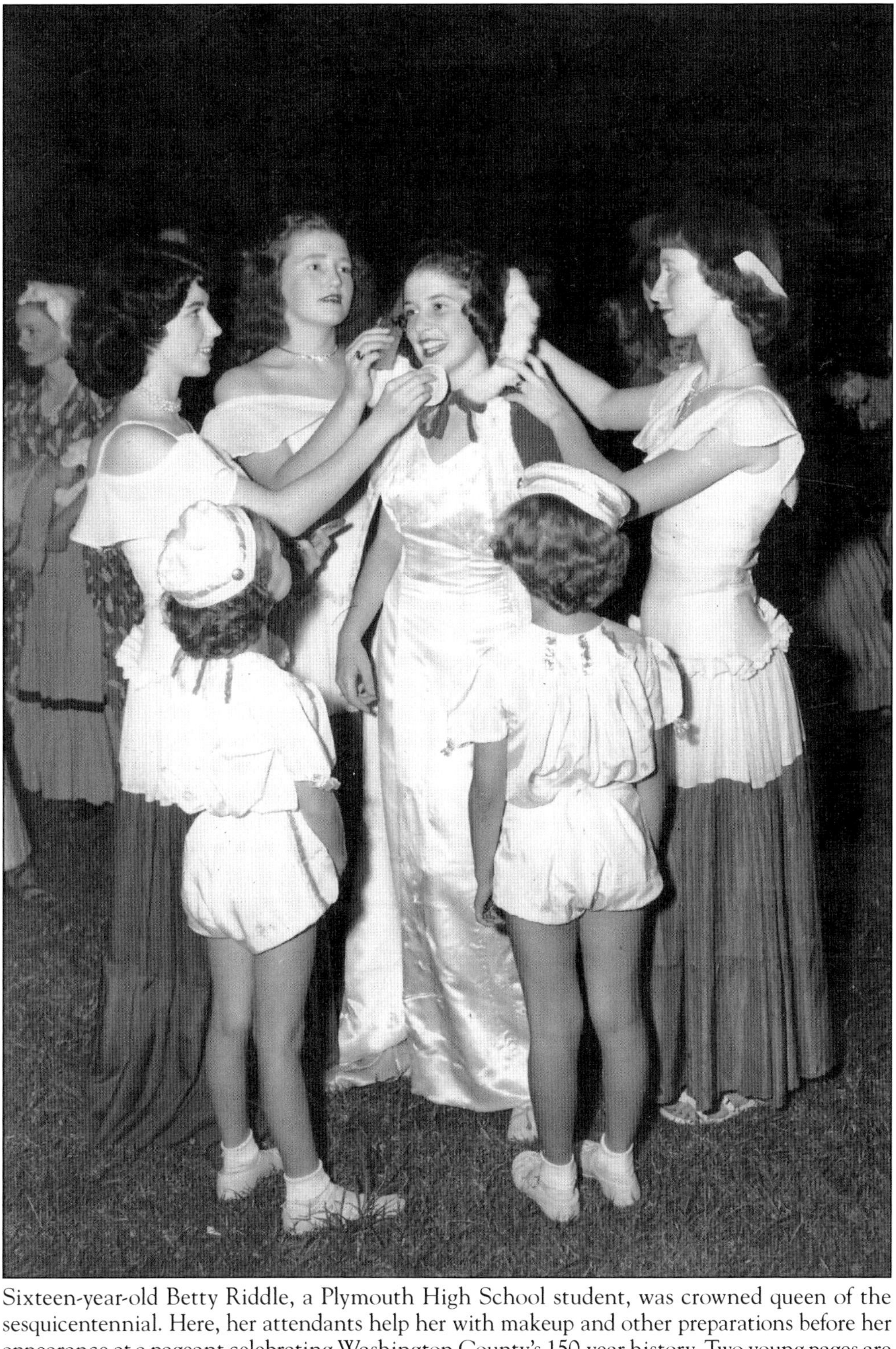

Sixteen-year-old Betty Riddle, a Plymouth High School student, was crowned queen of the sesquicentennial. Here, her attendants help her with makeup and other preparations before her appearance at a pageant celebrating Washington County's 150-year history. Two young pages are lost in admiration of the queen. (Photograph by Jack Weaver; courtesy of RRMM.)

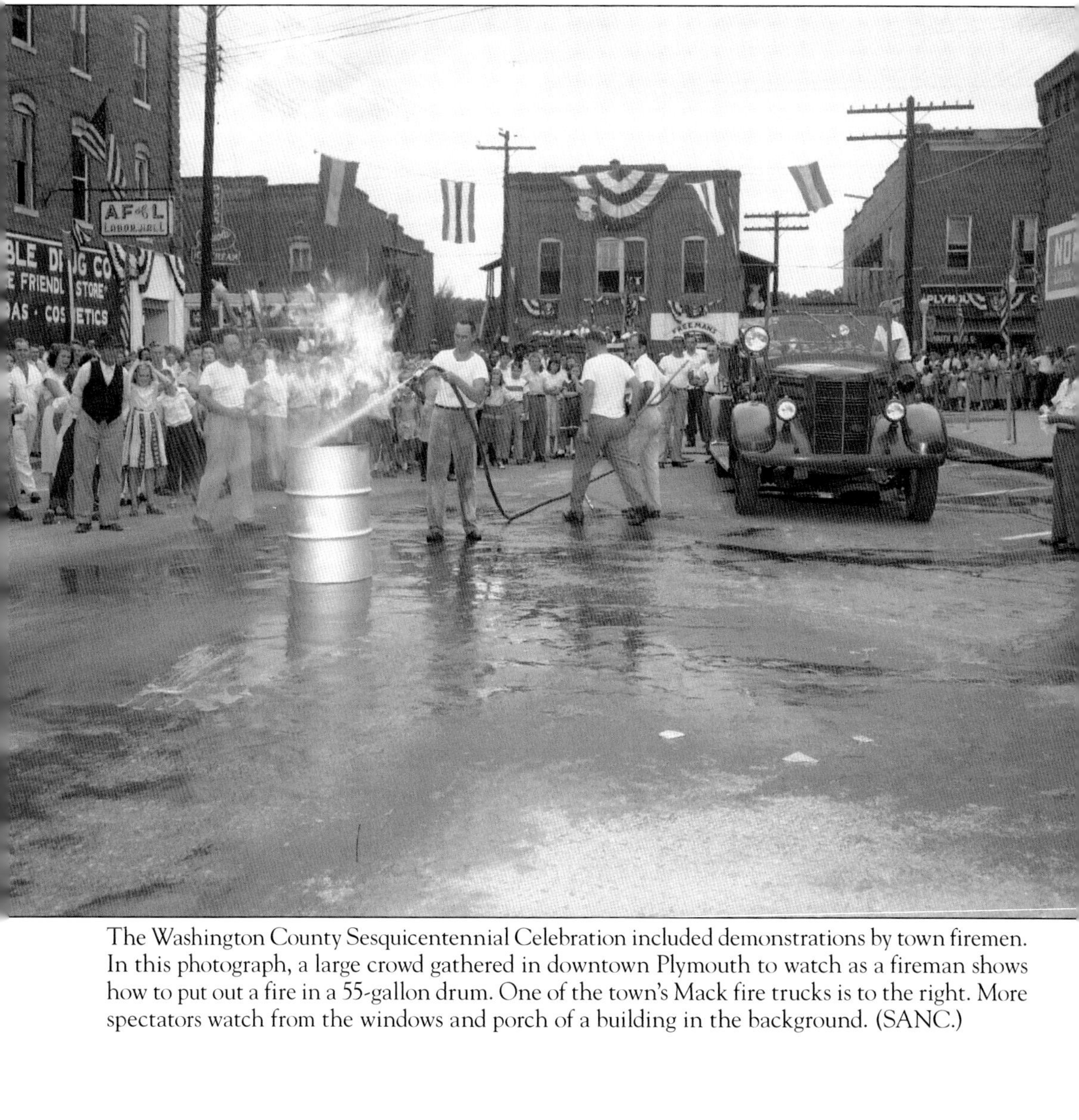

The Washington County Sesquicentennial Celebration included demonstrations by town firemen. In this photograph, a large crowd gathered in downtown Plymouth to watch as a fireman shows how to put out a fire in a 55-gallon drum. One of the town's Mack fire trucks is to the right. More spectators watch from the windows and porch of a building in the background. (SANC.)

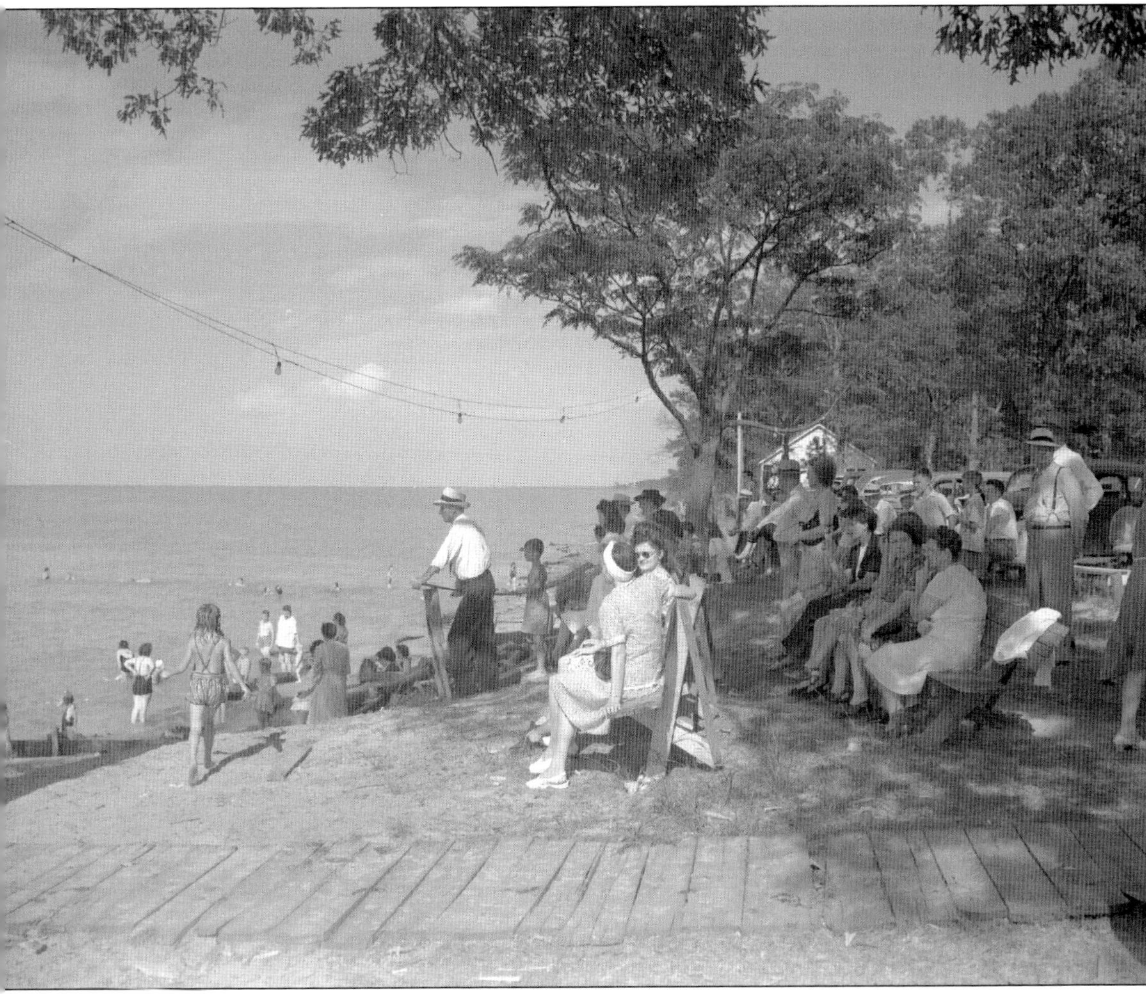

A small crowd gathers on the shore to watch the swimmers in the Albemarle Sound on a summer afternoon in 1945. Judging from the way people are dressed, it is likely that this photograph was taken on a Sunday afternoon, when people came straight from church services to Albemarle Beach. (SANC.)

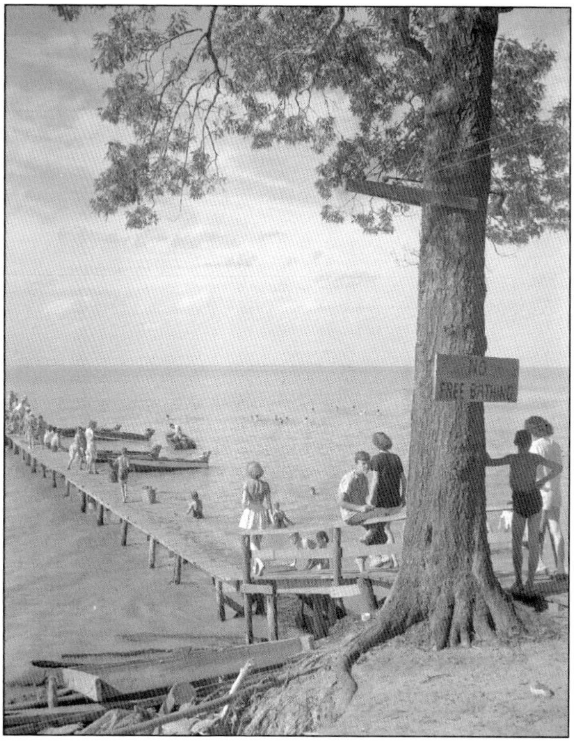

The Albemarle Sound is the largest freshwater sound in North America, but it also has been the old swimming hole for generations of Washington County residents. Seen here in July 1945, people are gathering at Albemarle Beach to swim and socialize on a hot summer afternoon. (SANC.)

Young swimmers play in the shallow water near the shore of the Albemarle Sound, while others just dangle their legs off the pier and watch the fun. Meanwhile, three young women, one of whom is holding a soft drink, stroll back to shore on the pier. (SANC.)

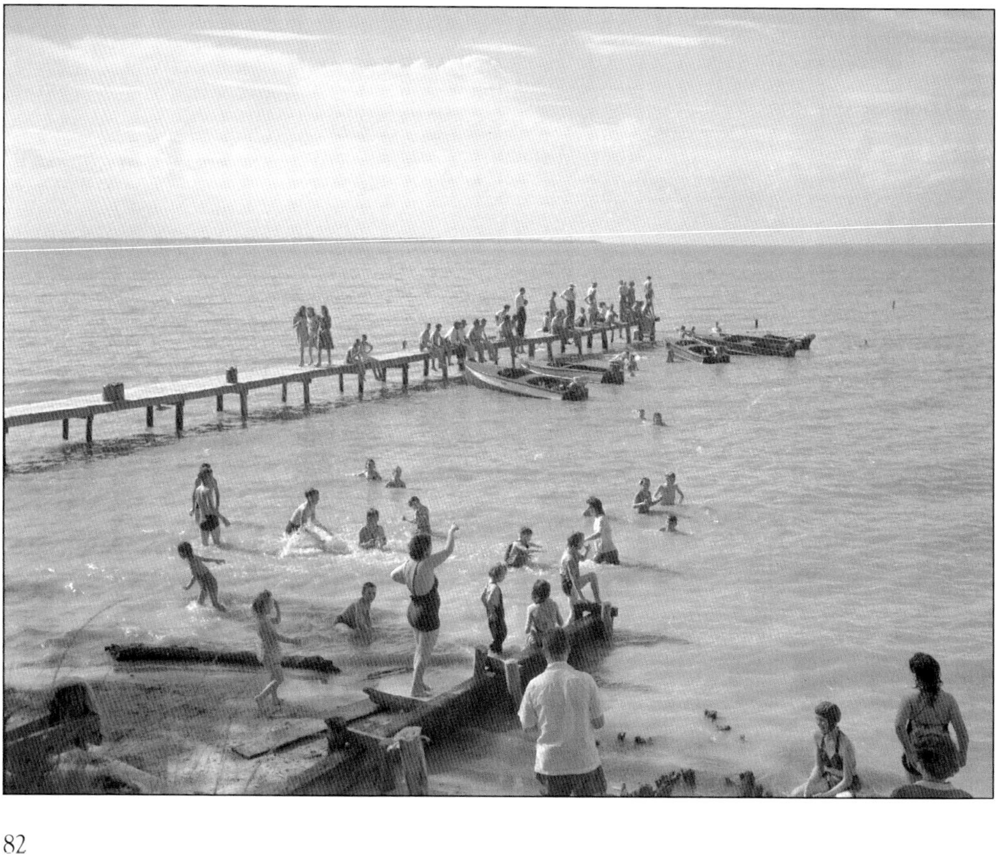

Pleasure boats named *Hon*, *Zip, Jr.*, and *Pet* are tied to the pier at Albemarle Beach in this July 1945 photograph. Water skiing was a hugely popular pastime on the Albemarle Sound, and a couple of these boats appear to have engines powerful enough to pull a skier. (SANC.)

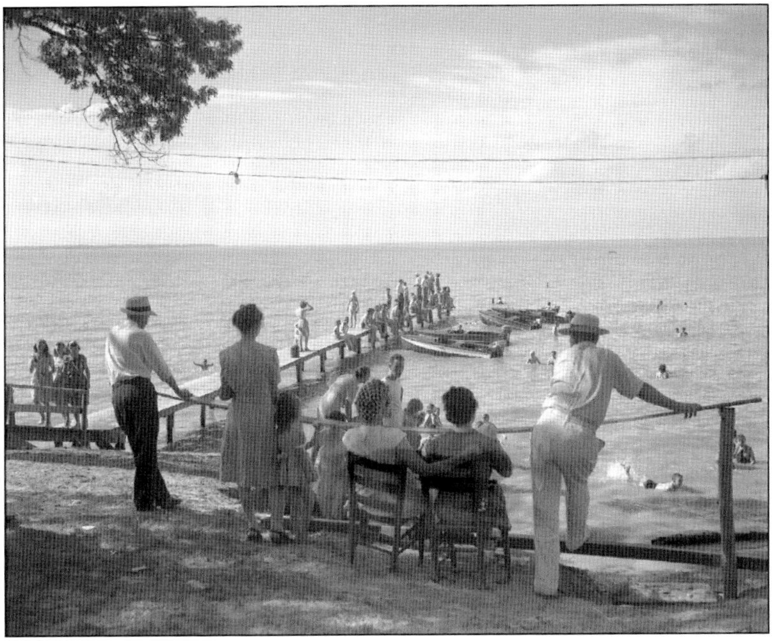

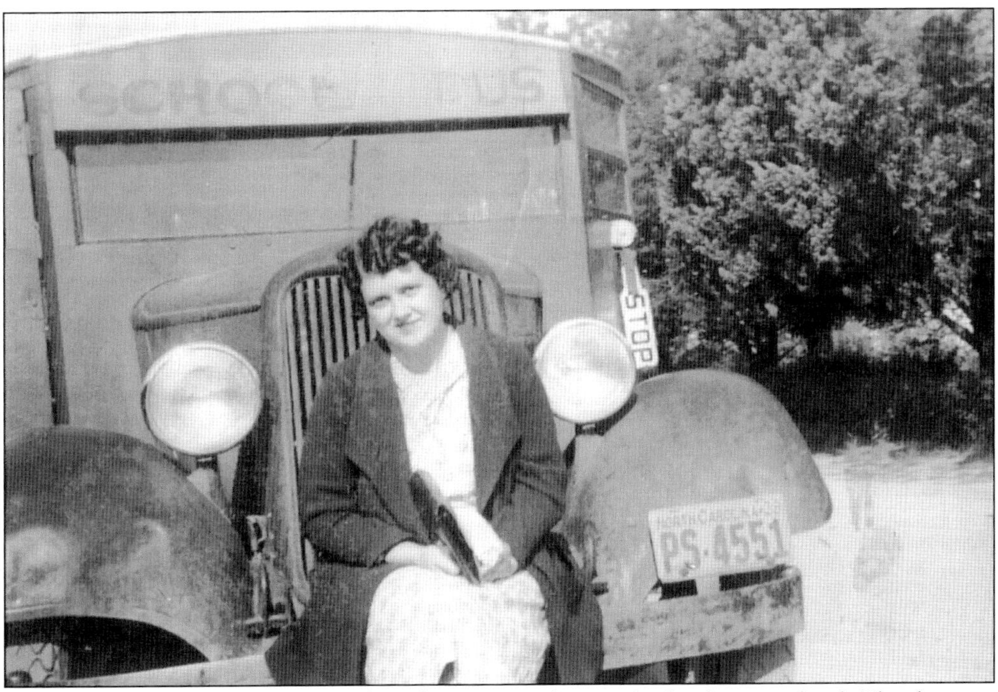

In 1938, many of the public school students in Mackeys rode this bus to school. The driver, a Mrs. Duncan, sits on her bus's front bumper and poses for a photo. Mackeys's high school closed in 1929, and students were sent to nearby Roper. (Mary Cotten Davenport.)

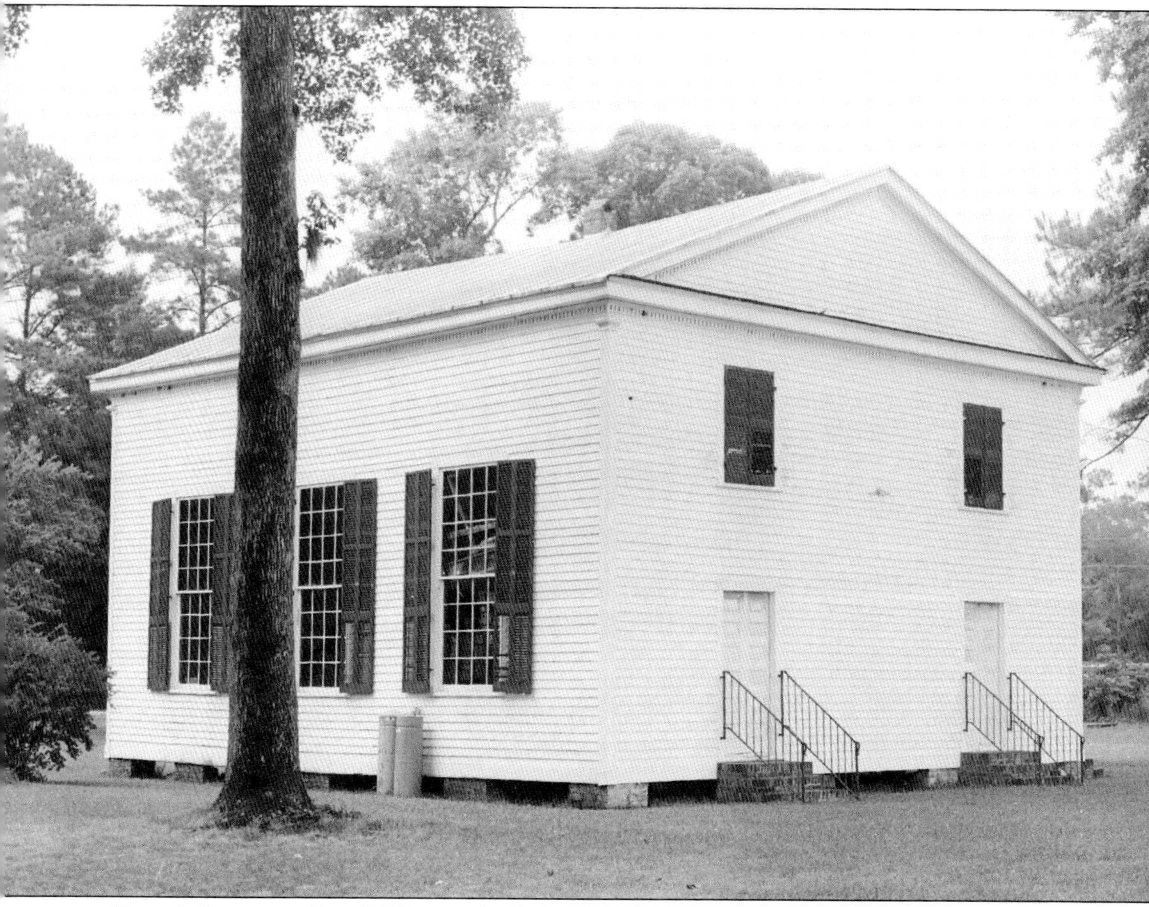

Slaves belonging to Joseph Norman built the church that became Rehoboth Methodist Church, east of Plymouth. The church, completed in 1853, was constructed of cypress and heart pine. Still standing, the building is considered to be among the finest examples of antebellum Greek Revival architecture in North Carolina. In 1939, Rehoboth became part of the Methodist Church. (NCSHPO.)

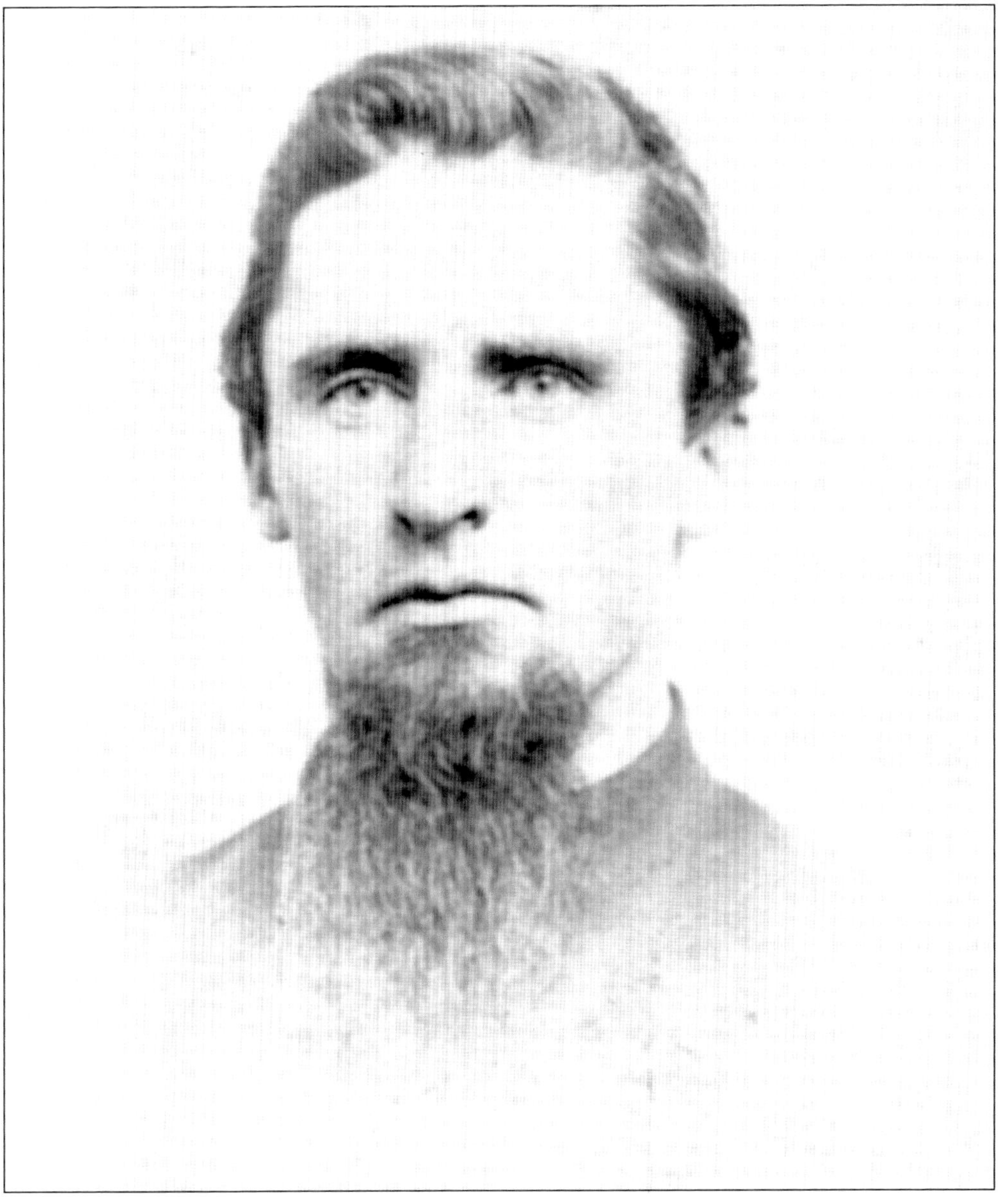

John L. Roper was 21 when he left Pennsylvania in 1856 for the California gold fields. He returned with a small fortune in 1861. When the Civil War erupted, he enlisted in the 11th Pennsylvania Cavalry and rose to the rank of captain. By the end of the war in 1865, he had acquired detailed knowledge of timber resources in southeastern Virginia and northeastern North Carolina. He is seen here in 1866, when he moved to Norfolk, Virginia, and started what would become the John L. Roper Lumber Company. By 1907, it was one of the world's largest timber operations, employing 3,000 workers, with sales offices in New York, Boston, Philadelphia, Pittsburgh, and other large northeastern cities. The company operated 12 sawmills and owned 800,000 acres of land, 150 miles of logging railroads, 23 logging locomotives, a dozen tugboats, and a trio of sailing schooners. Roper opened a large sawmill and lumber processing plant in Lee's Mill in Washington County in 1889, for which the residents were so grateful that they changed the name of the town to Roper. (Dr. A.L. Roper.)

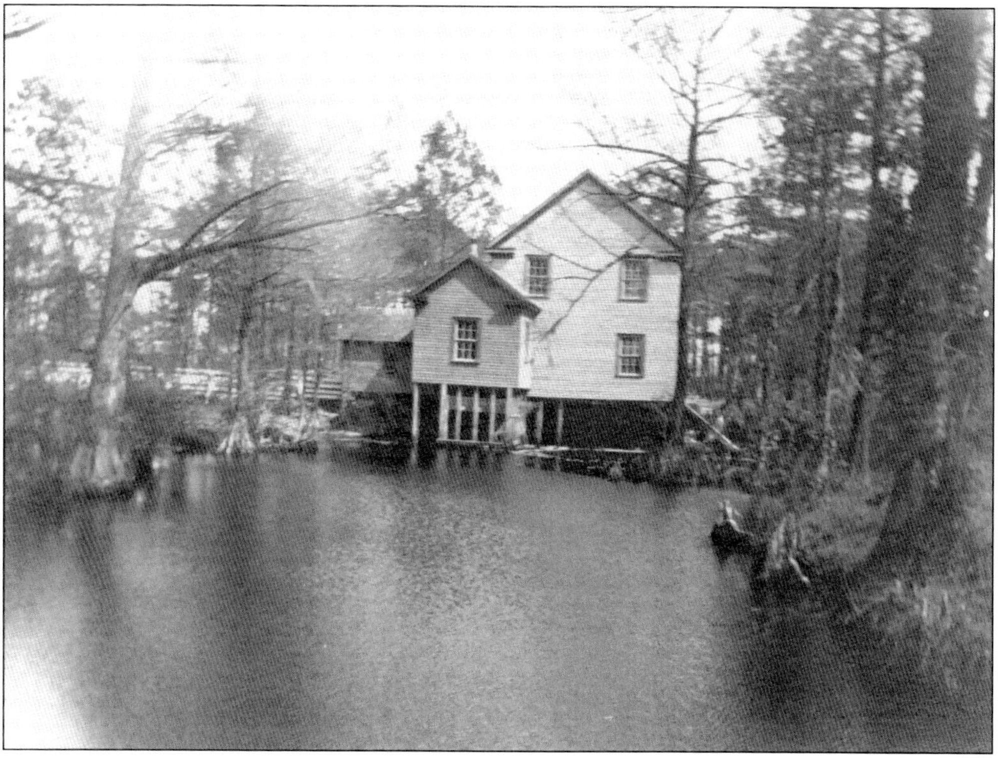

In 1702, Thomas Blount built a grist and lumber mill on Kendrick's Creek (later, Mackeys Creek) in what is now Roper. He also built a dam to provide power for the mill. Blount died in 1706. His widow married Thomas Lee, and the settlement around the mill became known as Lee's Mill. The mill and Mackeys Creek are seen here before 1921. (NCC.)

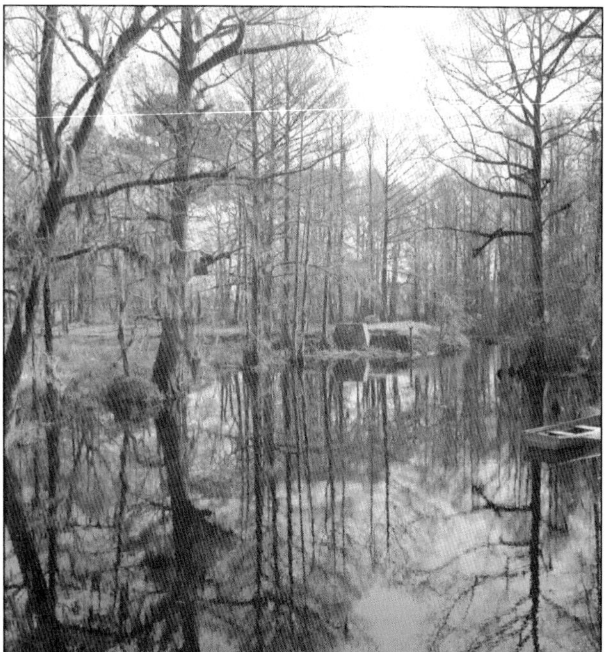

For 219 years, Lee's Mill operated in eastern Washington County. But the mill's dam on Mackey's Creek was a nuisance for local farmers. During heavy rainfall, the dam caused the creek to overflow its banks and flood farmers' fields, destroying their crops. In 1921, someone planted dynamite in the mill and blew it up. This 1938 photograph shows all that remained of the mill. (SANC.)

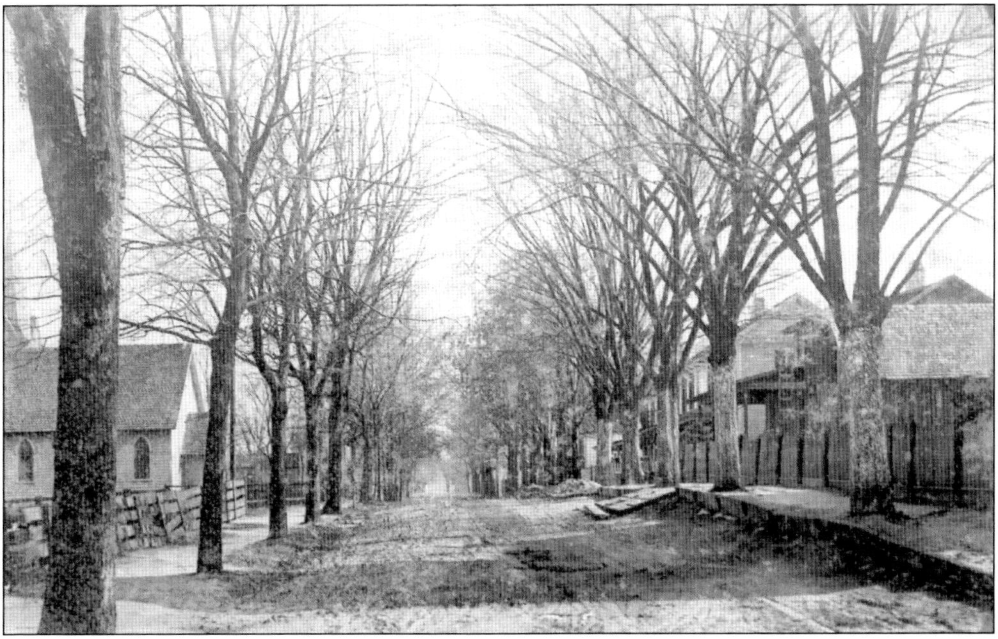

This c. 1900 view of Bousch Street in Roper shows the entrance to St. Luke's Episcopal Church, built in 1876, at far left. In 1975, the building housing an African American congregation at St. Anne's Episcopal Church collapsed. The St. Luke's congregation invited that of St. Anne's to join them, and the church became St. Luke's–St. Anne's Episcopal Church. (SANC.)

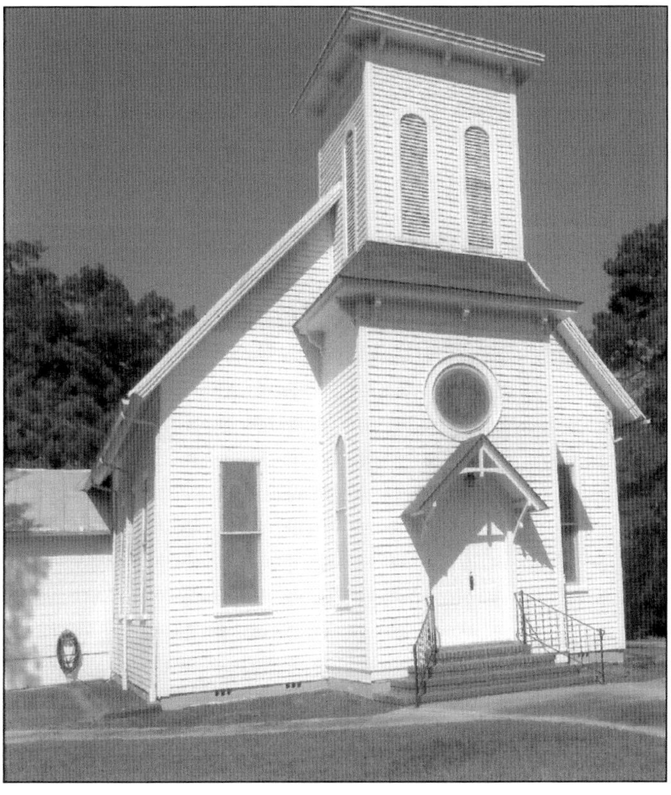

Hebron United Methodist Church was established in 1824. The church moved to downtown Roper in 1842, and the building was remodeled in 1886 with the help of the John L. Roper Lumber Company. (Author's collection.)

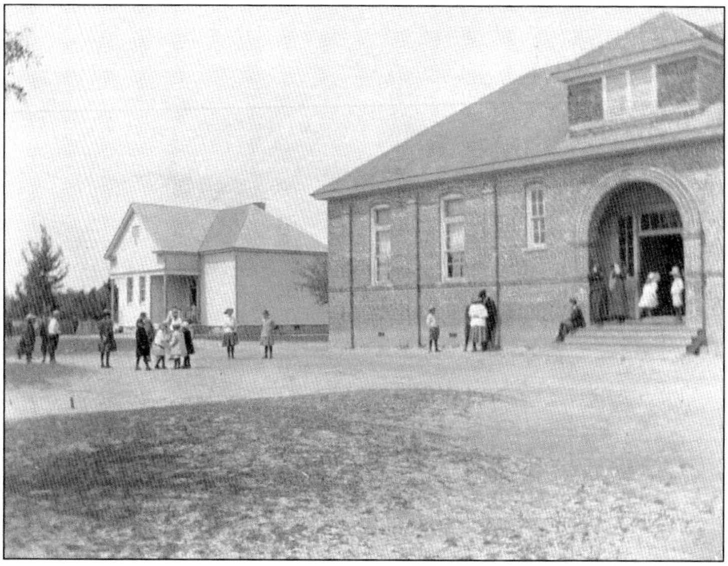

This four-room schoolhouse in Roper was built around 1904 to replace an inadequate frame building. In 1911, Washington County passed a special tax to improve schools, and the frame building in the background was built to provide more classroom space. In 1924, a new school replaced the brick building, and the frame building was sold and moved. (NCC.)

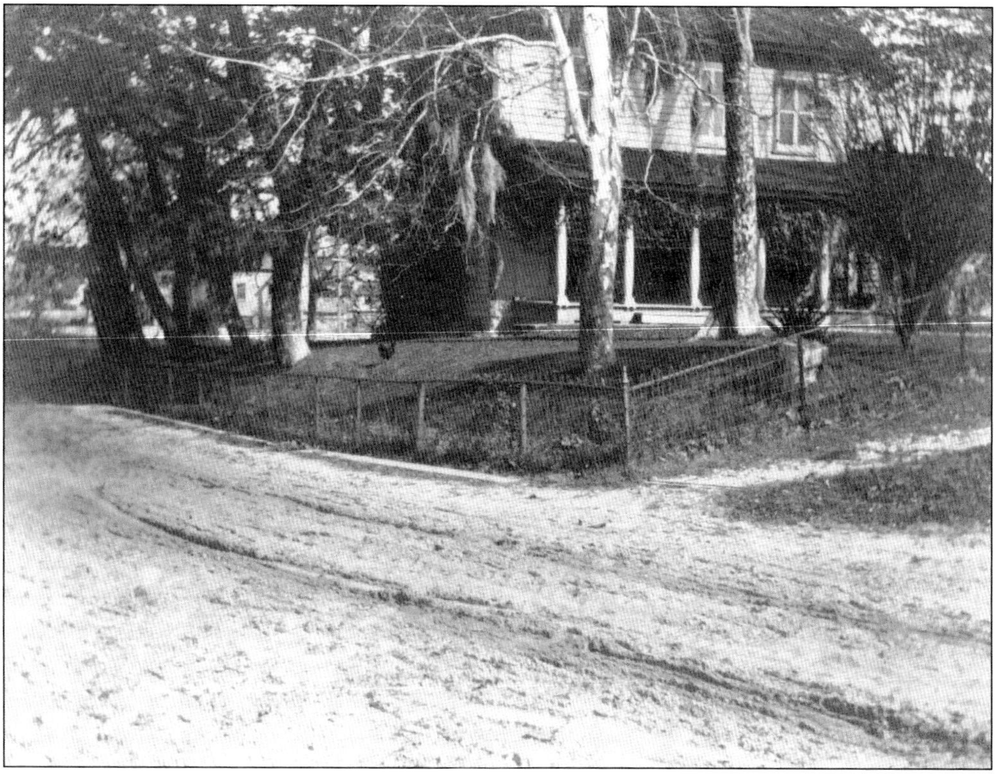

The Harrison-Blount House, also known as "Sleepy Hollow," was built around 1835 in Roper. The house was known for its beautiful setting overlooking Mackeys Creek, amid cypress trees draped with Spanish moss. Teachers of Roper schools often boarded at the house during the school year. The house still stands. (NCC.)

This photograph, probably taken between 1900 and 1910, shows a group of friends dressed in their Sunday best and posing on a bridge in Roper. The young woman second from right seems quite fond of the young man leaning on the bridge rail beside her. (NCC.)

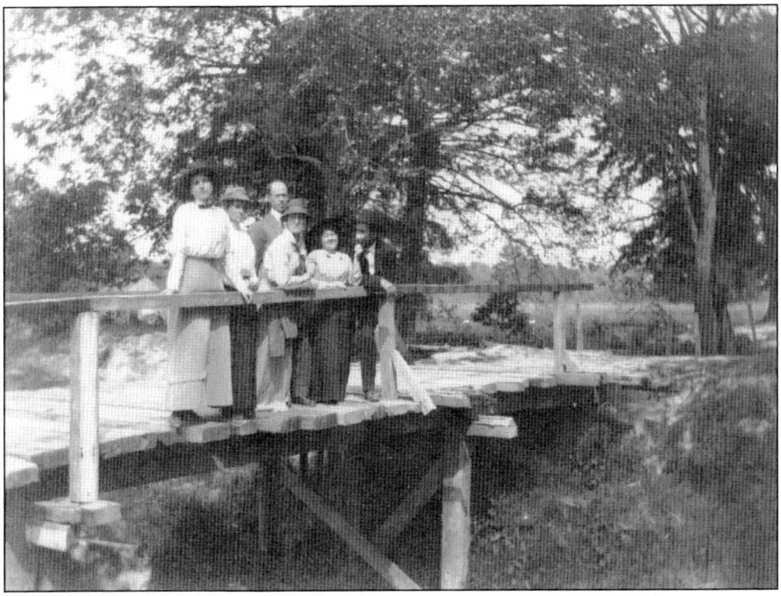

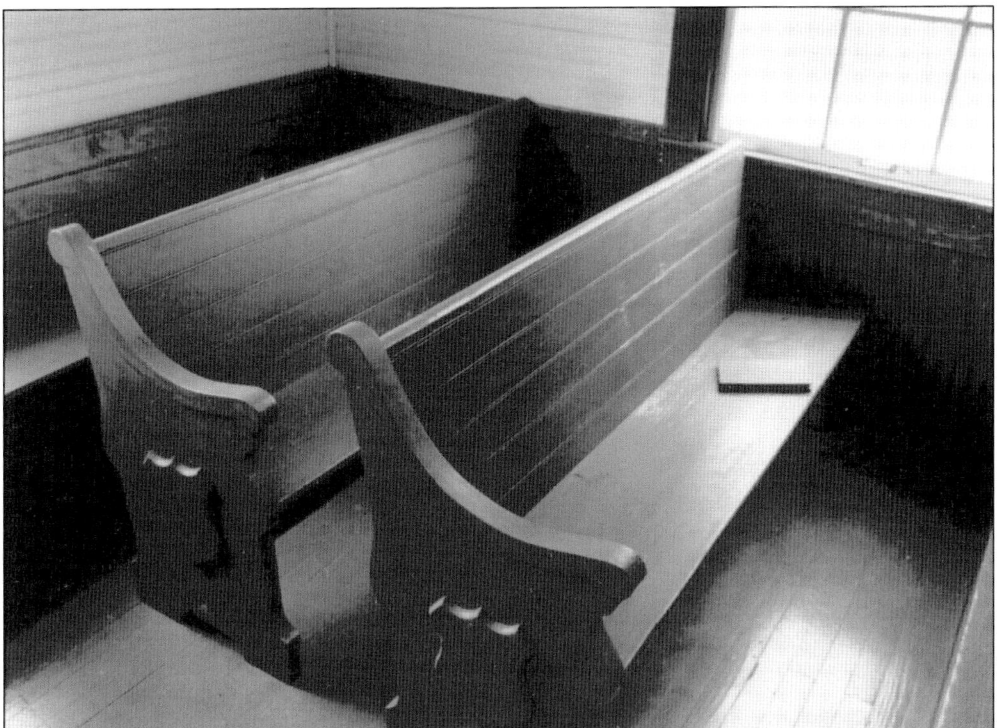

These two pews are found in the Concord Primitive Baptist Church, established in 1810 near the Washington County community of Cherry. The church's current building, constructed sometime around the turn of the 20th century, does not have electricity or running water. (Doward Jones Jr.)

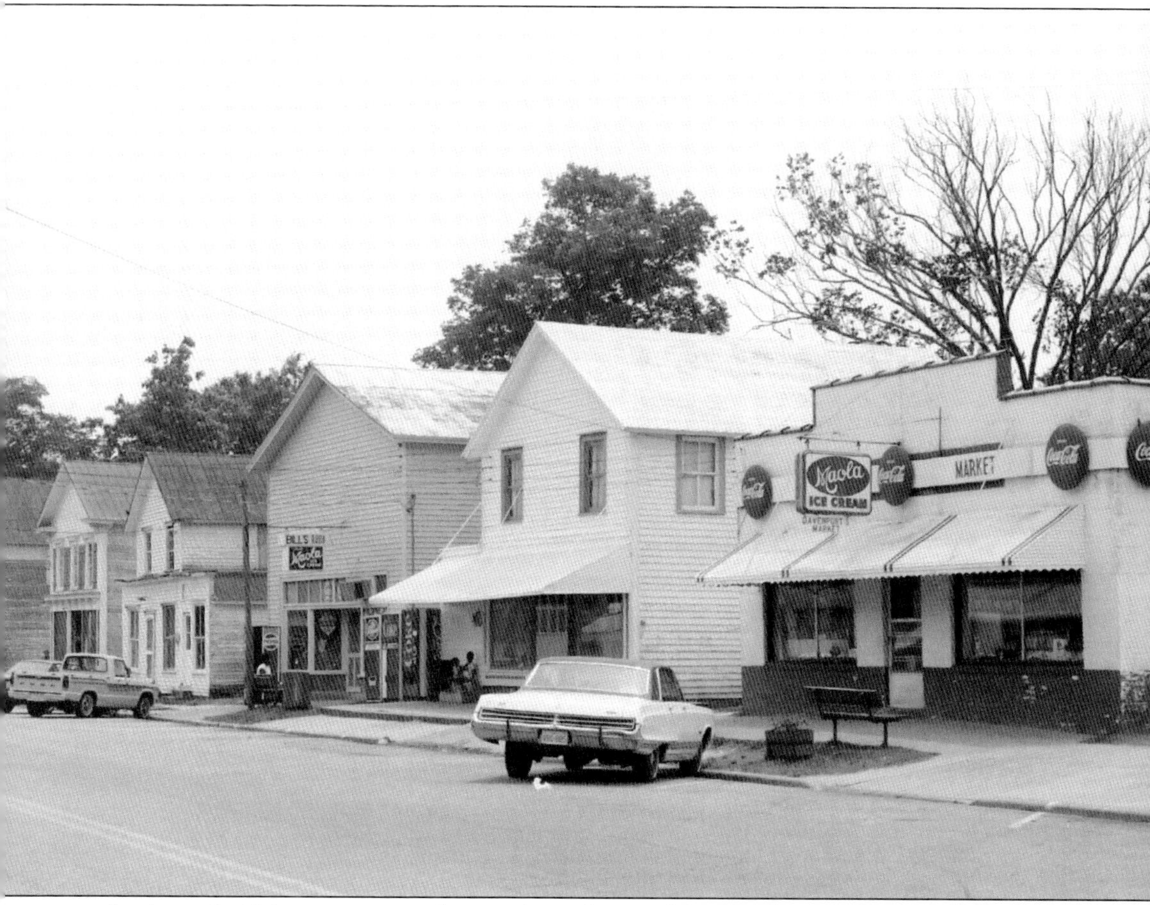

In the early 19th century, a settlement formed around St. David's Episcopal Church in eastern Washington County. The settlement was known as Cool Spring when a post office was built there in 1826. In 1874, the community was incorporated as Creswell in honor of postmaster general John A.J. Creswell. (NCSHPO.)

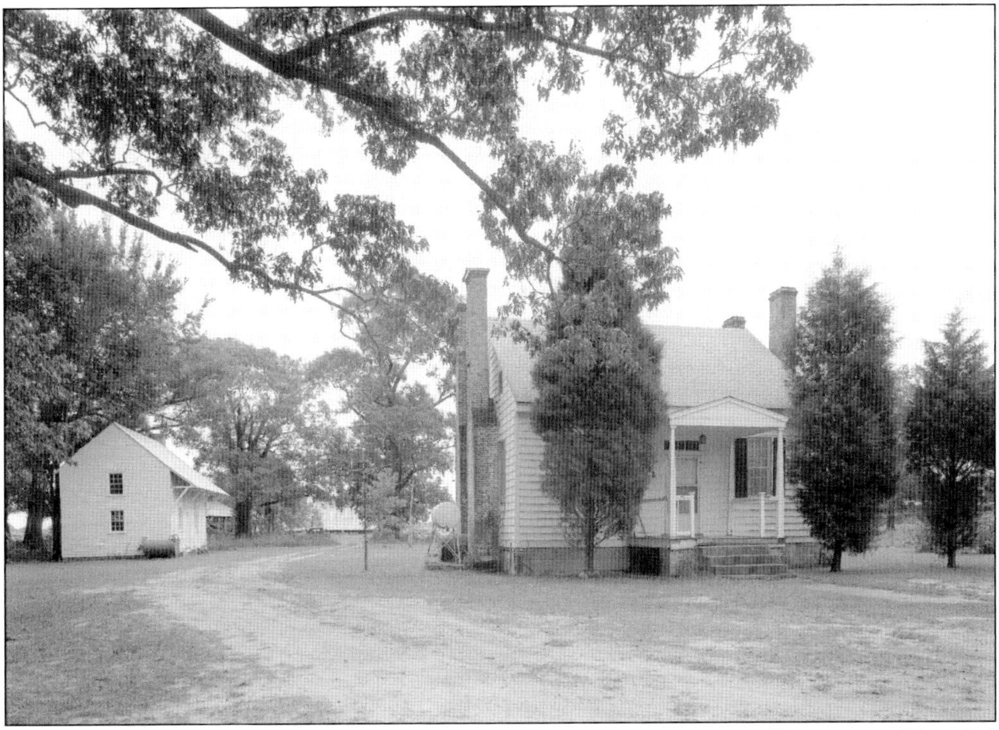

In 1789, Rev. Charles Pettigrew, an Episcopal priest, moved to western Tyrrell County and founded a plantation he called Bonarva. By 1797, Bonarva was thriving, so Pettigrew moved nine miles west and started a new plantation he called Belgrade. Two years later, Pettigrew's 60-acre spread became part of the newly created Washington County. The photograph above shows how modest Pettigrew's "plantation" actually was. Still, he was very comfortable in his new home. In 1803, Pettigrew gave Bonarva to his son Ebenezer Pettigrew and built a small chapel near Belgrade that became known as Pettigrew's Chapel. But Reverend Pettigrew, who had tuberculosis, died in 1807. Pettigrew's Chapel thrived, however, and in 1857, the congregation expanded the church, now called St. David's. The photograph below shows the church in 1964. (Above, NCSHPO; below, NCSUL.)

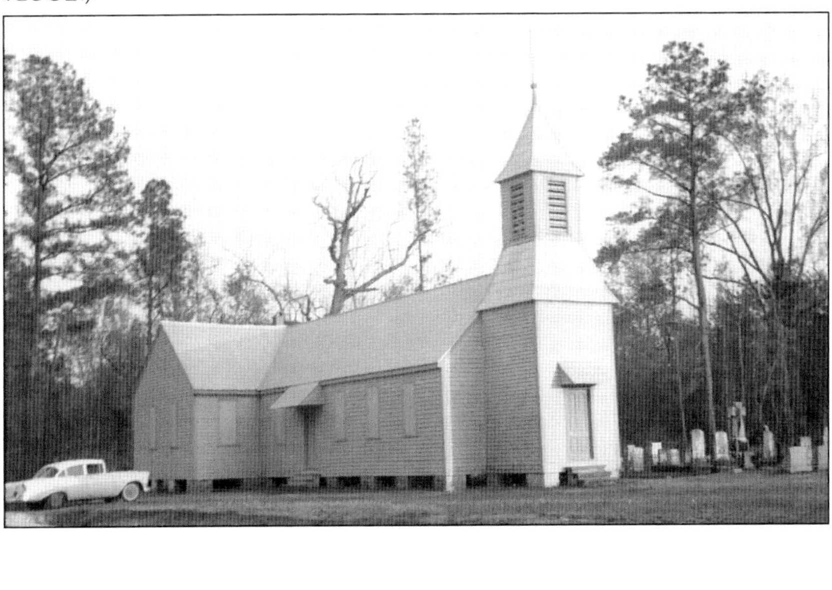

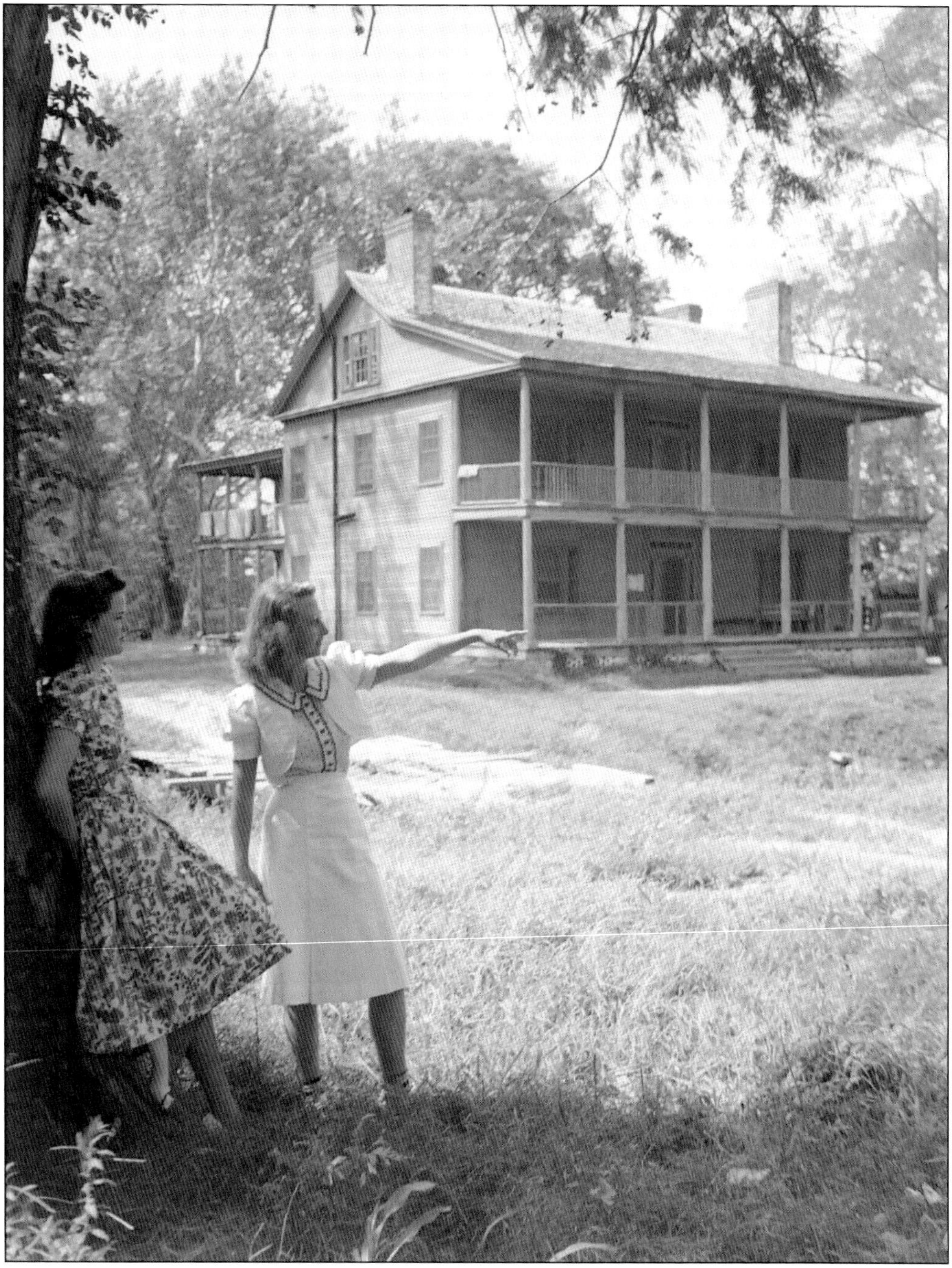

In August 1938, the North Carolina Department of Conservation and Development sent a professional photographer to document Somerset Plantation, near Creswell. The early-19th-century plantation had been deteriorating for some time, but the State of North Carolina had plans to restore it. The photographer brought two young local women—Jean Cox (left) and Mary Elizabeth Bray—to pose in his photographs. (SANC.)

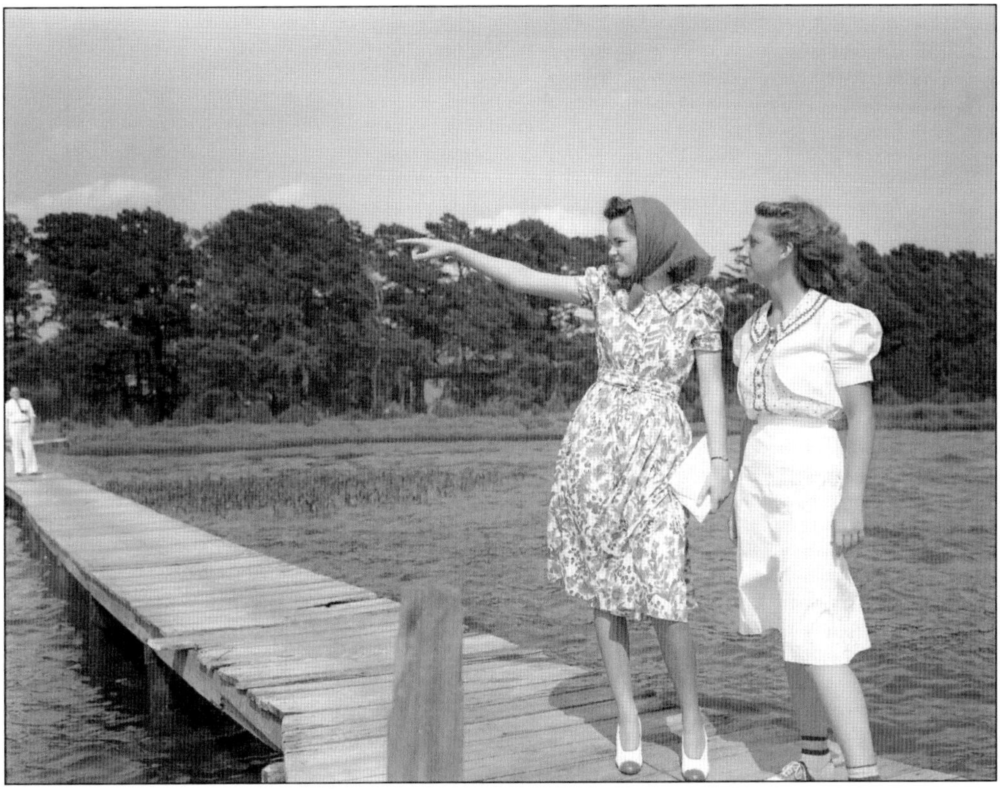

Mary Elizabeth Bray (right) and Jean Cox stand on a windswept pier in Lake Phelps, near Somerset Place, in 1938. This shallow lake in eastern Washington County covers 16,600 acres, making it the second-largest natural lake in North Carolina. Scientists are still puzzled about how the lake formed. Theories include a meteor strike, a long-ago glacier, or a peat fire. (SANC.)

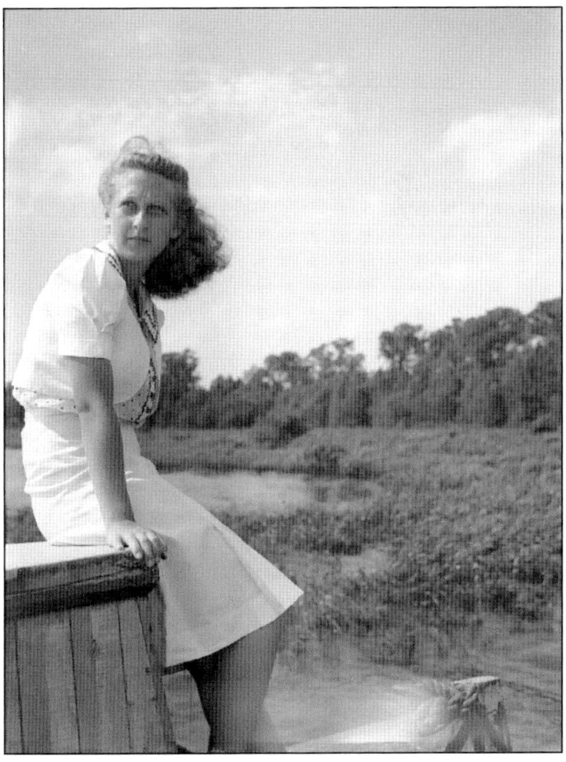

Mary Elizabeth Bray sits on the deck of a boat tied up on the shore of Lake Phelps, which archaeologists believe might have been formed more than 36,000 years ago. The waters are very clear because it is fed almost entirely by rainfall, and the low acidity of the water has preserved artifacts left by Native Americans from thousands of years ago. (SANC.)

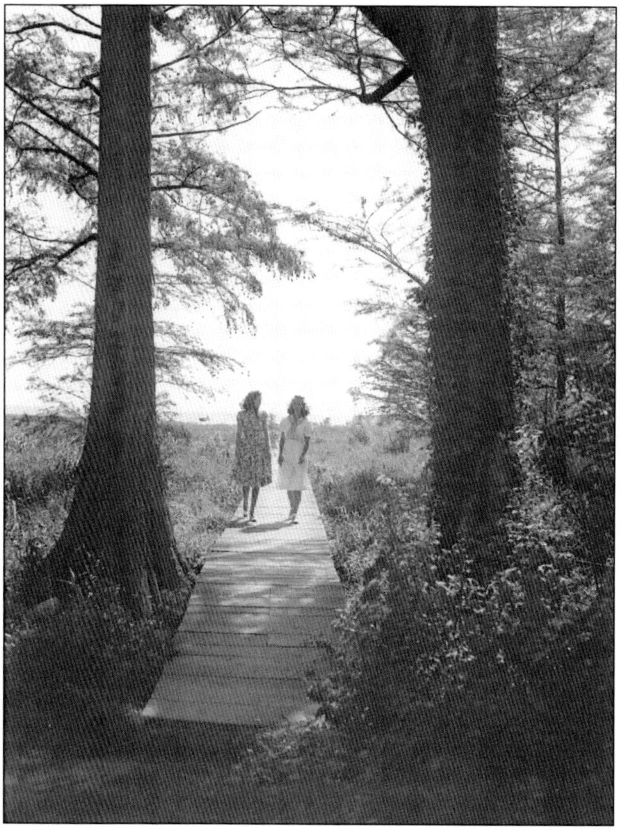

Seen here in August 1938, Jean Cox (left) and Mary Elizabeth Bray are framed by two large cypress trees as they walk on a boardwalk connecting Somerset Place plantation and Lake Phelps. Due to the discovery of dugout canoes older than the Egyptian pyramids, archaeologists believe that Native Americans lived on the shores of Lake Phelps about 12,000 years ago. (SANC.)

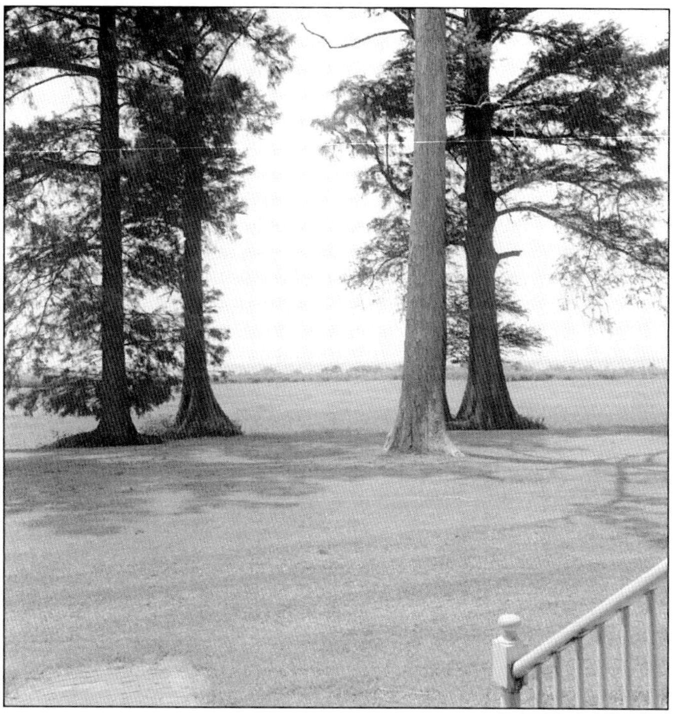

When the Josiah Collins family lived at Somerset Place in the mid-19th century, this was their view of Lake Phelps from one of the plantation's porches. While on a hunting excursion in 1755, Benjamin Tarkington climbed a tree and saw the lake, but Josiah Phelps claimed the right to name it because he was the first to wade into its waters. (SANC.)

By 1790, more than 160 slaves were working at Somerset Place, for which they had dug a six-mile canal from Lake Phelps to the Scuppernong River. The canal was used to transport crops to market and bring supplies and visitors to Somerset. In this 1938 photograph, an unidentified man stands next to a lock that allowed lake water to flow into the canal. (SANC.)

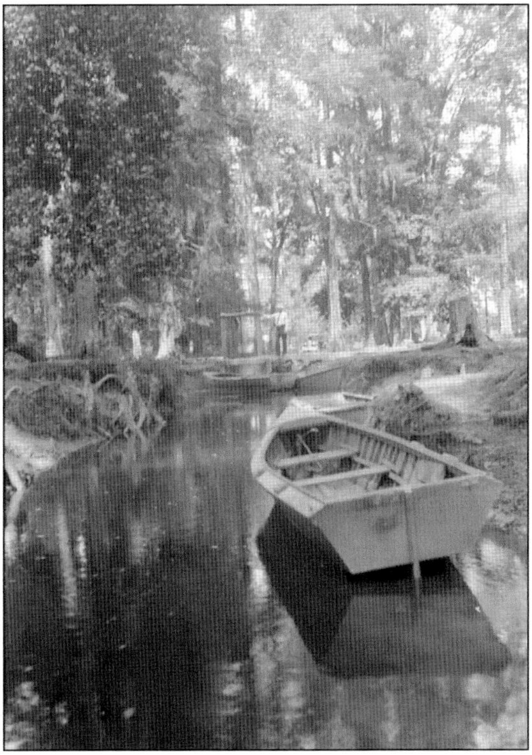

Jean Cox (right) and Mary Elizabeth Bray survey the crops at Somerset Place in 1938. The plantation produced rice, oats, wheat, corn, flax, cotton, hay, turnips, peas, Irish potatoes, and sweet potatoes. By 1850, there were 276 slaves living at Somerset. Enslaved field hands usually worked more than 300 days per year; they were given around 60 days off, including Sundays. (SANC.)

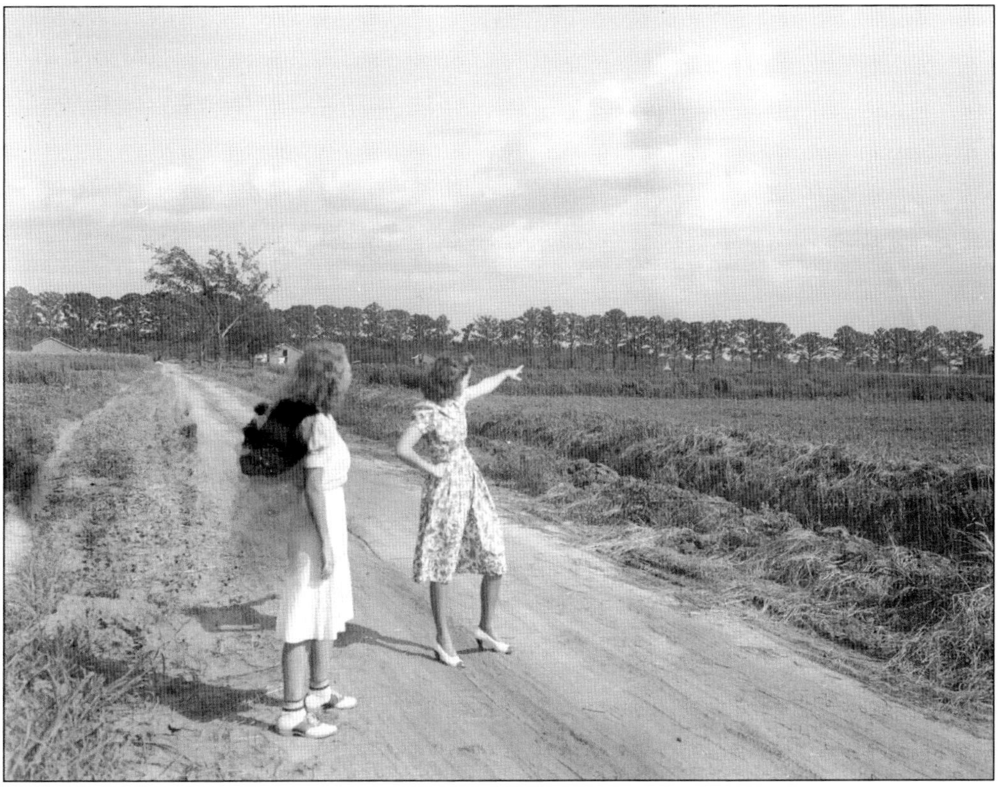

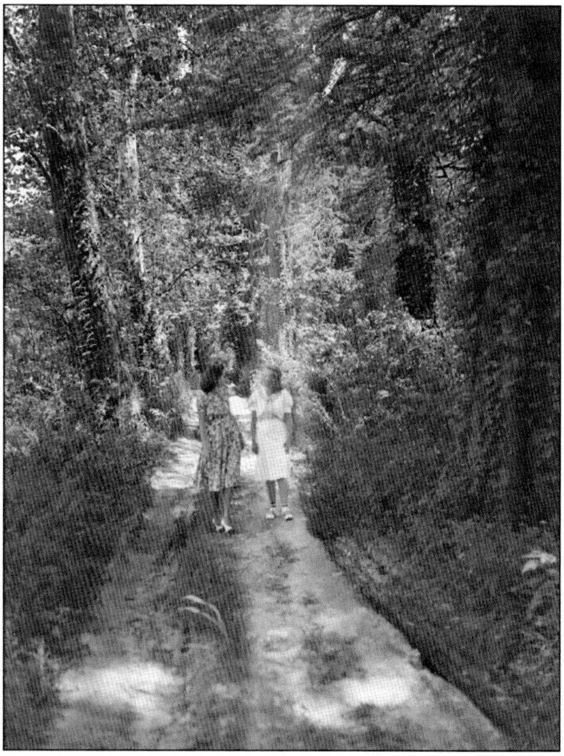

Jean Cox (left) and Mary Elizabeth Bray walk along one of the 19th-century carriage roads near Somerset Place. One such road connected the Collins family with their nearest neighbors, the Pettigrews, at Bonarva Plantation in nearby Tyrrell County. James Johnston Pettigrew, who later became a general of the Confederate army, was born at Bonarva on July 4, 1828. (SANC.)

Jean Cox (left) and Mary Elizabeth Bray walk along a carriage road near the Collins family's 19th-century residence at Somerset Place. When this photograph was taken in 1938, the buildings were showing signs of deterioration. But state officials were organizing an effort to restore the main house and outbuildings as a state historic site. (SANC.)

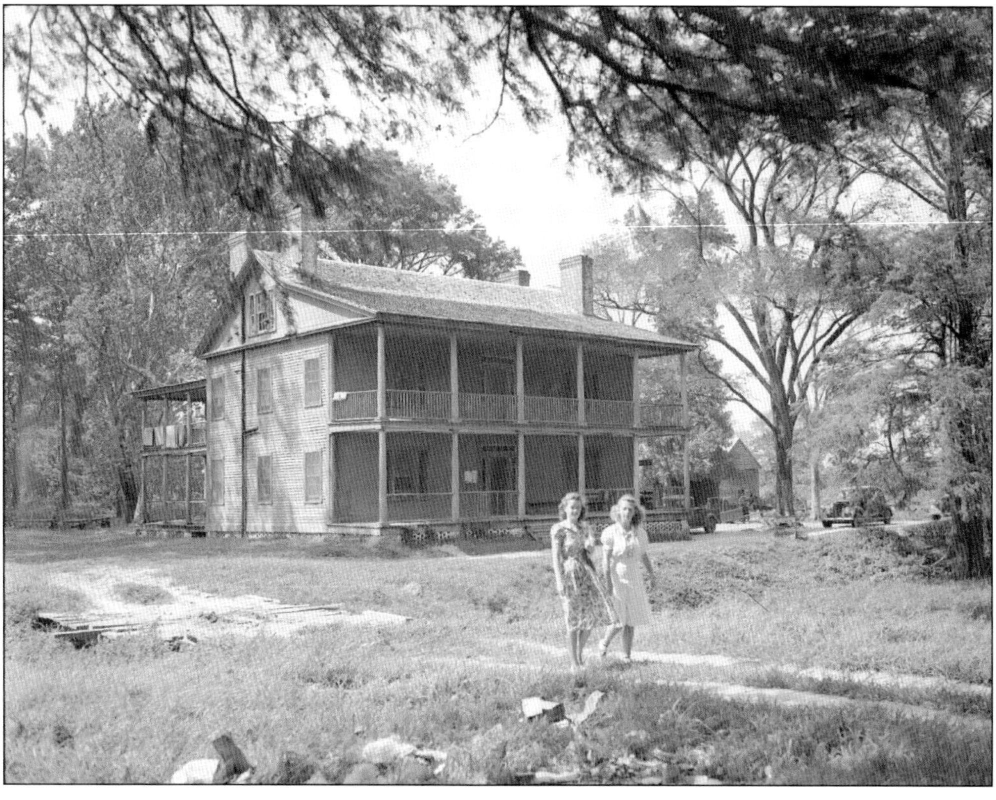

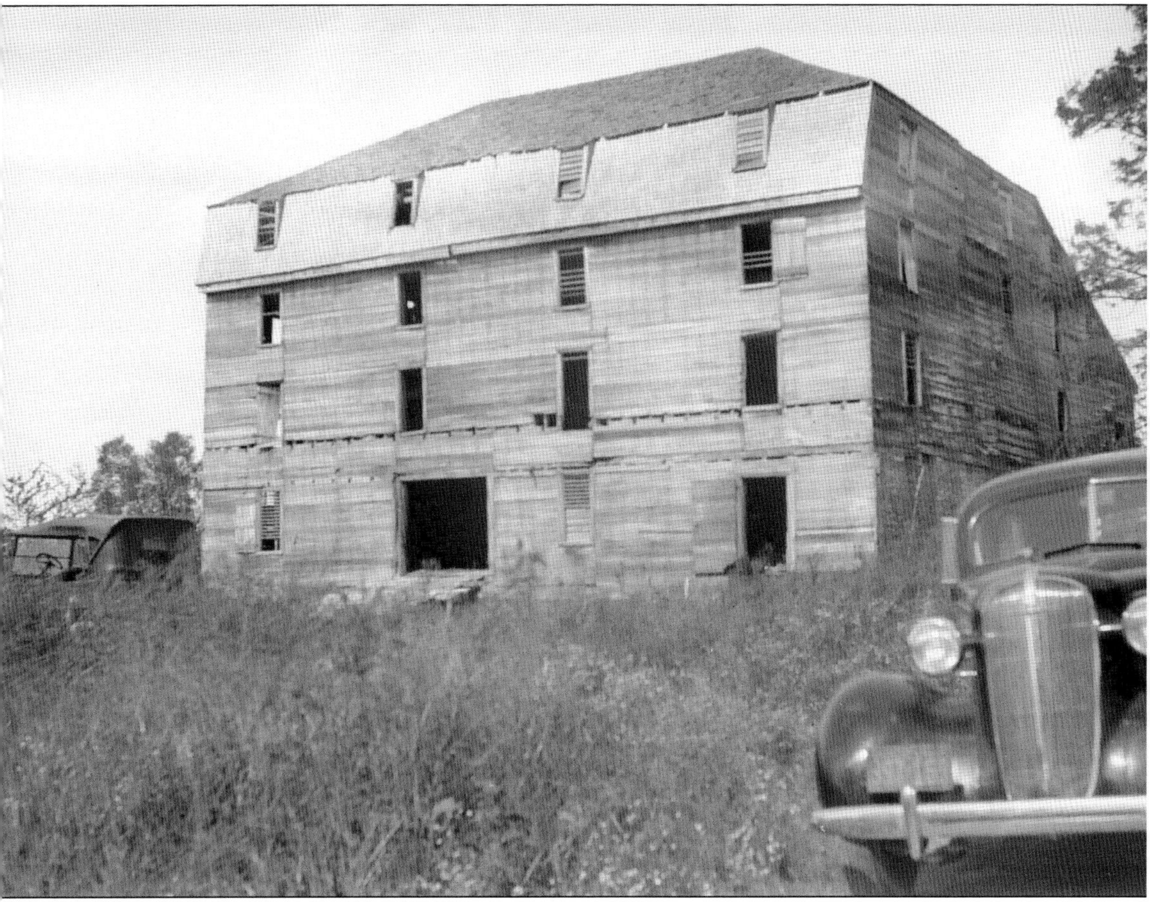

In 1784, Edenton merchant Josiah Collins formed the Lake Company with Nathaniel Allen and Dr. Samuel Dickinson. Together, they bought 100,000 acres around Lake Phelps for farming and lumbering. By 1790, slaves had built this unusual four-story barn that housed equipment and farm animals on the first floor. Rice, corn, hay, and other crops were stored on upper floors. The barn burned down in 1949. (SANC.)

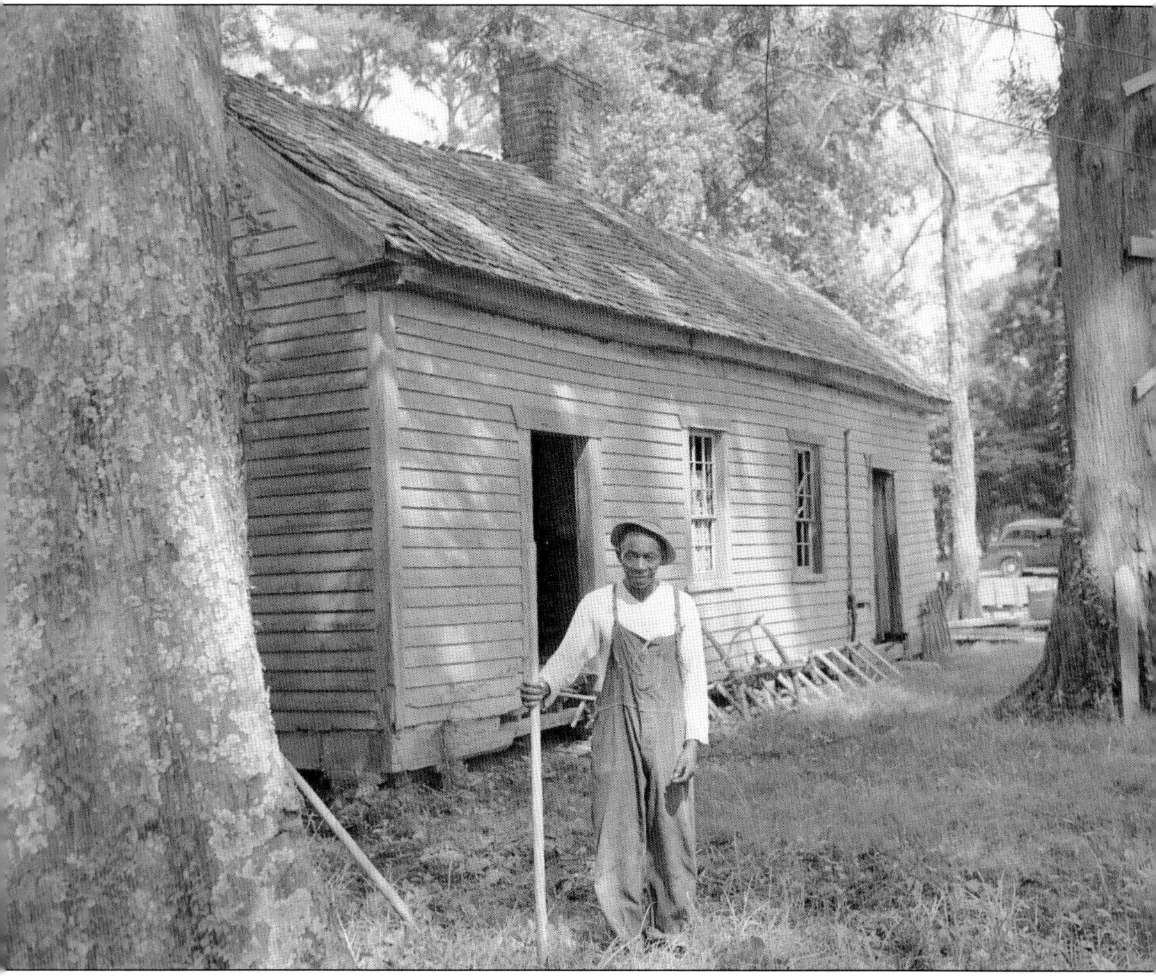

In this 1938 photograph, a caretaker stands near one of the dilapidated buildings that housed slaves at Somerset Place. At one time in the mid-19th century, there were about two dozen small cabins housing slaves. In some of the cabins, 12 to 15 people lived in one room. (SANC.)

By the early 1950s, the state's efforts to preserve and restore Somerset Plantation were yielding results. The main house had been repaired, along with a new coat of paint, and archaeologists began excavating the grounds, which uncovered the foundations of slave quarters and other outbuildings. (SANC.)

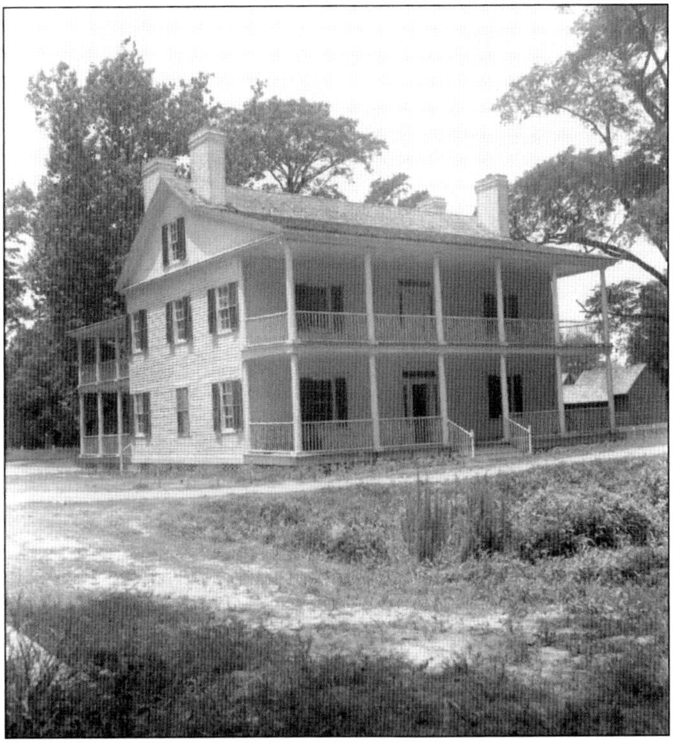

Here, a car drives on an old carriage path, past cypress trees and fields once cultivated by slaves, en route to Somerset Place in 1938. Now 74 years after the end of the Civil War, the old plantation and its outbuildings were falling into disrepair. (SANC.)

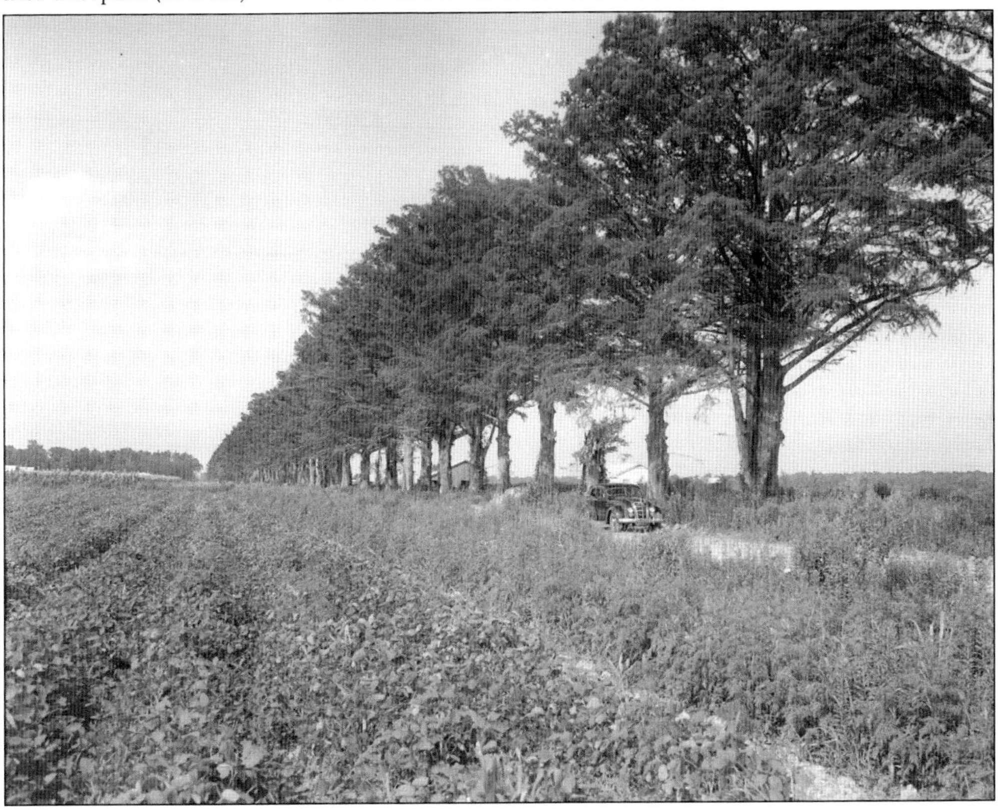

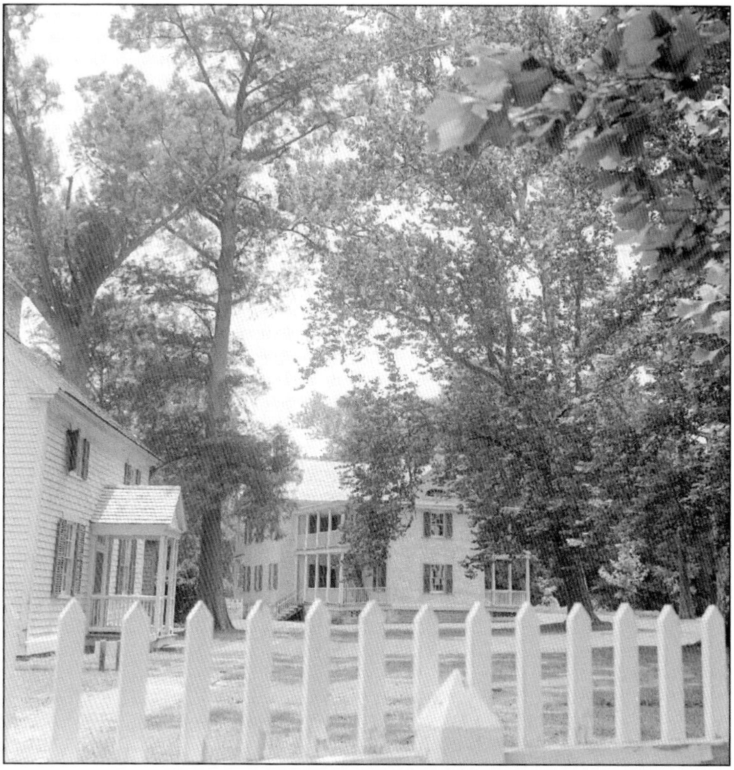

By the 1960s, progress had been made in restoring Somerset Place, both inside and out, and in 1969, it became a North Carolina State Historic Site. This photograph shows the Colony (at left) and the main house restored from their dilapidated condition of the 1930s. (SANC.)

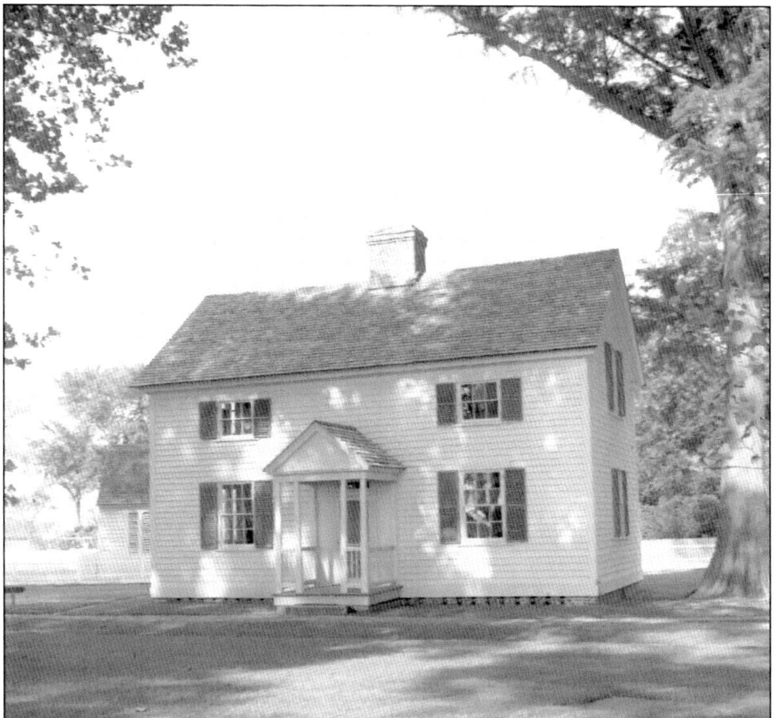

This two-story frame house, known as "the Colony," was built in 1841 near the main house, where the Collins family lived. Before the Civil War, the sons of Josiah Collins III lived in this house, which doubled as their school and the residence of ministers and tutors who taught the Collins children. (SANC.)

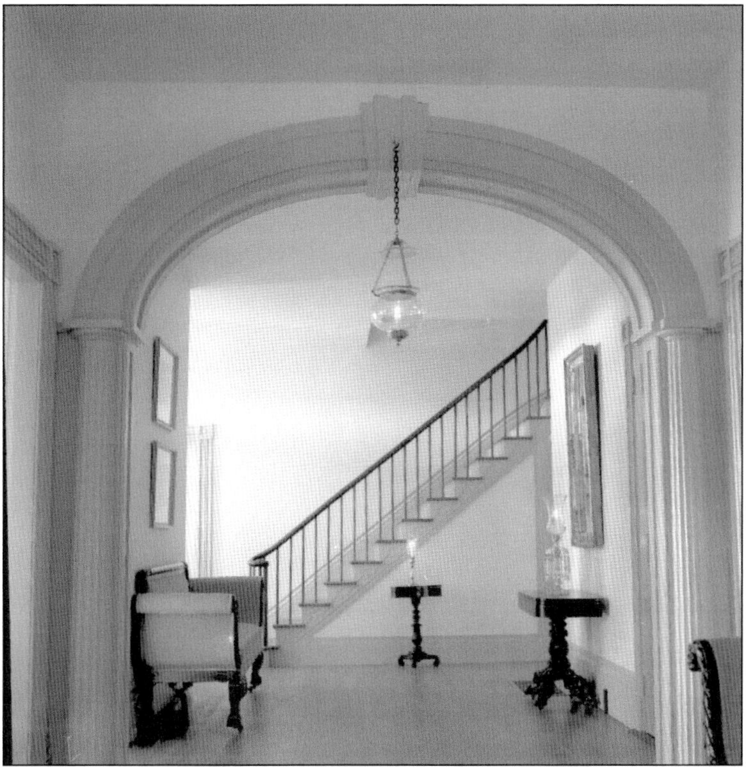

The main house at Somerset Place was one of the finest homes in northeastern North Carolina when Josiah Collins III and his family lived there before the Civil War. Seen here is the entrance hall of the main house after it had been restored and named a state historic site. (SANC.)

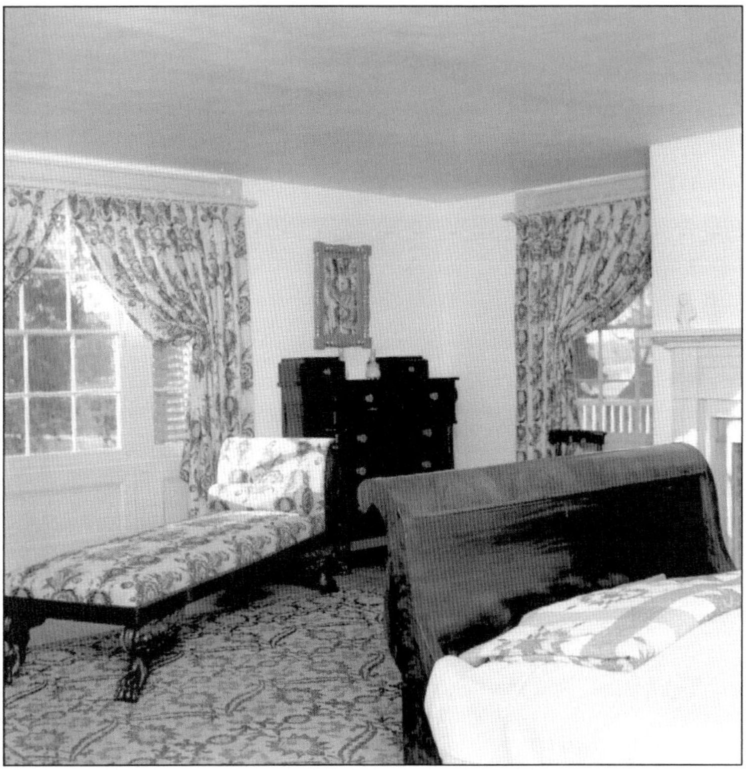

The master bedroom of the main house at Somerset Place was restored to its approximate appearance when Josiah Collins III and his family lived there before the Civil War. Although the house was far from cities and towns, it was quite comfortable for its time. (SANC.)

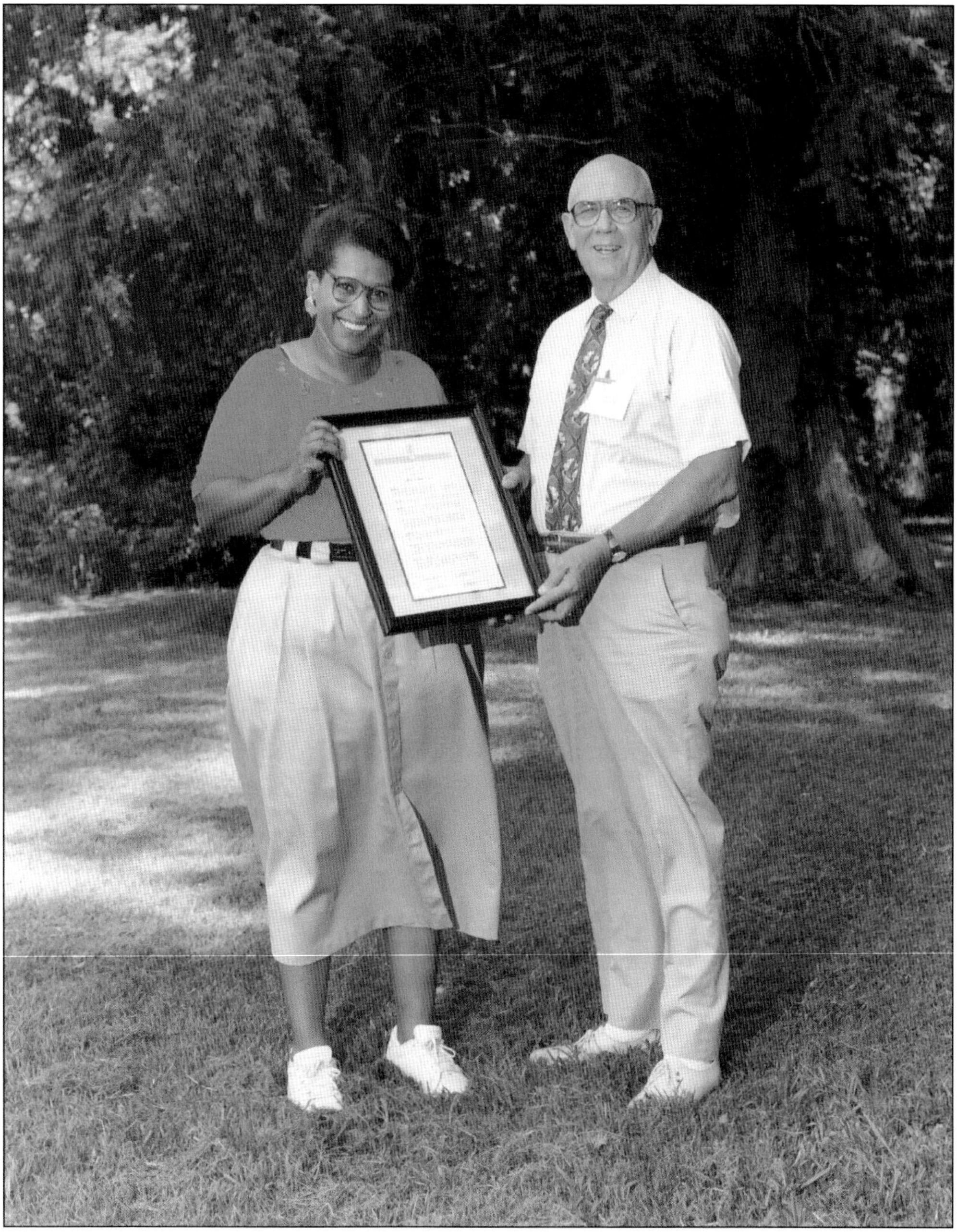

Dorothy Spruill Redford (left) is descended from slaves who lived and worked at Somerset Place before the Civil War. She spent 10 years researching the genealogy of the enslaved community there. Her groundbreaking work led to a series of gatherings, or "homecomings," of descendants of the enslaved community at Somerset. Seen here in 1991, Redford presents an award to state representative Howard Chapin for his support of projects at Somerset Place. (SPSHS.)

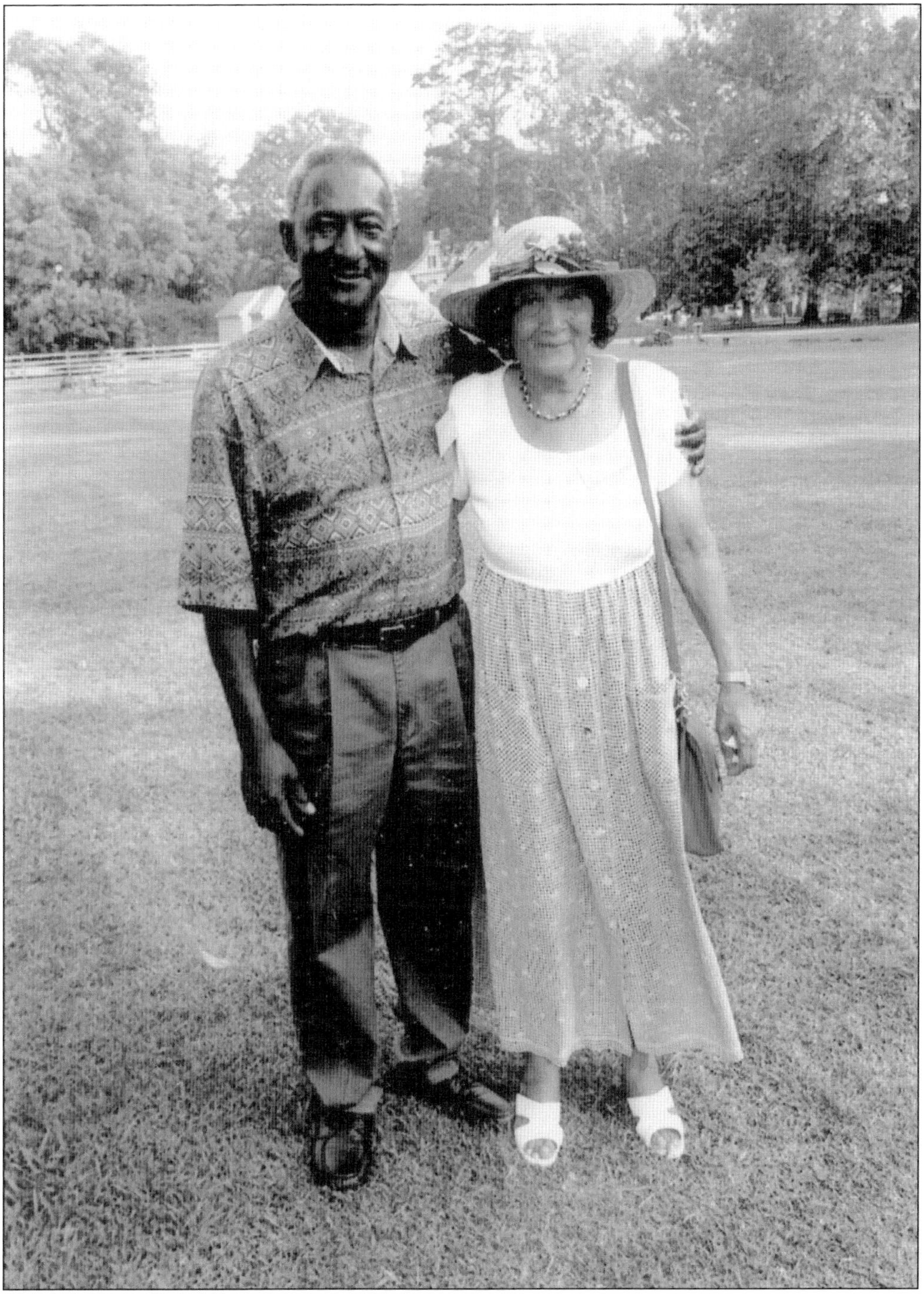

The annual homecomings at Somerset Place drew people from all over the United States who were descended from slaves who built, lived, and worked at Somerset Place before the Civil War. This photograph shows descendants Haywood McKinley Leigh, 65, and his mother, Sarah Brown Leigh, 91. The homecomings also attracted author Alex Haley and North Carolina governor Jim Martin. (SPSHS.)

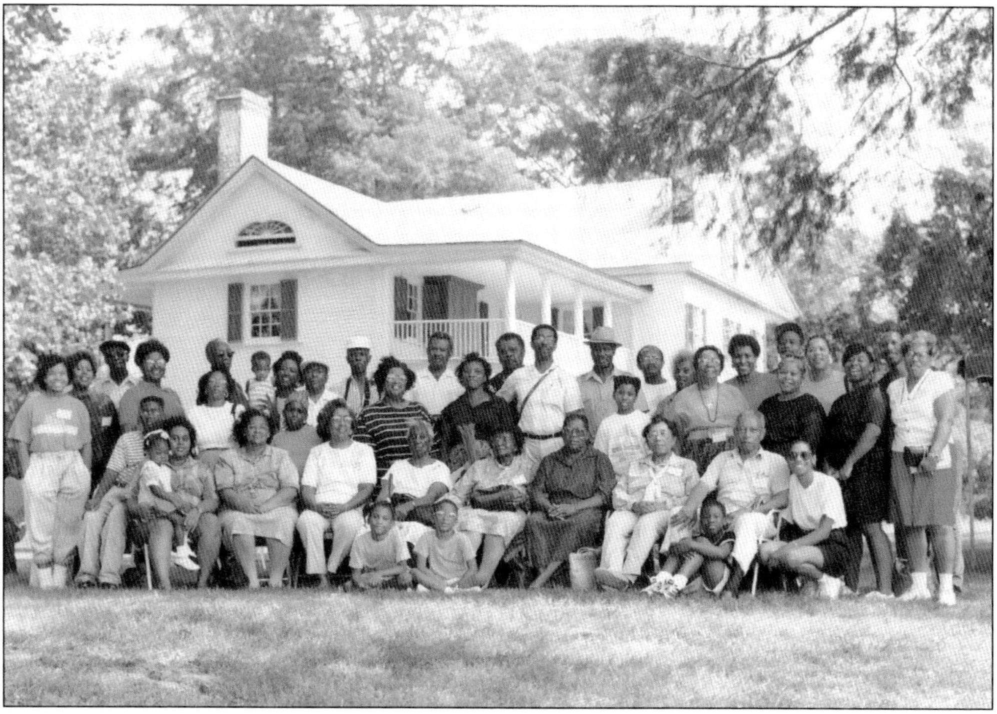

Dorothy Spruill Redford's painstaking research brought hundreds of descendants from Somerset's enslaved community together for homecomings in the 1980s and 1990s. Detailed records kept by the Collins family before the Civil War helped Redford in her research. The Littlejohn family attended the Somerset homecoming in 1991. (SPSHS.)

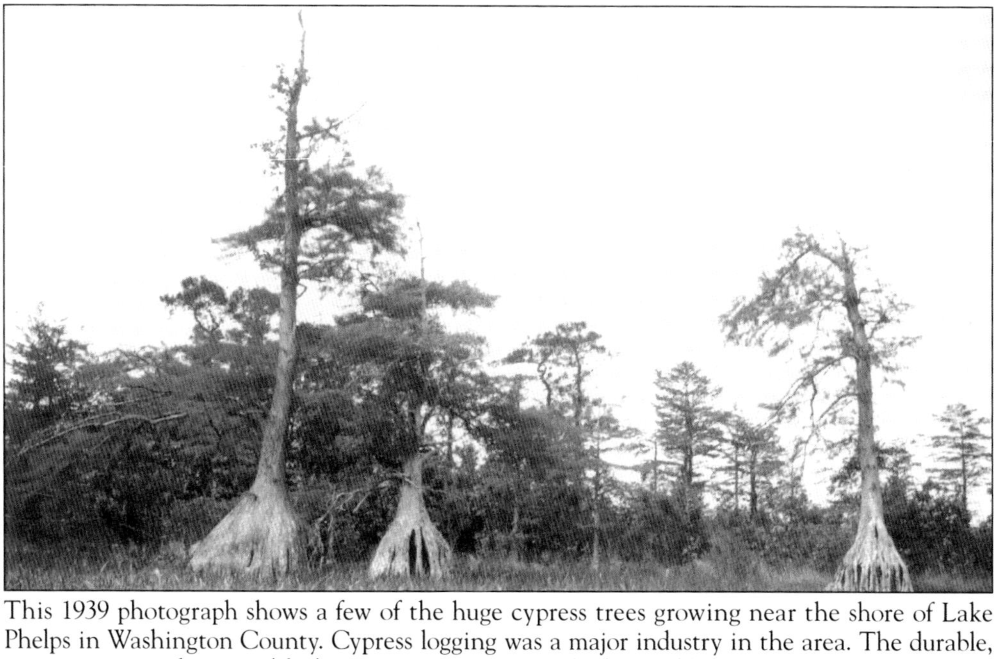

This 1939 photograph shows a few of the huge cypress trees growing near the shore of Lake Phelps in Washington County. Cypress logging was a major industry in the area. The durable, rot-resistant wood was used for housing construction and other building, as well as for long-lasting cypress shingles. (SANC.)

Three

Personalities

Many vibrant, talented, and accomplished people have left their marks on Plymouth and Washington County.

Some were players in historic events that affected the course of history for both North Carolina and the nation. They included people such as Confederate general Robert Hoke, who became a serious annoyance to the Union's efforts to retain control of North Carolina's coast near the end of the Civil War. Jack Lucas, a determined US Marine with a fiery temperament, won the nation's highest military honor for his remarkable bravery during the Battle of Iwo Jima in World War II.

Others took their immense talents to larger stages and arenas, earning the acclaim of huge audiences. Plymouth native Augustin Daly was celebrated as a playwright and producer in the United States and Europe in the late 19th century. Charles Bowser, a standout athlete at Plymouth High School in the 1970s, went on to stardom on the football field with Duke University and, later, the Miami Dolphins of the National Football League. And even though John L. Roper never lived in Washington County, his influence on the local economy was so great that a small town changed its name to honor him.

Some are remembered for their leadership in local affairs. And still others are remembered simply for being a familiar face on Water Street in Plymouth or one of the other Washington County communities.

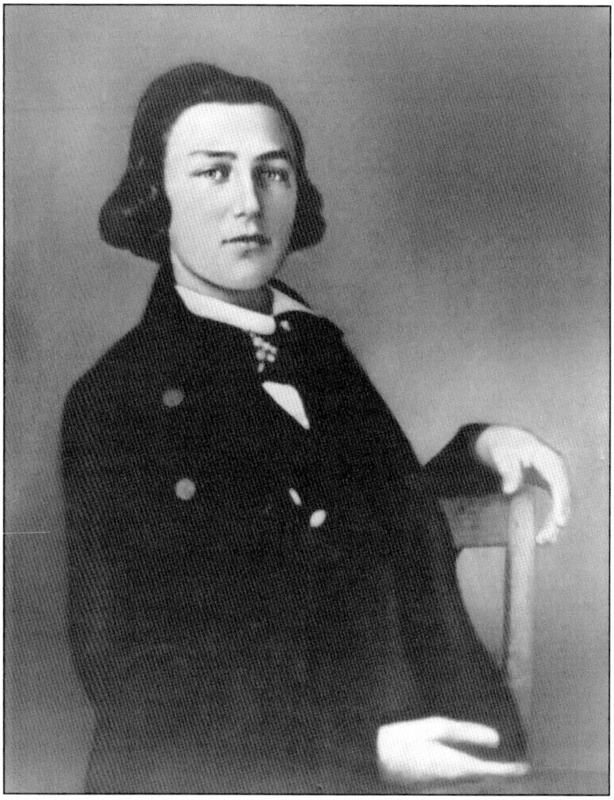

Alfred Franklin Garrett spent much of his life in a house his father had built around 1750. The house still stands near Plymouth on higher ground known as Garrett's Island, which borders swamps and a creek. A successful businessman in the mid-19th century, Garrett built a town house in Plymouth and lived in the Garrett's Island house during the summer. He also served in the Civil War. (Mary Cotten Davenport.)

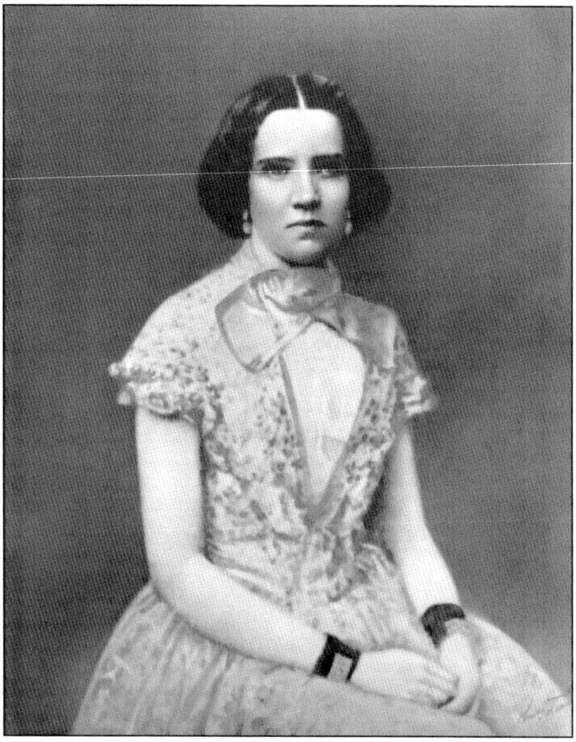

Mary Eliza Cotten became Alfred Franklin Garrett's third wife in 1854. Before she married Garrett, however, she had a friend named Lorenzo who greatly admired her. In July 1850, Lorenzo, in the florid style of the day, wrote in Mary's autograph book, comparing her to "an angel that had missed its way on some minor mission Heaven had bade it go." (Mary Cotten Davenport.)

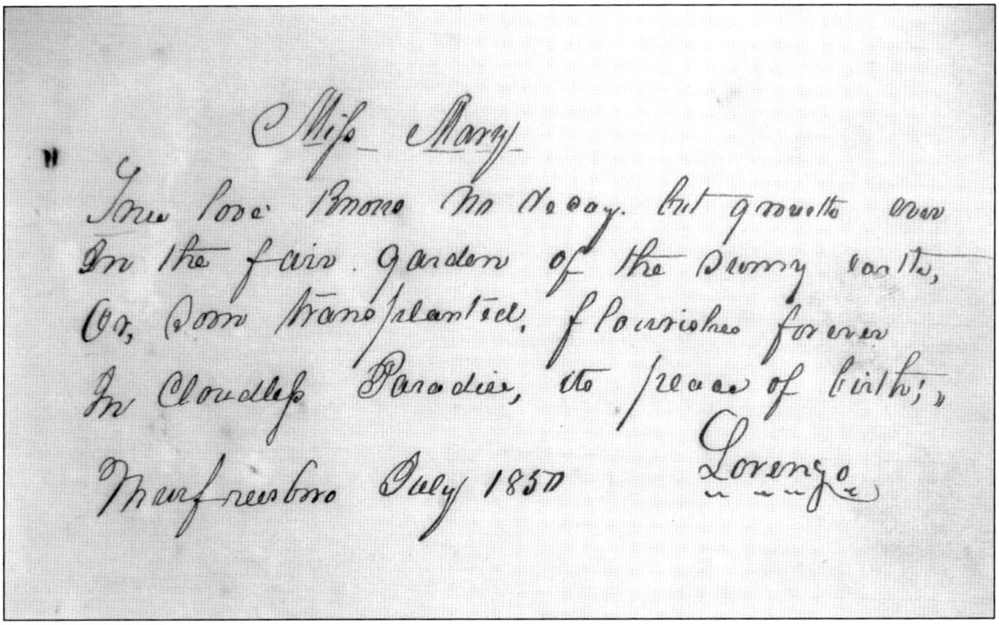
Miss Mary
"True love knows no decay. but groweth ever
In the fair garden of the sunny earth,
Or, soon transplanted, flourishes forever
In Cloudless Paradise, its place of birth;"
Lorenzo
Murfreesboro July 1850

In the mid-19th century, young ladies often kept autograph books with them to collect signatures and flowery prose from their friends and admirers. In July 1850, Mary Eliza Cotten Garrett visited a friend named Lorenzo in Murfreesboro, about 50 miles upriver from Plymouth. Lorenzo wrote several entries in Mary's autograph book, including this statement: "True love knows no decay." (Mary Cotten Davenport.)

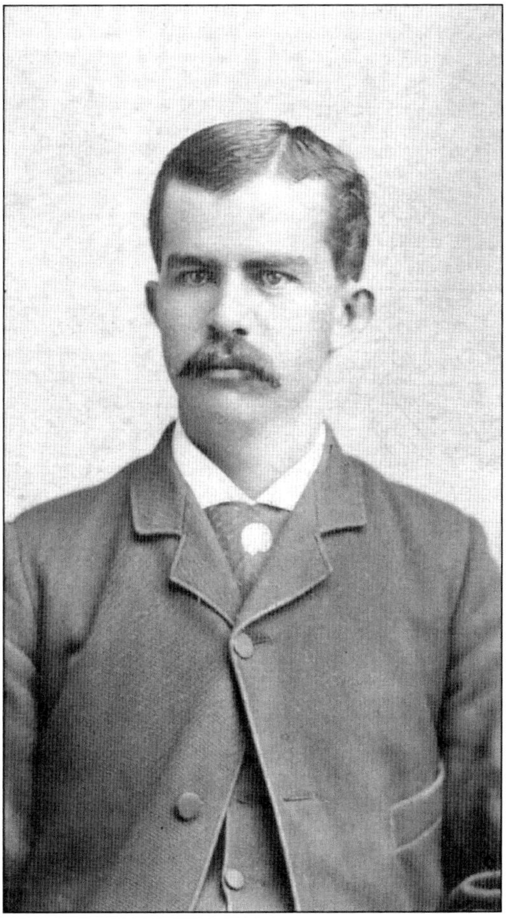

Born in Bertie County, Stuart Lawson Johnston graduated from the University of North Carolina at Chapel Hill in 1859. During the Civil War, he served as a captain in the 17th North Carolina Regiment, then went on to practice law in Plymouth after the war. Johnston is buried in the Grace Episcopal Church cemetery in Plymouth. (Mary Cotten Davenport.)

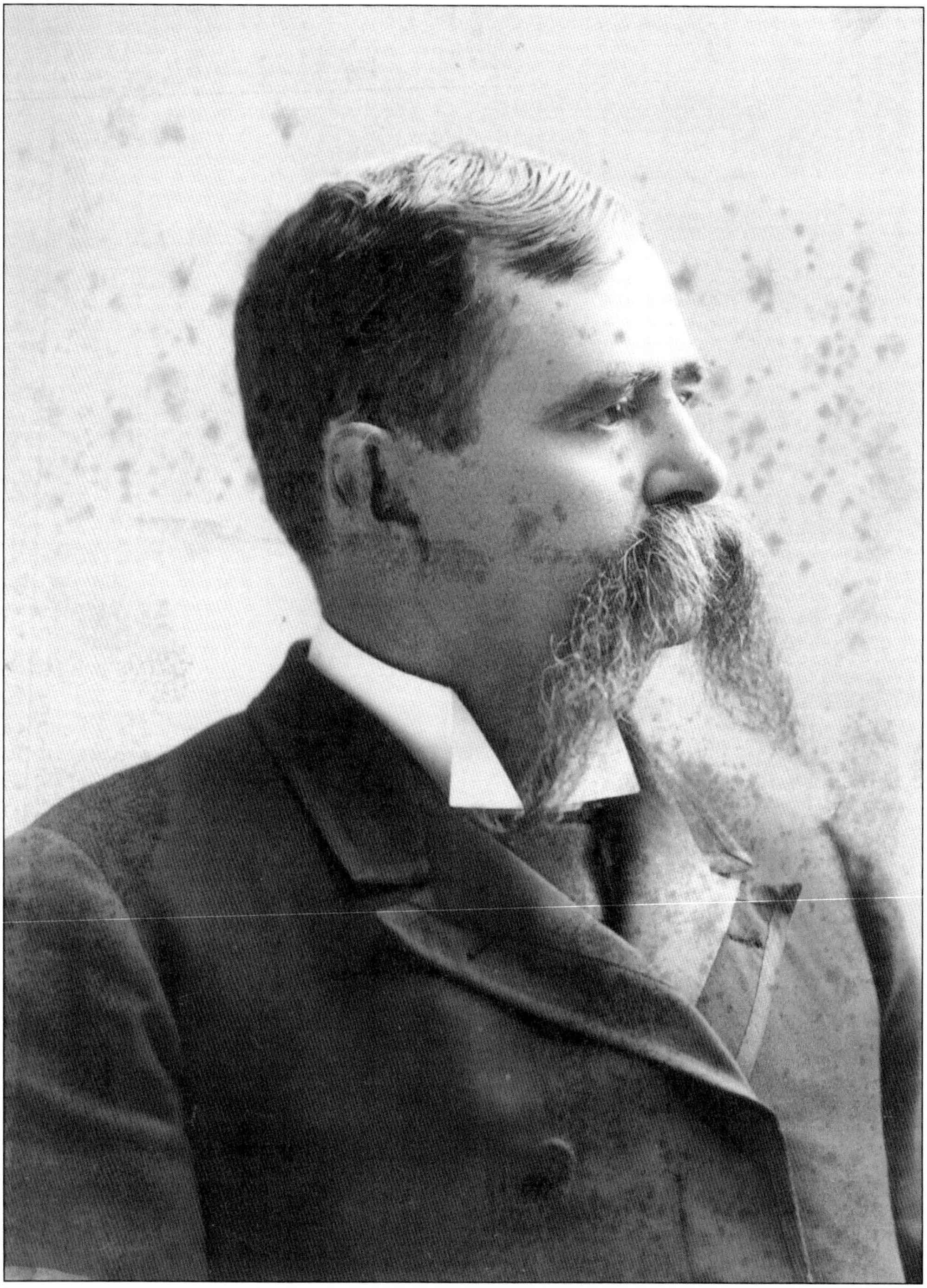

Louis Charles Latham was born in Plymouth in 1840. He graduated from the University of North Carolina in 1859. His studies at Harvard University were interrupted by the outbreak of the Civil War in 1861. Latham joined the Confederate army and rose to the rank of major. He returned home after the war and began a political career that included serving in the state legislature. (Albert Jones.)

Born on July 28, 1838, Plymouth native Augustin Daly (right) was the son of Denis Daly, an Irish sailor, and Elizabeth Duffey. In 1838, Denis Daly set up a shipping business in Plymouth. When Denis died in 1841, Elizabeth moved Augustin and his infant brother to Norfolk, Virginia. Daly became a world-famous playwright and producer. By the late 19th century, he owned a theater on New York's Fifth Avenue. In the photograph below, Daly (seated third from right) is reading a play to his theater company in New York. His death in Paris in 1899 made headlines in the United States and Europe, and his funeral was held in New York's famous St. Patrick's Cathedral. (Both, Photography Collection, Miriam and Ira D. Wallach Division of Art, Prints and Photographs, The New York Public Library, Astor, Lenox, and Tilden Foundations.)

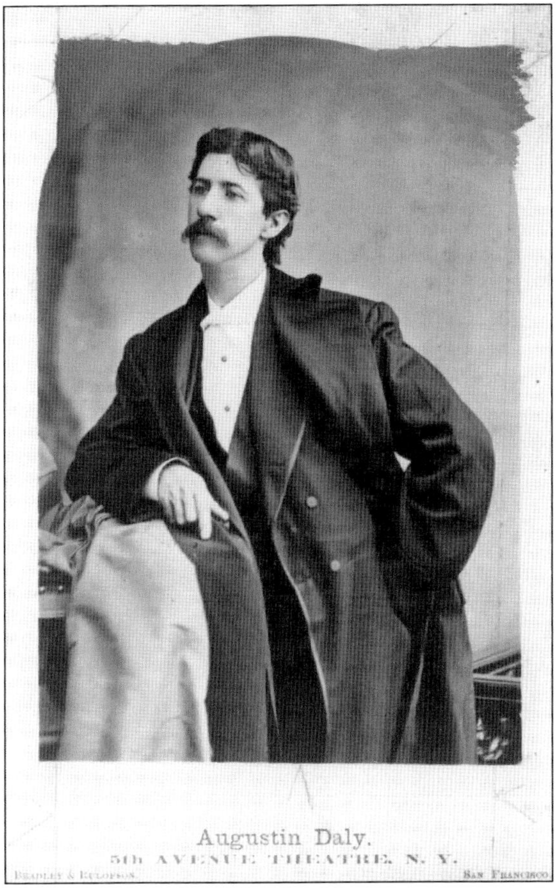

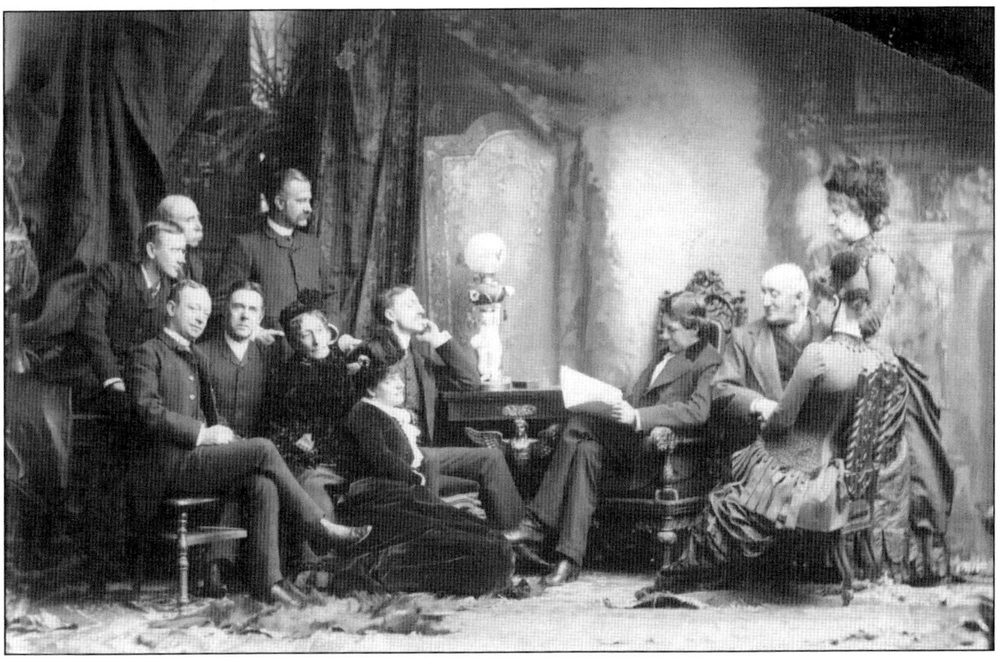

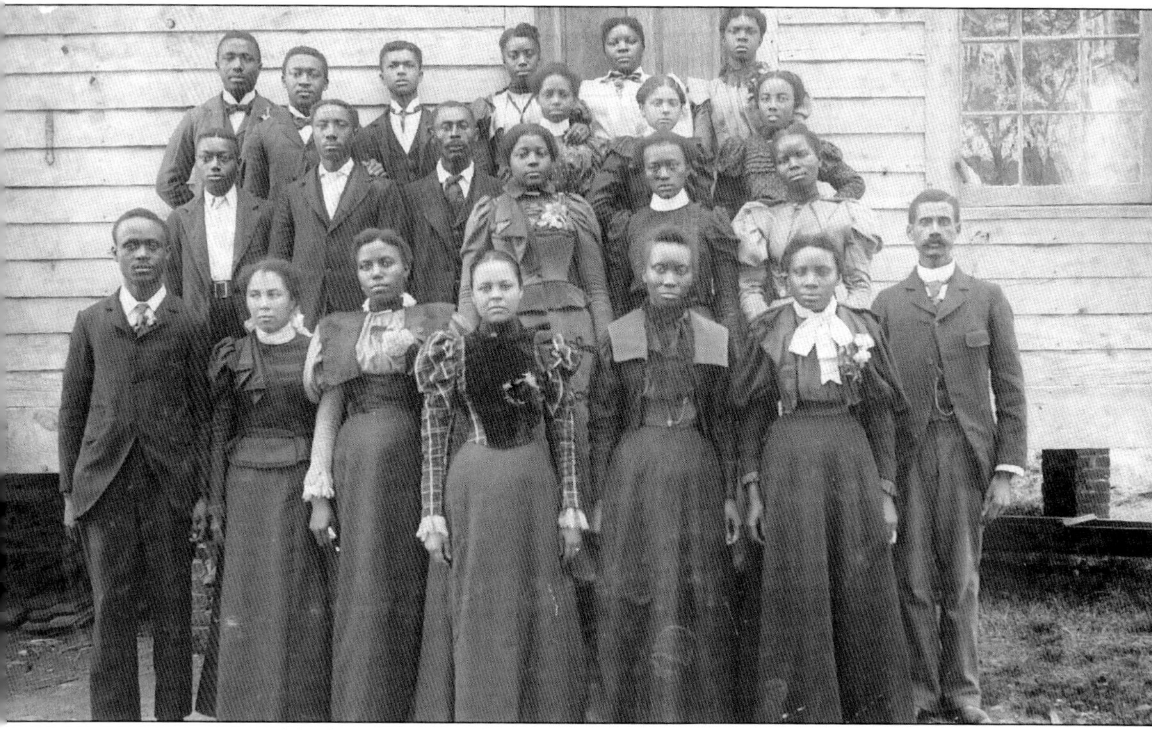

Peter Moore paid for his education through manual labor. In 1889, he became assistant principal at the State Normal School in Plymouth. In 1892, he became principal of the new State Colored Normal School in Elizabeth City (now Elizabeth City State University). In this photograph of the Elizabeth City faculty, Moore is seen at the far right, just behind the first row. (ECSUA.)

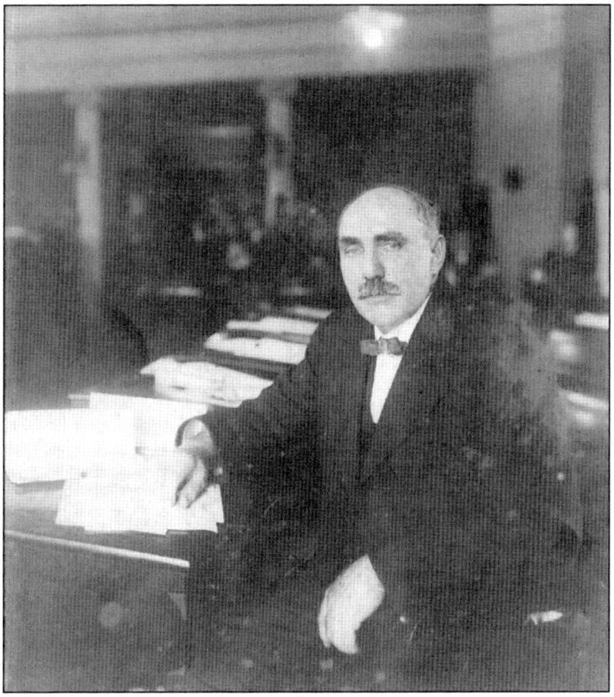

William S. Davenport was born in Tyrrell County in 1859. He married Henrietta Blount in 1883 and became a farmer in Mackeys. In the *Roanoke Beacon* of December 6, 1889, it was said that Davenport "holds more positions than any other man within our knowledge—he is a merchant, postmaster, express agent, steam boat clerk, freight agent and farmer." In 1917, he was elected to the North Carolina Senate. (Mary Cotten Davenport.)

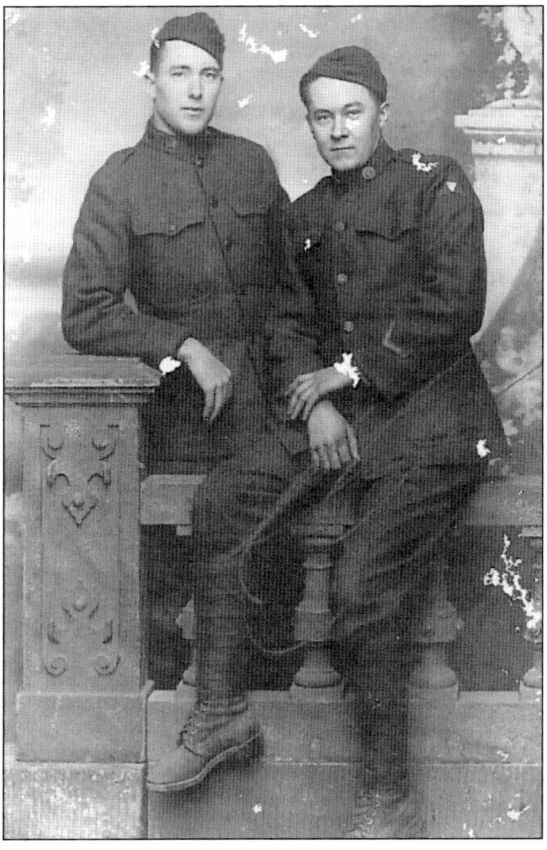

Renold S. Davenport (left), with an unidentified friend, served as an Army medic during World War I. A memorial plaque in Mackeys Methodist Church, where he attended, notes that Davenport entered the Army on April 1, 1918, spent 12 months "overseas," and was discharged on August 9, 1919. The plaque notes that he died on March 8, 1920, "of diseases contracted while in the service of his country." (Mary Cotten Davenport.)

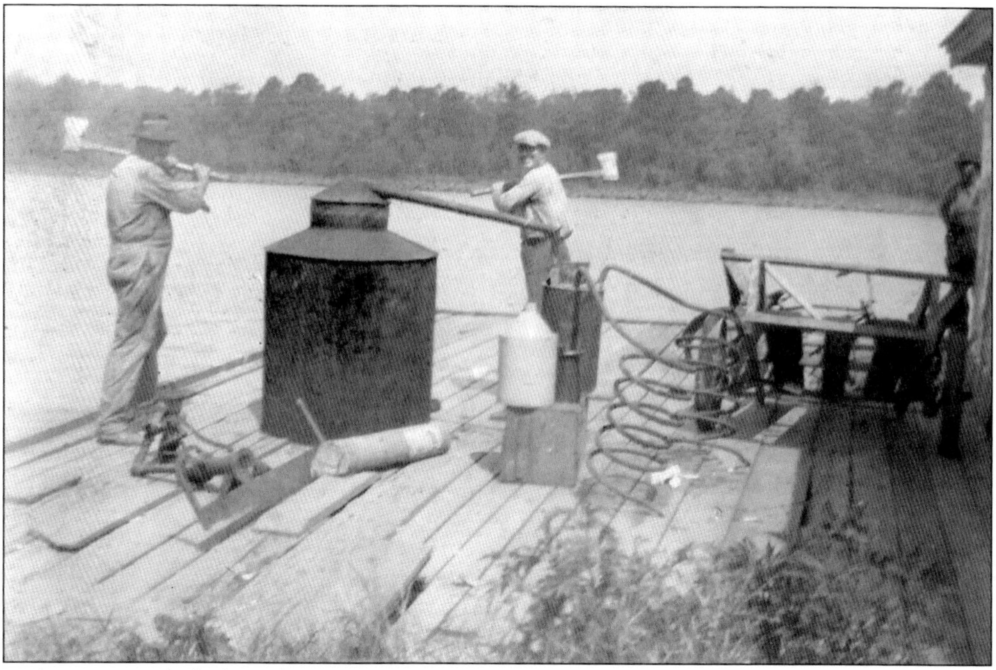

Making untaxed whiskey, also known as moonshine, has a long history along the Roanoke River. Moonshiners were especially busy during Prohibition, from 1920 to 1933, when it was illegal to produce, transport, or sell alcoholic beverages in the United States. In this 1928 photograph taken somewhere on the Roanoke in Washington County, revenue agents pose for a moment before smashing a still. (PPCWM.)

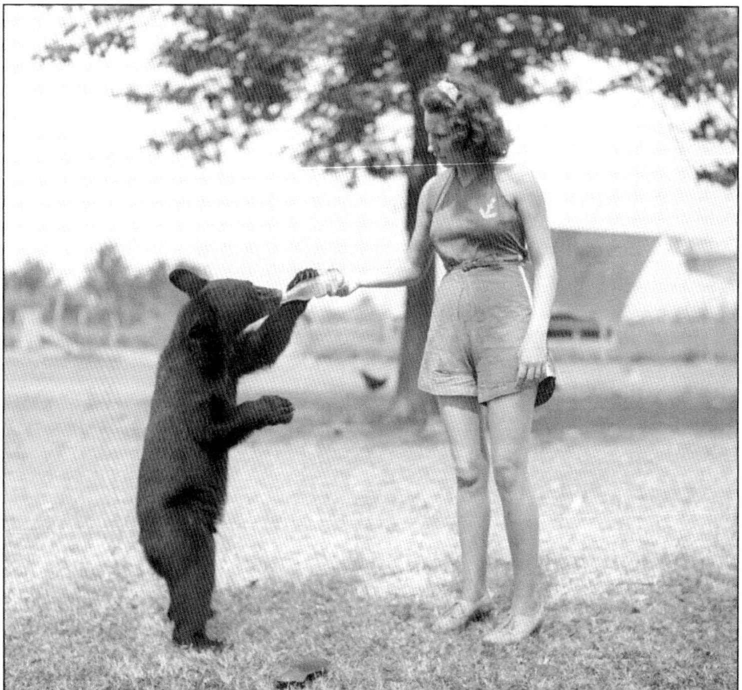

In this 1938 photograph, a young woman is sharing her soft drink with a small—and tame—black bear. But the friendly young bear had many larger, fiercer relatives nearby. Thousands of black bears live in the swamps and woods of Washington County. Their average weight ranges from 300 to 500 pounds, making them among the largest in the United States. (SANC.)

Benjamin W. Robertson grew up on a farm near Plymouth and entered the US Army Air Corps in 1942, a few months after graduating from Plymouth High School. He became a gunner on a B-17 bomber. In March 1944, Robertson's plane was shot down over Nazi Germany. He parachuted out of the plane, but German civilians captured him and sent him to a POW camp. (Mary Cotten Davenport.)

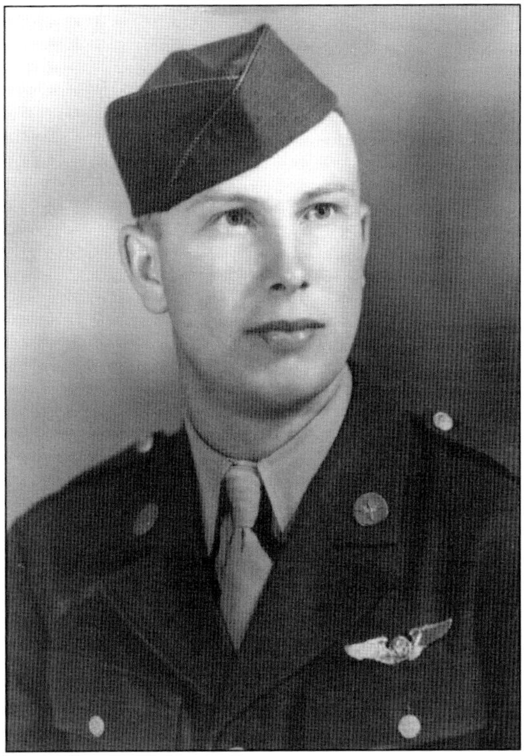

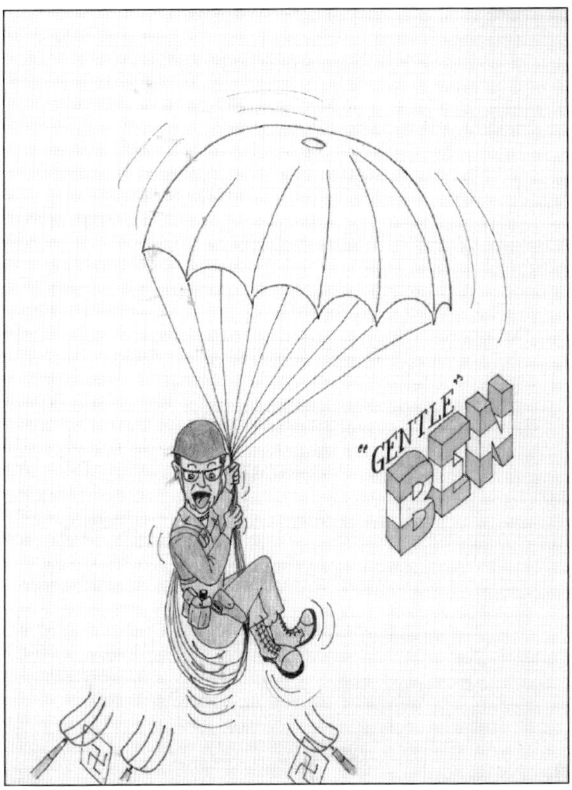

Benjamin W. Robertson drew this cartoon on graph paper, depicting the reception he received from German civilians after he had parachuted from a B-17 bomber shot down over Nazi Germany in March 1944. Robertson spent a year in a POW camp. His weight dropped from 215 pounds to 150. American soldiers freed the prisoners in April 1945, shortly before the war in Europe ended. (Mary Cotten Davenport.)

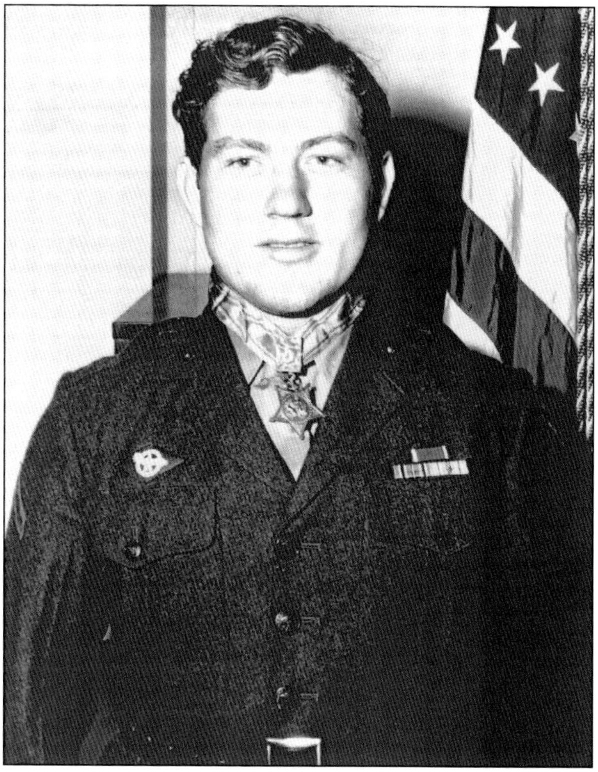

Plymouth native Jack Lucas lied about his age to join the US Marines and stowed away on a troop ship to take part in the Marines' invasion of Iwo Jima in February 1945. During a fierce firefight with Japanese troops, Lucas threw himself on two live grenades to protect his fellow Marines. Although riddled with shrapnel from his head to his thighs, he somehow survived the explosion. Lucas, 17 at the time, was awarded the Congressional Medal of Honor, with which he is shown. (D.K. Drum.)

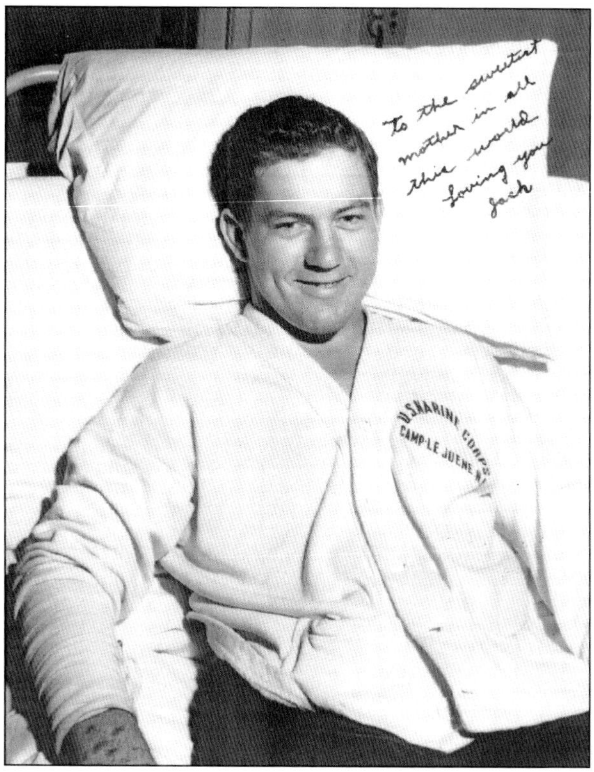

It took Jack Lucas a long time to recover from the wounds he sustained when he threw himself on two live grenades to protect fellow Marines during the Battle of Iwo Jima in February 1945. Lucas sent this photograph to his mother that shows him in the hospital at Camp Lejuene, North Carolina. Note the scars from shrapnel wounds visible on his right forearm. (WCL.)

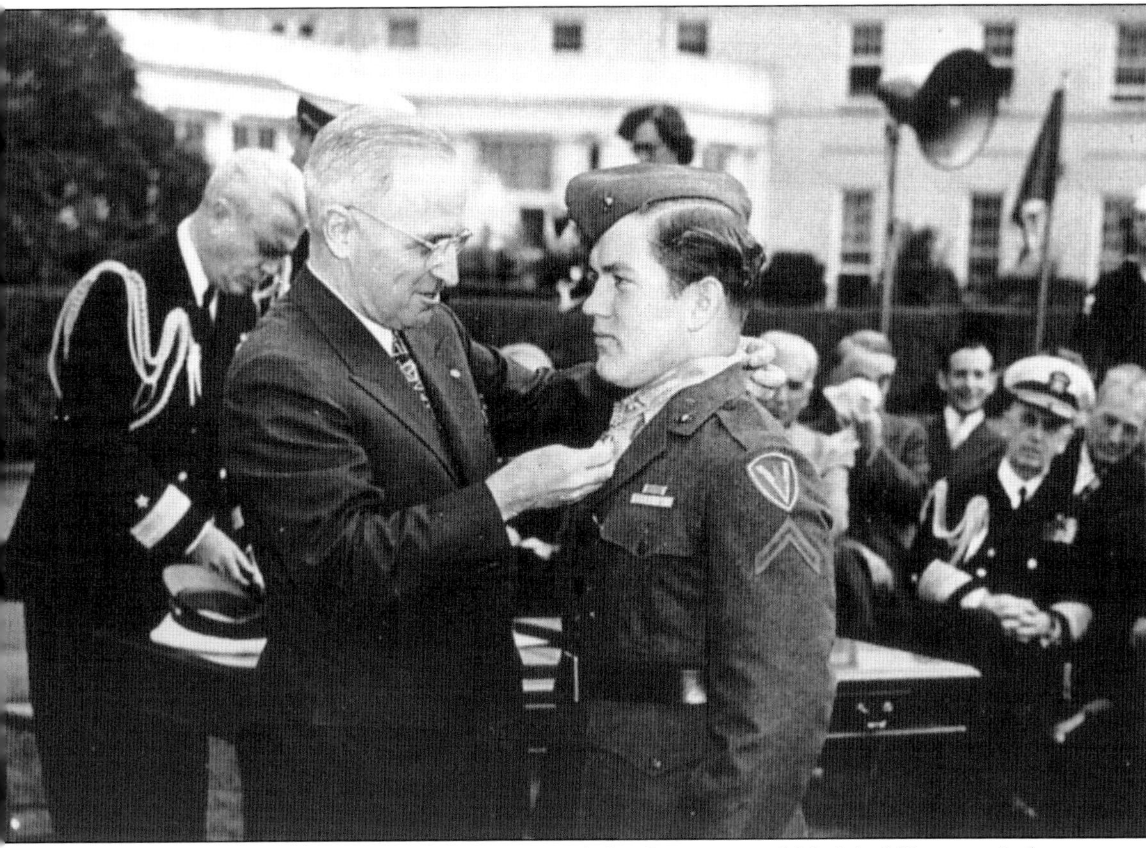

On October 5, 1945, Pres. Harry Truman presented the Congressional Medal of Honor to Jack Lucas during a ceremony at the White House in Washington, DC. Lucas later said that he managed not to wince when President Truman accidentally touched one of the still-healing wounds he had received when he threw himself on two live grenades during the Marines' invasion of Iwo Jima in February 1945. (D.K. Drum.)

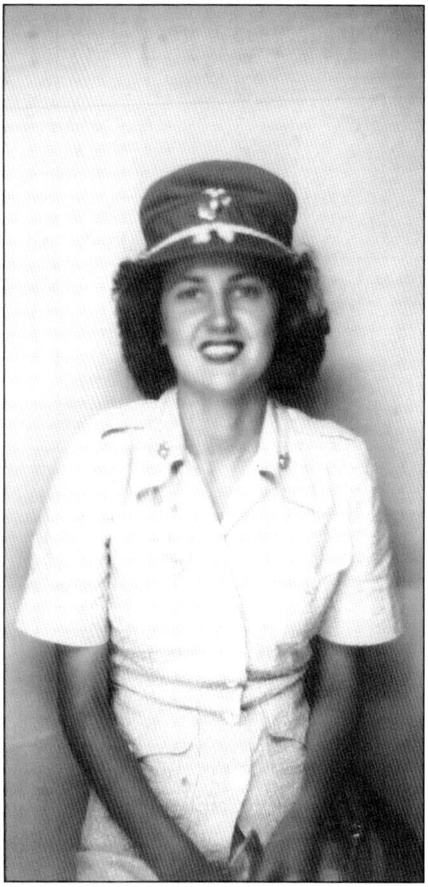

Mary Cotten Davenport grew up in Mackeys, North Carolina, and graduated from Plymouth High School. At the age of 23, she enlisted in the US Marine Corps in 1943, during World War II. She served as a clerk typist until she was discharged in February 1946. After the war, she married Benjamin W. Robertson, who had survived a year in a German POW camp. (Mary Cotten Davenport.)

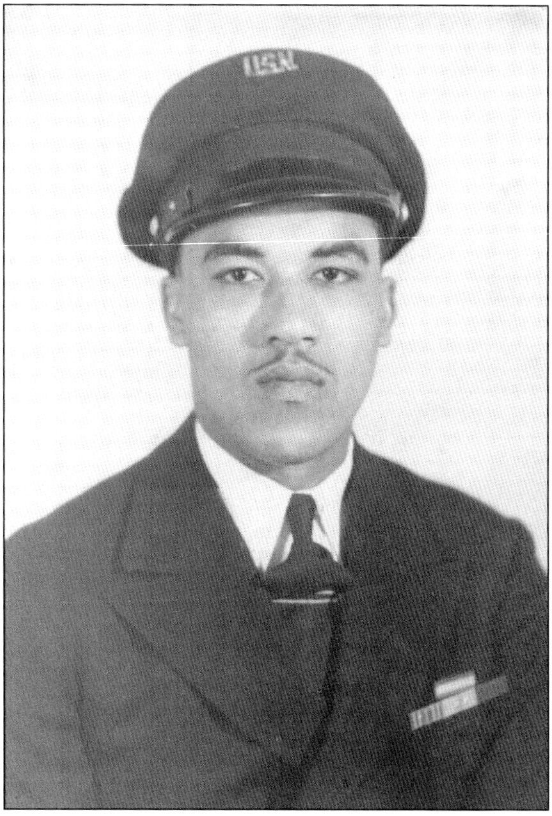

Melvin Cordon served in the US Navy aboard the aircraft carrier USS *Enterprise* during World War II and saw combat in the Pacific. After the war, he earned a degree from North Carolina A&T College and became a teacher, eventually teaching agriculture in Washington County schools. After retiring in 1983, he served on the Plymouth Town Council. A park in Plymouth is named in his memory. (Undine Cordon.)

Alton Baker worked at the North Carolina Pulp Company, which later became Weyerhaeuser. When the paper mill's labor force was unionized in 1938, separate union chapters were created for African American and white workers. Baker became president of the black unionized workers in the late 1940s and served as their president into the 1950s. (Merion Anderson.)

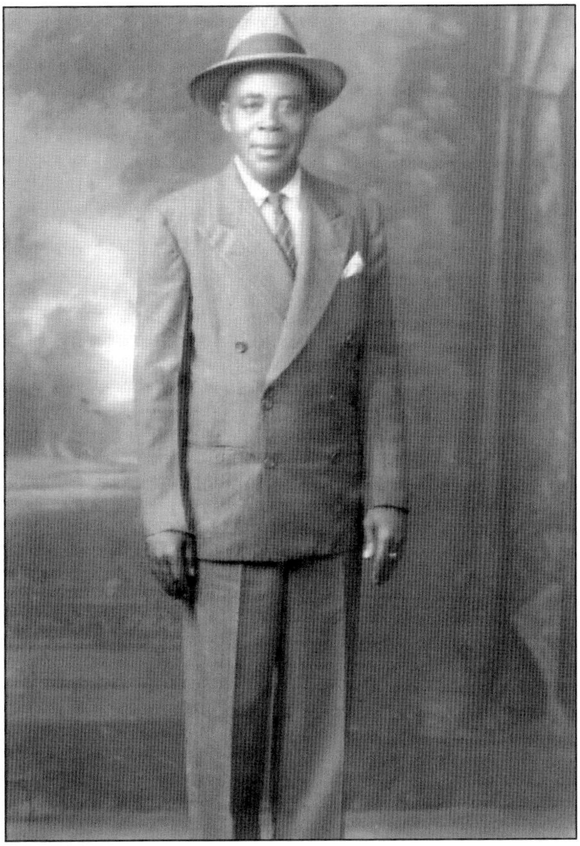

This eighth-grade class from 1946 included, from left to right, (first row) Wyoming Smithwrith, Chester Lee Holley, John Downing, Luetta Heckstall, Novella Johnson, Freddie Johnson, Sarah Channel, Gracie Hyman, Ernest Jennette, and Berlain Smith; (second row) Merion Baker, Mary Heckstall, Margarite Taylor, Savannah Mitchell, teacher Mrs. McLean, Anna Ruth Barnes, Mary Jordan, Lena Heath, and Martha Hocutt. (Merion Anderson.)

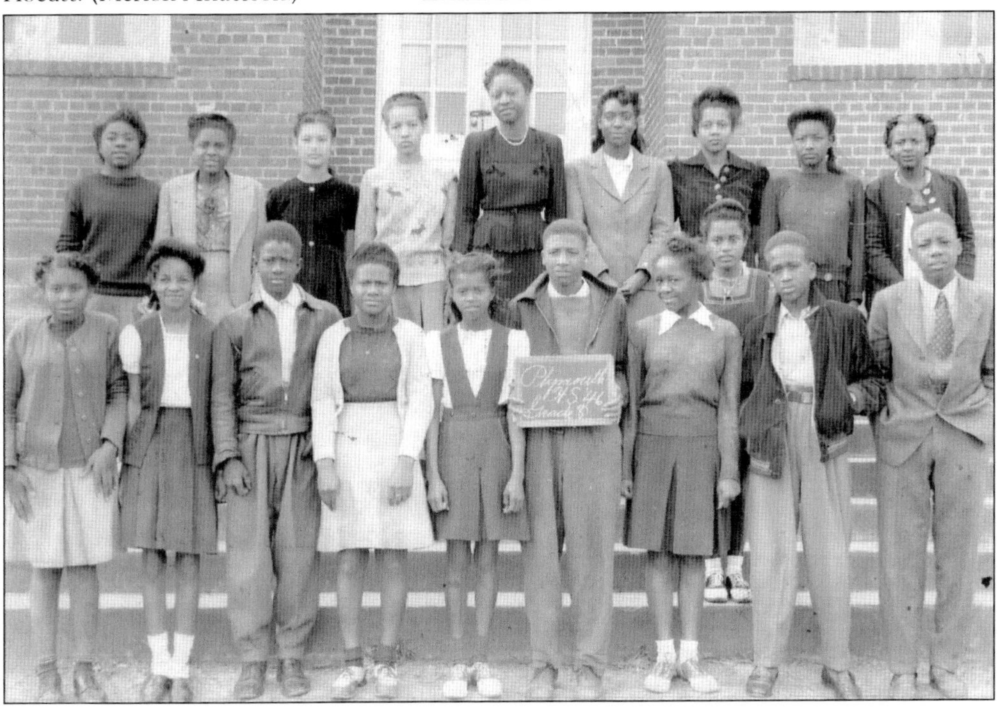

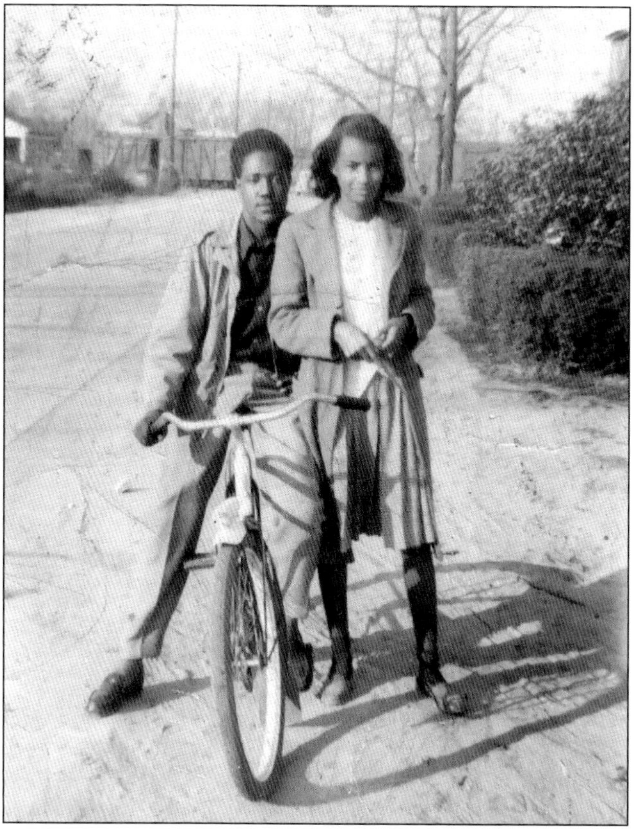

Two young friends paused for a few moments to pose for this photograph, which was shot in Plymouth around 1944. Sitting on the bicycle is James Jordan. With him is his friend Mary Louise Wiggins. Jordan and Wiggins attended Washington County's segregated public schools. (Merion Anderson.)

Before Washington County schools were integrated, African Americans attended separate schools in Plymouth. This photograph shows the basketball team for the black Plymouth High School in 1947. From left to right are (kneeling) Joseph Wingate, Harry Lee Hedgepeth, and Maurice Baker; (standing) coach Charles Bell, Robert Barnes, ? Goodman, Richard Stewart, Wallace Minor, Joseph Belcher, and Horace Simon. (Merion Anderson.)

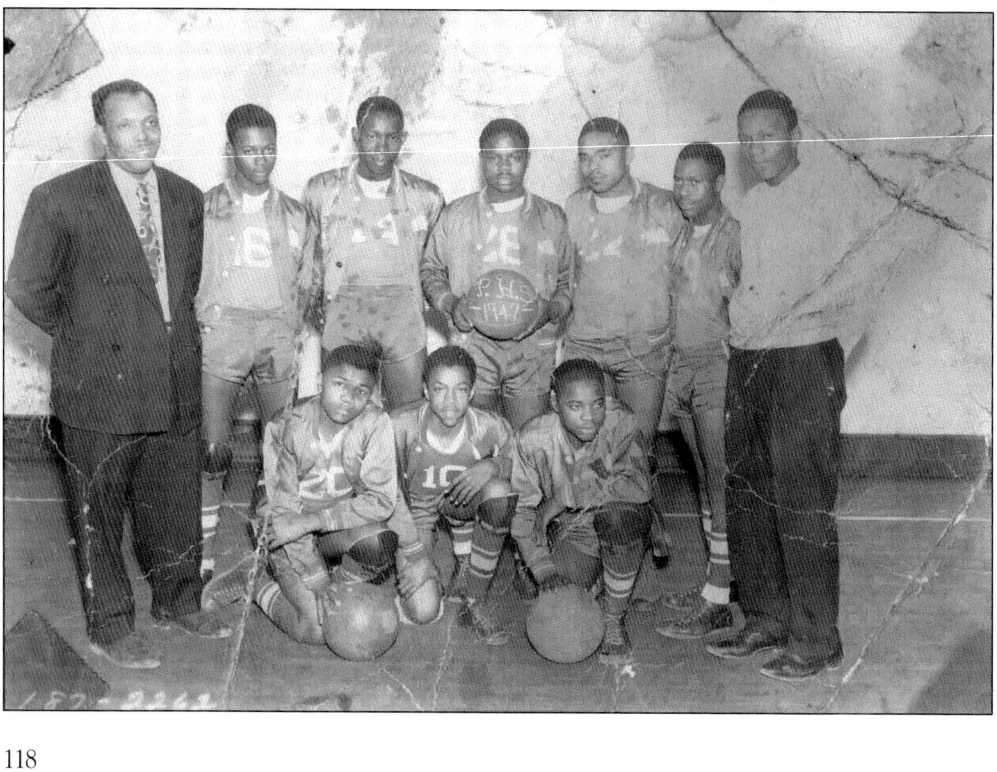

Caredwyn Phelps is the only woman to represent Washington County in the North Carolina State Legislature. Phelps, a Pennsylvania native, was married to Dr. J.M. Phelps of Creswell when he was serving in the legislature. Dr. Phelps died of a heart attack on March 26, 1961. Four days later, Governor Terry Sanford appointed Phelps to finish her husband's term. (NCSSO.)

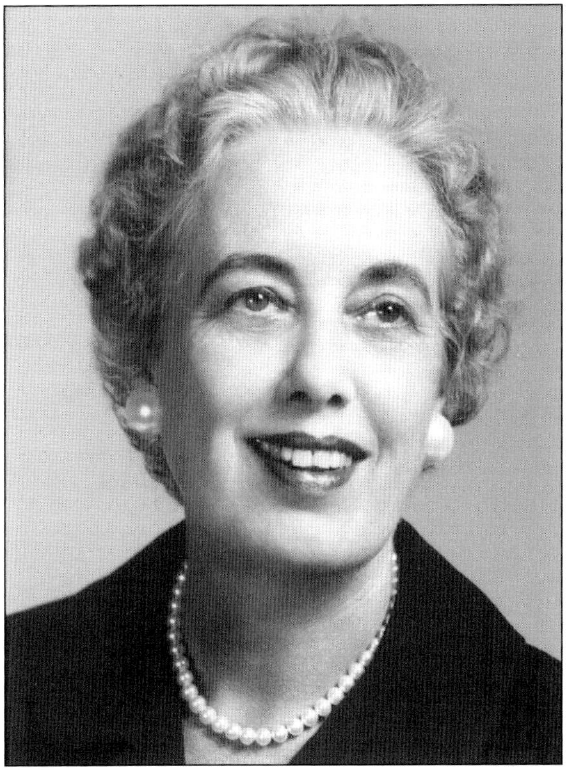

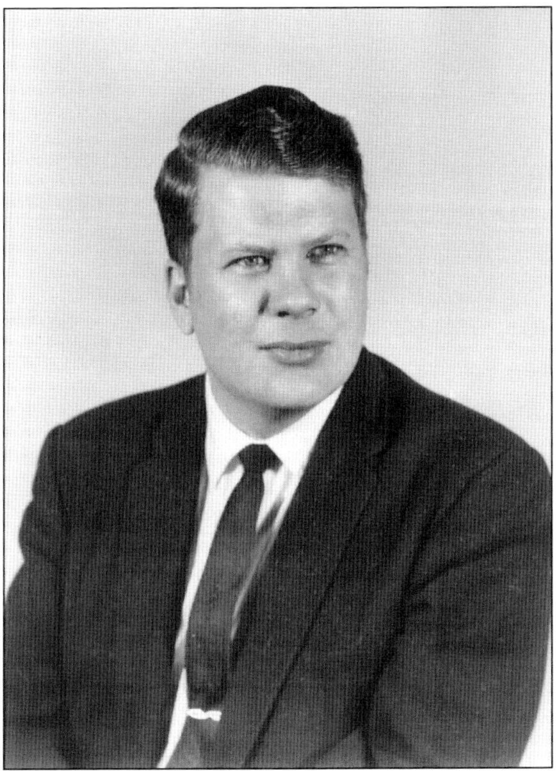

Born in Roper, Carl Bailey graduated from Plymouth High School in 1942. He served in the US Army Air Corps during World War II. He graduated from the Wake Forest College School of Law in 1950 and married Jarahnee Hinson of Plymouth in 1957. He represented Washington County in the North Carolina House of Representatives from 1963 to 1965. (NCSSO.)

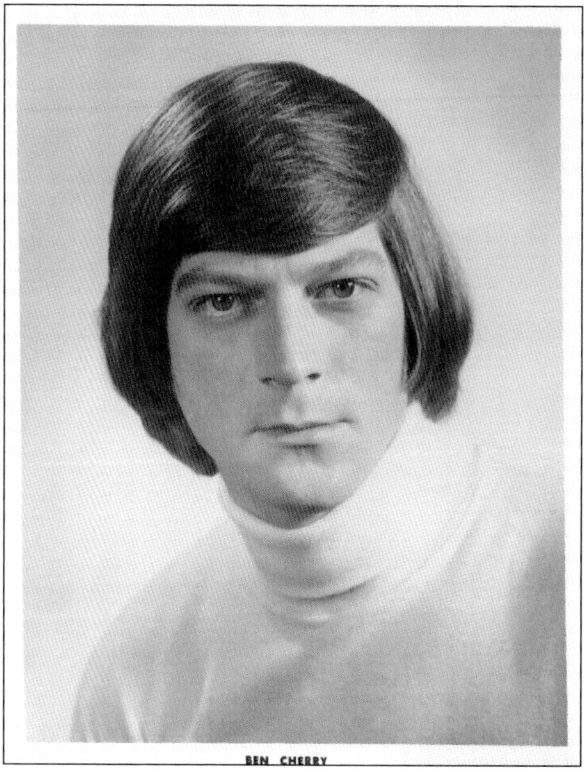

Plymouth native Ben Cherry graduated from East Carolina University and went to New York to pursue an acting career while working as a page and tour guide at NBC in the early 1970s. During a visit home, however, Cherry learned that his mother had cancer, and did not return to New York. But he found a way to use his acting skill. (Ben Cherry.)

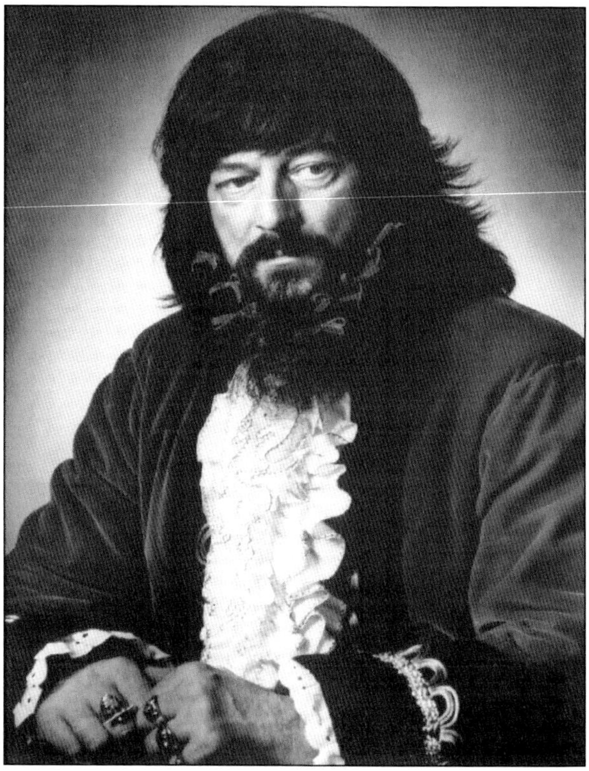

In 1718, the infamous pirate Blackbeard lived briefly in Bath, a small town in northeastern North Carolina, near Plymouth. So when Plymouth actor Ben Cherry (pictured) decided to impersonate the legendary pirate, he was, in a sense, taking on the role of a local legend. Cherry made a career as a Blackbeard impersonator, bringing the legendary pirate to life across the United States and Caribbean. (Ben Cherry.)

Charles Bowser graduated from Plymouth High School in 1978 and accepted a football scholarship to Duke University. He became a fixture as linebacker for the Blue Devils, setting school records for sacks. Here, Bowser takes down an opposing ball carrier during a game at Duke's Wallace Wade Stadium. (Charles Bowser.)

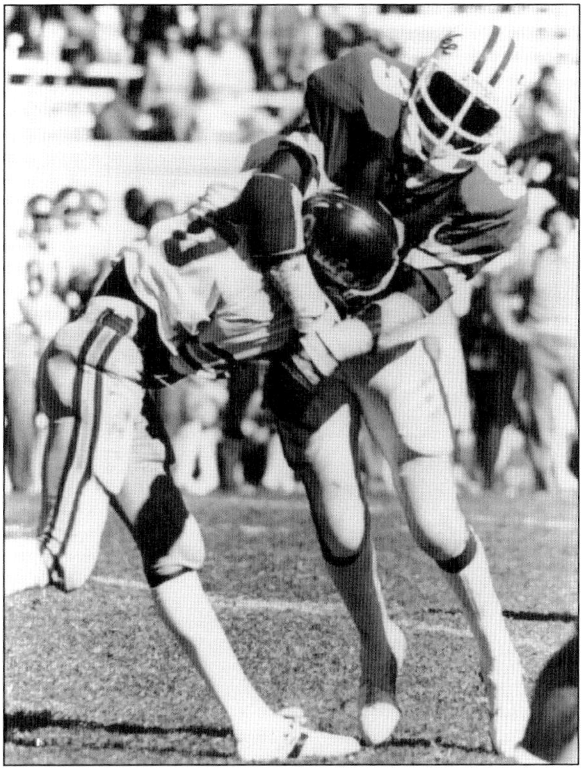

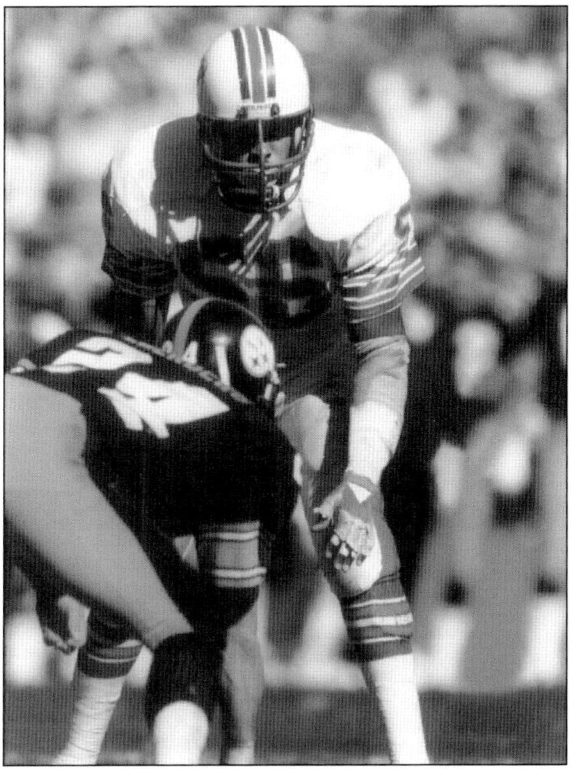

The Miami Dolphins selected Bowser in the 1982 NFL draft. In 1984, he became a starting linebacker and, with nine sacks, was ranked second on the team. He also started at linebacker in the 1985 Super Bowl, when the Dolphins lost to the San Francisco 49ers, 38-16. An injury cut short Bowser's NFL career, however, and he retired after the 1985 season. (Charles Bowser.)

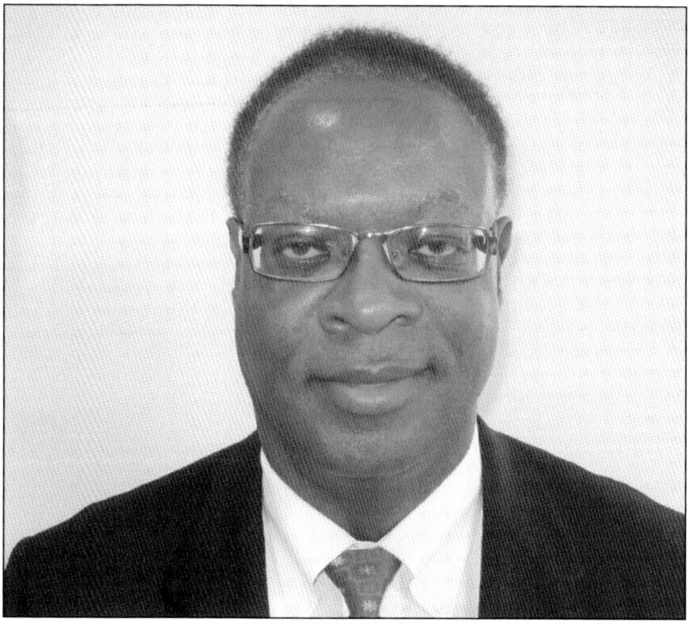

Plymouth High School, Duke University, and NFL standout Charles Bowser became active in hometown affairs upon retiring from professional football after the 1985 season. The former Miami Dolphins linebacker conducted annual football camps in Plymouth for young players and helped Plymouth High School win two North Carolina Class 1-A state football championships. (Charles Bowser.)

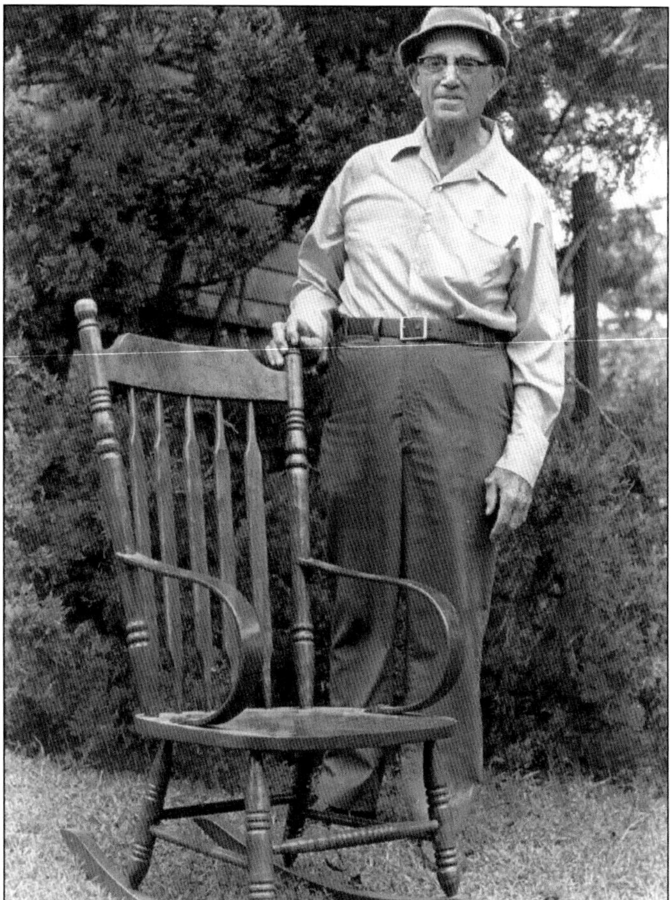

In addition to working as postmaster of Plymouth during the 1960s and 1970s, Corbet Swain was known for his hand-built rocking chairs, one of which is shown here, as well as his "gentlemen's oyster roast" every year at his home on Main Street. (Doward Jones Jr.)

Boots Garrett's smile and friendly demeanor made him a familiar sight on Water Street in downtown Plymouth in the 1970s and 1980s. (Doward Jones Jr.)

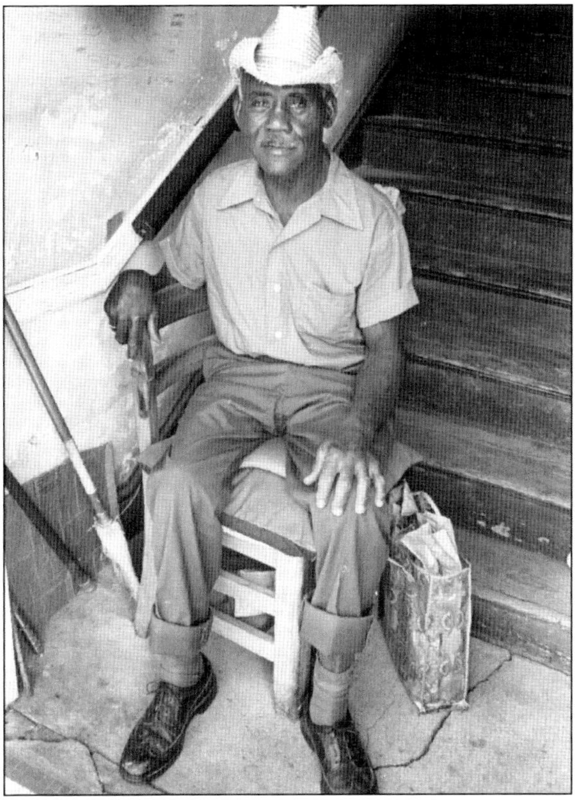

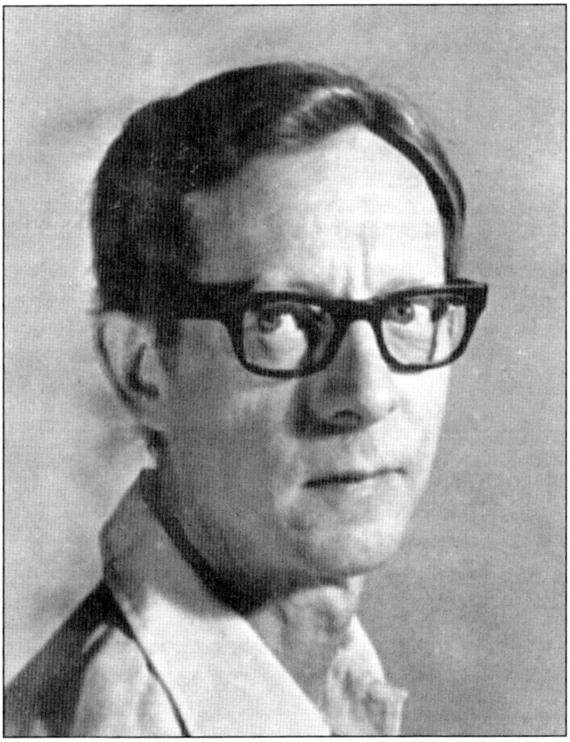

Born in Plymouth in 1929, Gene Harris received his only painting lessons from a local artist in the early 1950s and went on to paint sensitive and occasionally ethereal landscape and wildlife paintings. With 26 of his paintings, he illustrated his second book, a history of eastern North Carolina titled *Eden: Coastal Carolina*, published in 1978. (Doward Jones Jr.)

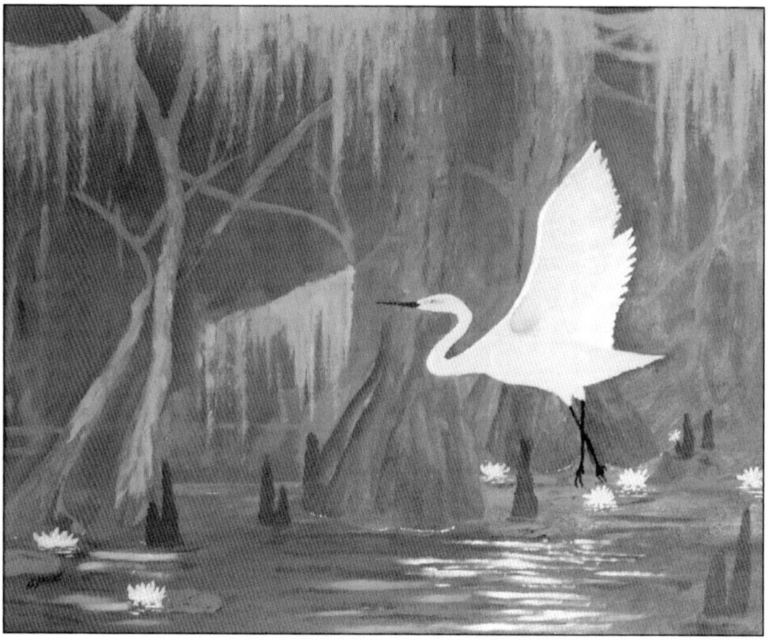

Plymouth artist Gene Harris painted this northeastern North Carolina landscape showing an egret in a cypress swamp. (Doward Jones Jr.)

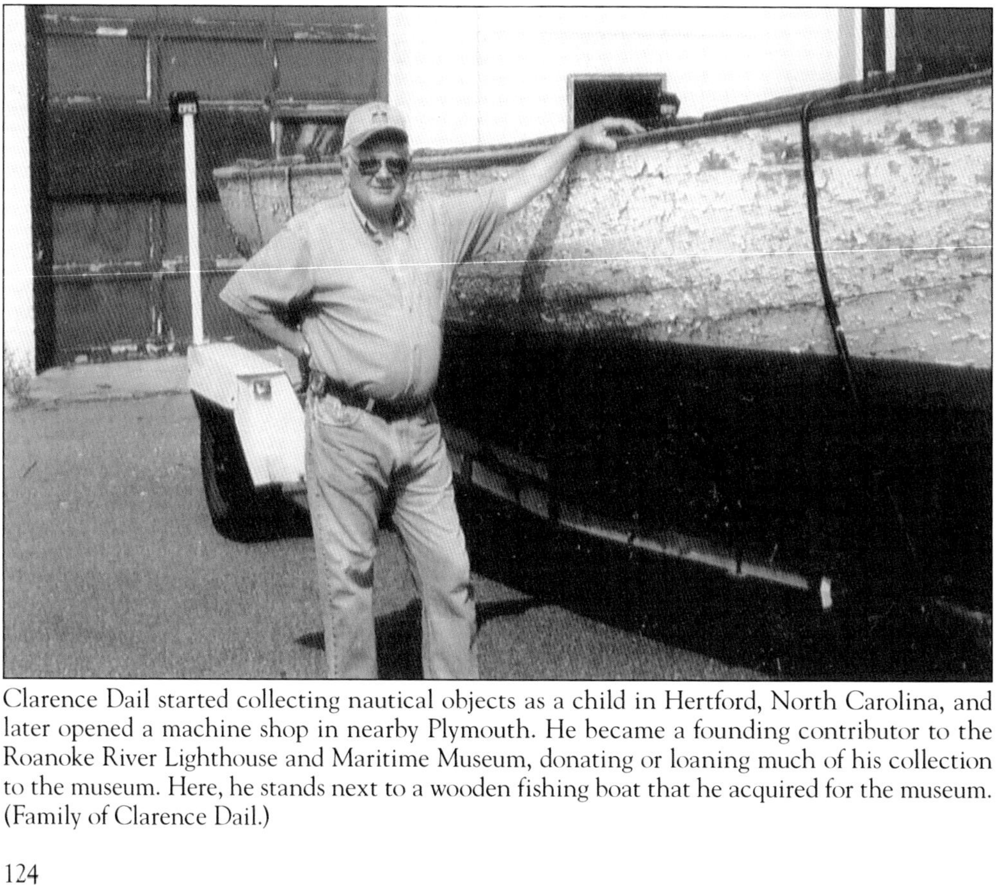

Clarence Dail started collecting nautical objects as a child in Hertford, North Carolina, and later opened a machine shop in nearby Plymouth. He became a founding contributor to the Roanoke River Lighthouse and Maritime Museum, donating or loaning much of his collection to the museum. Here, he stands next to a wooden fishing boat that he acquired for the museum. (Family of Clarence Dail.)

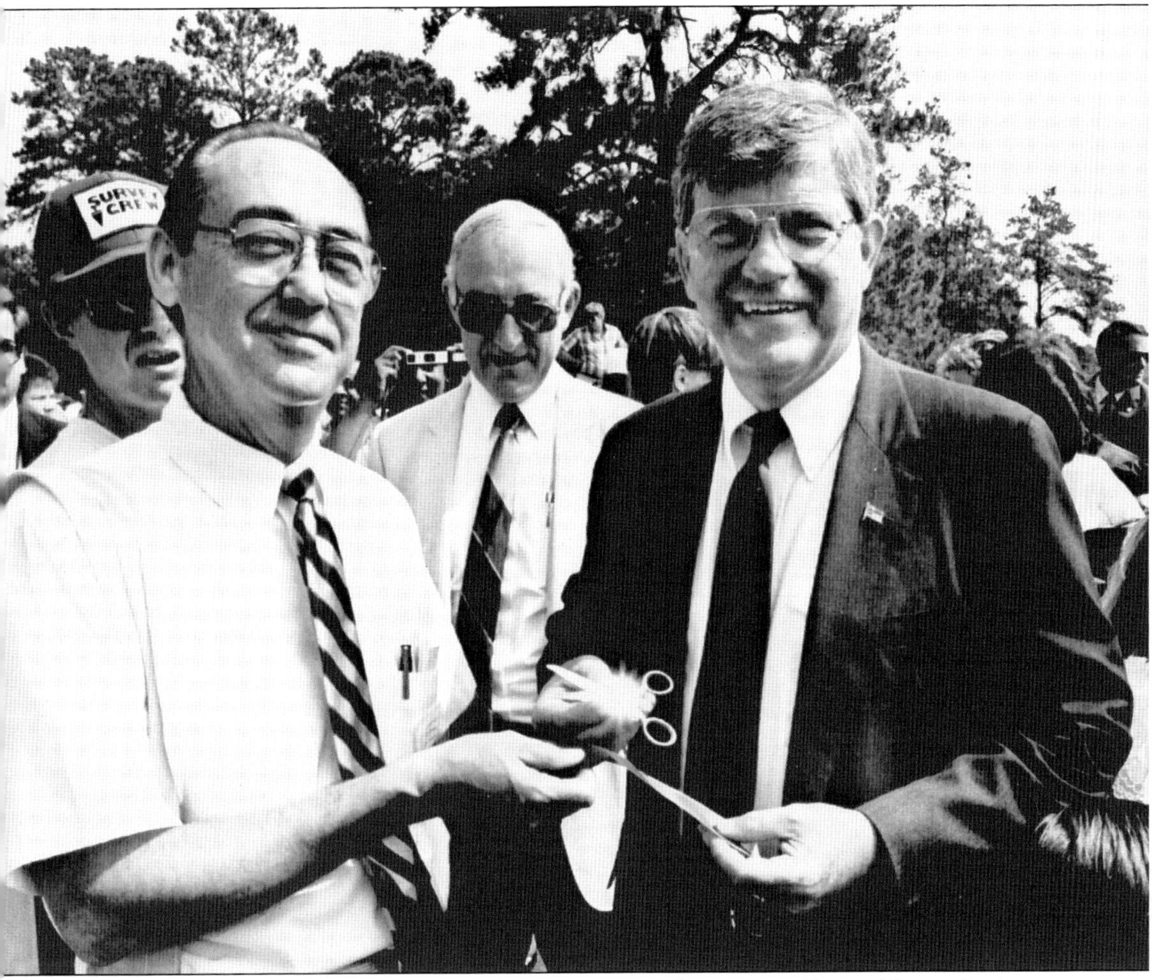

North Carolina governor Jim Martin (right) gives a pair of scissors to Doward Jones Sr. for a ribbon-cutting ceremony to open the new bridge across the Albemarle Sound in 1990. The governor thought Jones, the publisher of Plymouth's *Roanoke Beacon* weekly newspaper, should do the honors because he had long pushed for a new bridge over the sound. (Doward Jones Jr.)

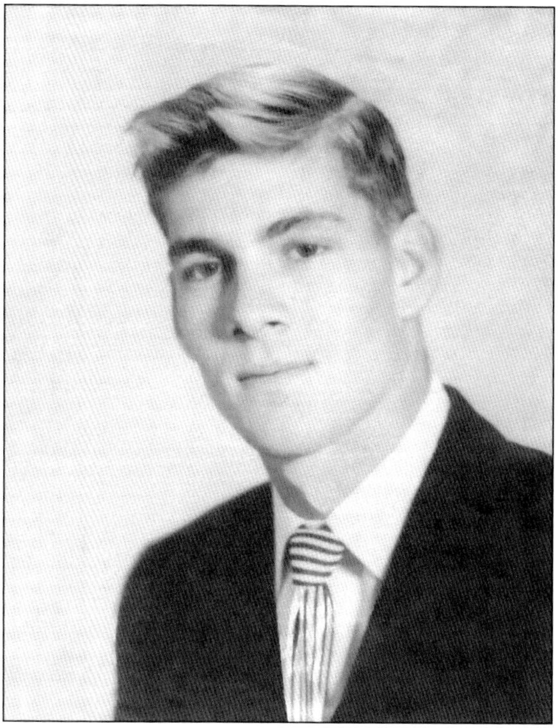

The late Harry Lee Thompson was born into an old Bertie (pronounced "Ber-tee") County family. Although he spent most of his life in his hometown of Windsor, he became a fixture in Plymouth and Washington County as curator of the Port o' Plymouth Civil War Museum. Thompson is seen here as a young man when he was a student at Duke University in 1953. (The Thompson family.)

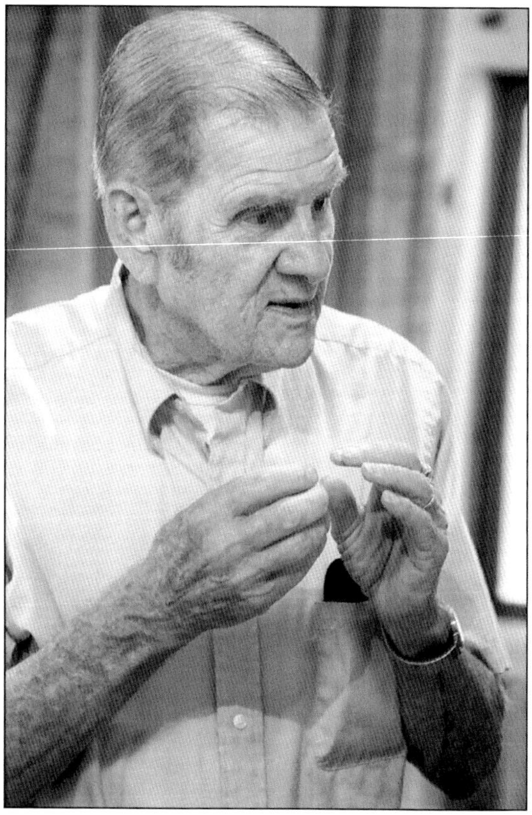

Thompson was curator of the Port o' Plymouth Civil War Museum from 1983 until shortly before his death in 2013. In addition to becoming known for his passion for local history, his enthralling tales, and his folksy, unpretentious demeanor, he was recognized as an authority on eastern North Carolina history. Thompson also established a tool museum in his hometown of Windsor. (Doward Jones Jr.)

Bibliography

"A Trip Through the Varied and Extensive Operations of the John L. Roper Lumber Co. in Eastern North Carolina and Virginia." *American Lumberman*. April 27, 1907.

Harris, G.G. *Eden: Coastal Carolina*. Plymouth, NC: Somerset Publications, 1978.

Lucas, Jack H. and D.K. Drum. *Indestructible: The Unforgettable Story of a Marine Hero at the Battle of Iwo Jima*. Cambridge, MA: Da Capo Press, 2006.

Modlin, Betsy B.L., ed. *Washington County, NC: A Tapestry*. Winston-Salem, NC: The Josten Printing Company, 1998.

Pierce, Greg. *A Synthesis of the Prehistoric Archaeological Investigations of Lake Phelps, Washington County, North Carolina*. Master's thesis, Department of Anthropology. Greenville, NC: East Carolina University, 2010.

Redford, Dorothy Spruill. *Generations of Somerset Place: From Slavery to Freedom*. Charleston, SC: Arcadia Publishing, 2005.

Trotter, William R. *Ironclads and Columbiads: The Civil War in North Carolina, The Coast*. Winston-Salem, NC: John F. Blair, publisher, 1989.

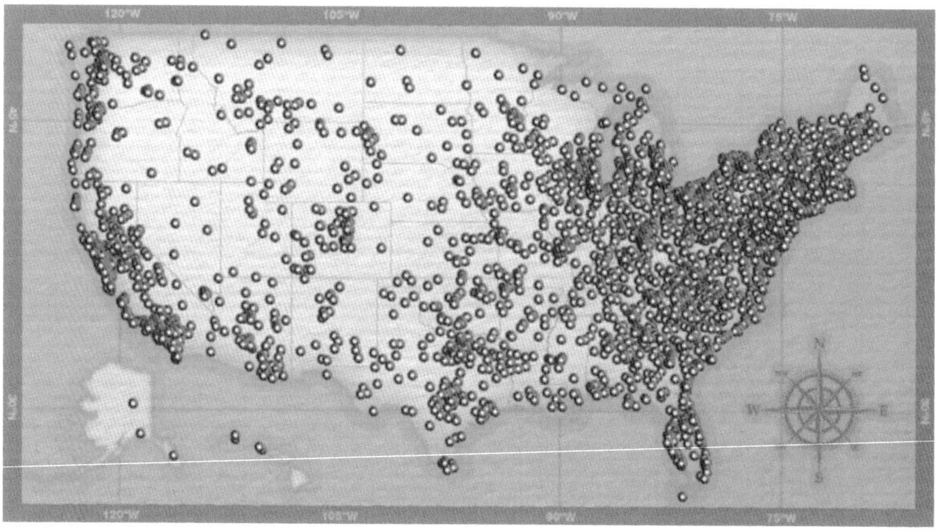

Consistent with our mission to preserve history on a local level, this book was printed in South Carolina on American-made paper and manufactured entirely in the United States. Products carrying the accredited Forest Stewardship Council (FSC) label are printed on 100 percent FSC-certified paper.